From Dot
To Cleopatra

▲

From
D O T
To
CLEOPATRA

———

Alun Buffry

FRONTIER 2000 SERIES

Frontier Publishing
Windetts, Kirstead, Norfolk
NR15 1BR

This paperback edition 1997

First Published in Great Britain by
Frontier Publishing 1997

Copyright ©Alun Buffry 1997

ISBN: 1 872914 09 8

This book is sold subject to the condition that it shall not, by way of trade or otherwise, be lent, re-sold, hired out, or circulated without the publisher's prior consent in any form of binding or cover other than that in which it is published and without a similar condition including this condition being imposed on the subsequent purchaser.

Typeset by T&O Graphics, Broome,
Bungay, Suffolk

PRINTED IN GREAT BRITAIN
Redwood Books, Trowbridge, Wiltshire

CONTENTS

Introduction
1 WHEN WAS DOT? 7
2 FACT, THEORY AND FICTION 16
3 THE ANCIENT EGYPTIANS 31
4 GODS AND GODDESSES 46
   LIST OF MAIN EGYPTIAN GODS 49
5 DIVINE PLAY 55
6 TOMBS, PYRAMIDS AND MUMMIES 69
   LIST OF EGYPTIAN PYRAMIDS 83
7 THE GREAT PYRAMID OF CHEOPS : FACTS ...84
8 A MILLENNIUM AND A HALF 97
9 MOSES, MAGIC AND WRITING 106
10 THE EIGHTEENTH DYNASTY 116
11 RAMESSES THE GREAT, THE 19TH DYNASTY? 132
12 MORE RAMESSES 139
13 THE LATE PERIOD AND THE GREEKS 146
14 THE PTOLEMIES 152
15 CLEOPATRA, JULIUS AND MARCUS 157
16 DAILY LIFE IN ANCIENT EGYPT 179
   VISITING THE MONUMENTS TODAY 191
   Glossary 212
   PHAROAHS IN ORDER OF DYNASTY 214
   ALPHABETICAL LIST OF PHAROAHS 219
   Booklist 224
   Acknowledgements 228
   Index 228

Introduction

I fell deeply in love with the monuments and ancient culture of Egypt upon my first visit to that land of happy peoples. That first visit was to see the Great Pyramid, although my two week holiday gave me adequate time to visit many monuments and sites I had never even heard of until then. Since that day the fascination has continued to grow, as I personally learn more and more. Even whilst writing this book new discoveries have been made at Giza, Alexandria and Luxor.

I felt a need to collect together as much information on the Pharaohs and their monuments, as I could get. I decided to attempt to build a database. The problem that I immediately encountered was that the information seemed scattered throughout many volumes of work as the artefacts of Ancient Egypt are themselves scattered throughout the world's museums and private collections. I soon discovered that 'classical;' Egyptologists do not agree even amongst themselves, as to dates, events, places and names. Furthermore, a new breed of Egyptological Scientist, the likes of John West were arriving in Egypt and making discoveries and theories which were blowing the classic theories apart (a fact still stubbornly denied by many). Collecting and collating data was very hard work.

Of course the reading of endless lists and tables appeals to comparatively few people, whereas the 'magic' of the Ancients appeals to more. I decided to attempt to present the information, without prejudging one theory above another, in a work which would be readable and enjoyable to the lay person, yet containing the wealth of data required by 'more scholarly' students of the Ancient.

I have tried to write this book so that each chapter covers one essential aspect or period of history and prehistory. Naturally this involves a certain amount of repetition; that itself is a 'symptom' of Ancient Egypt – the same styles, artworks, ceremonies and beliefs repeated over three thousand years.

I hope that you enjoy this book, which I hope also will inspire you to visit that wonderful land and stand where Pharaohs once stood.

1

WHEN WAS DOT?

Since the dawn of intelligence on Earth mankind must have looked at the many wonders of nature and pondered on our origins. From the tiniest grains of sand to the tiny twinkling stars in the night sky, the miracle must have started somehow, in the time I have called 'Dot'. Millions of diverse creatures and plants, massive mountains, terrifying storms, sunshine, rain, snow and hail, volcanic eruptions and hurricanes all reveal power beyond imagination. Mankind himself, said to be the crown of creation, encountered the enigma of the joy and cruel sadness reflected in the lives of individuals and their environment. Nature, or God, must have seemed both creator and destroyer, bringer of life and of death. Perhaps the greatest question of all, 'who are we?', was amongst those asked of tribal elders and wise men.

Whether or not these elders and priests ever knew the answers is not known to us today. In fact today we are still pondering. Surely, however, such comprehension would be beyond the tribes and any answers would have been symbolic and mythological in kind. The creator would be personalised in order to receive the worship and adoration of the people. The tribal leaders may well have reserved the true meaning (or lack of it) for their initiates, retaining power for themselves. Today we can read many stories and 'scientific' explanations for our origins, maybe choosing for ourselves what to believe or disbelieve, or maybe keeping our confused small minds open, awaiting a sudden revelation. The choice is yours.

The period covered between the year 'Dot' and the life of Cleopatra, is, of course, huge. Cleopatra falls within what we call 'history', the year Dot is most definitely pre-historic. History began in the times of the Pharaohs. History consists of what was written down at the time or shortly afterwards and our interpretation of it, affirmed or denied by other evidence such as other accounts and archaeological finds such as mummies and artifacts from the past.

What adds to our confusion about the so-called truth of our past, is the fact that ancient civilisations had a different concept of the passage of time and dating. Before the birth of Jesus Christ, or at least about the time of the birth of someone with a similar name, we call BC, 'Before Christ' and since then we term AD or Anno Domini meaning 'after the Lord'. Obviously before Christ the people did not know of BC or AD and had dating systems based on something else. The Ancient Egyptians appear to have started their calendar from the year in which the Pharaoh ascended the throne, so to speak. When a Pharaoh died a new Pharaoh took control and this was year '1' again. Although there is some evidence as to the order of the Pharaohs (such as who was who's son and the dating of tombs and inscriptions) there remains a great deal of confusion as to exactly who was exactly when! Although the ancients, who were keen astronomers, left many inscriptions, there remains much confusion in their interpretation. Added to this is the probability that it was the victors of wars and battles who wrote the surviving accounts of events. Furthermore, since some Pharaohs tried to wipe out all trace of their predecessors and even claim monuments as their own, by re-inscribing them, the confusion is even greater. This happened to many inscriptions of the Pharaohs Hatshepsut and Akhenaten, where the attempts at eradicating their names were unsuccessful. In any such attempts which may have been successful all trace of the Pharaoh may be lost for ever; the period of his or her reign has been filled by other names. Once again we sense uncertainty about history. There remain arguments over dates, even today, amongst Egyptologists and, as more and more is found, dating systems have to be revised. One such revision occurred when it was discovered that a certain tomb had been sealed before the time of the occupant's predecessor.

All this uncertainty may be off-putting to some, but to others, like the author of this work, it is the essence of the fascination of watching the entanglements and unravelling of Egyptology. To many Egyptologists it is simply annoying and they refuse to accept the changes. An example of this is the work of John Anthony West on the Sphinx. With the help of

Professor Schoch of Boston University, a geological expert, he examined the weathering on the surface of the rock from which the Sphinx was made and compared these to other dated rockfaces in the surrounding area. West concluded that the type of weathering on the Sphinx is different from that of surrounding tomb and enclosure walls and that the weathering of the Sphinx seemed like water damage. This created an anomaly since we know that there has been no heavy rain or flooding since the accepted time of the carving of the giant figure. West postulates that the monument is eight to ten thousand years older than previously thought. This suggests the existence of a terrestrial (or extra-terrestrial) civilisation from a time we know nothing about and would cause history to be rewritten. This is not pleasing to the classic Egyptologists!

Although history is said to have been "invented" by Manetho only a few thousand years ago, the term history usually applies from several thousand years before that, at the time of the appearance of writing. The times before writing was used, we regard as prehistory. Prehistory is even more uncertain than history. With history it is often a case of whether or not we believe an account; with prehistory our belief or disbelief is consistent with modern theories and religions.

Men, biologically quite similar to us, lived a long time before the Pharaohs. These men lived in communities; they hunted, farmed, fought battles and worshipped their gods and goddesses. Finds of bones and other artifacts are used to try to consolidate, create or destroy theories, in conjunction with other finds. The 'oldest man' has been unearthed several times (not the same one!). Archaeologists are still trying to link up the various finds and trace them back to discover our true origins; they have not yet succeeded; evolution is still very much a theory. Our concepts of prehistoric man and his world remain somewhat haphazard, as are the discoveries. If, for instance, we unearthed bones one million years old beside ancient tools, we could suppose that the man used the tools. That is not to say that those tools were necessarily always used since then; they may have been reinvented more than once. If we were to unearth million-year-old bones next to a wristwatch or wheel, we would assume that the proximity of the finds was accidental. We can only guess sometimes.

It is not the purpose of this work to discuss geology, archaeology, astronomy or cosmology beyond that known about by the Ancient Egyptians and so I intend to jump back through time to the very beginning, the year 'Dot'. What can we possibly 'know' of that time, before time itself existed, if you excuse the word "time"? It is certainly not my intention to guide you towards or away from any particular belief or religion. But I must say that religious beliefs do not necessarily negate scientific evidence. Neither does scientific evidence necessarily disprove beliefs. If a religion leads us to believe that the world was created at such and such a time (like 4004BC), yet geology suggests that the earth is very much older as is mankind as a race, then this conflict can be brushed aside by accepting that whenever it was made it was made to look older! Maybe it was made last week and we were all given memories and histories and geology and so on. Maybe a stupid idea, maybe not. Whatever we think, we know we are here to enjoy existence and part of that can be the fun and excitement of choosing the set of ideas we personally feel best suits the evidence.

The universe looks very big and very old and nobody can be blamed for wondering where it came from in the first place, the year Dot. All the ideas of how it may have started and what happened at the beginning, are of three basic types – a supernatural act of creation, a result of laws of physics or a perpetual existence.

Perpetual existence is the basis of a now rarely accepted scientific theory called the 'Steady State Theory'. This postulated that the universe has always existed and that it is constantly expanding, everything always moving away from everything else, leavings gaps in space which are constantly being filled from elsewhere with matter. Thus when we look out into space it appears that we are at the centre and that everything, all the stars and galaxies, is moving away from us; incidentally the further away it is the faster it seems to be moving, which may suggest acceleration which would need some sort of accelerating force. This type of theory leaves a lot of questions unanswered and has lost its popularity amongst cosmologists.

The 'Big Bang Theory' is more popular and based on observation as well as the known and maybe not yet known laws of physics. This theory looks back through time and attempts to trace the course of the expansion of everything back to one extremely dense primordial point or singularity, of almost infinite mass and with gravitational forces so great that matter as we know it would not have existed; all the atoms and particles would have existed as potentials only. This singularity is said to have been the centre of the universe with all space and time within it and the centre of the present universe is in fact everywhere within it, with nothing outside of it. There is complicated mathematics which support this theory to some extent and observations of a background radiation, cosmic noise, which is believed to be an echo of the original explosion (or at least the most recent one). What, though, caused this primordial singularity to explode? A singularity has no physical dimensions, it is a point. And why did it 'wait' until then? The Big Bang theory says that the explosion was an inevitable result of scientific laws. Of course the laws may have been created, or the Big Bang caused, by some supernatural being or God, so once again there is room for religion. A popular extension of the Big Bang is the idea that before the expansion there was a compression and before that an expansion. That is the theory of an oscillating universe. In other words we are back to a modified version of "it's always been here". In any case, whether this is the first or the fifth (or whatever) expansion there is no clue to any previous universe. Yet other theories based on working mathematics and probabilities suggests that the universe is splitting off as we make decisions or events occur. They say that we follow one particular universe where everything is how we experience it, whereas different decisions would have taken us through different but parallel universes. For example, if today you pick the red coat to wear, in another universe you would have picked the green one! This, of course, is simplifying it ridiculously, as its hardly any big Universal issue whether you coat is red or green, that is, of course, unless the red coat causes the death of the man who was to save the world, or something like that.

The theories and mythologies which hold that the universe was created are of more interest in this work. Modern and ancient religions alike are based on the existence of a God or Creator. The question of "Well, who created God?" can be neatly side-stepped because the words 'Creator' and 'Creation', in these religious senses, are mutually exclusive. If God was created, then He (or She) is part of the creation and not The Creator at all. There are many ideas and beliefs and theologies about who the Creator is, where He is, or why and how He did it. Then again many religions prohibit or discourage questioning – "ours is not to ask". At the basis of all these religions is a supposed Divine Act of some sort. In Genesis we are told that God said "Let there be Light" and there was light. In the New Testament Saint John reiterates that the creative act was one of speech : "In the beginning was the Word and the Word was with God and the Word was God ... All things were made by Him". In other religions the act of creation is said to have been one of spitting, vomiting, urinating, masturbating or copulating, to produce either the world direct or lesser gods with creative powers of their own. All the mythologies of Ancient Egypt are of this type. Of course there is no evidence supporting this type of belief, which is not considered necessary as the basis is faith. This book will be concerned with only the gods and goddesses of Ancient Egypt and how they affected the people of that time.

However the universe came in to existence, one thing is sure. We are here and we can look back in the attempt to unravel the past, thus embarking on a fascinating journey of our own. What we pull out of it is up to us. To do this, first we must once again jump through time, billions of years, to the appearance of man.

Now remember that most of this is still guesswork based on archaeological finds, with a lot of people spending a lot of time trying to piece it all together. Men had still not invented writing so there aren't any books to tell us what was really going on. What has been found buried in the earth are the remains of simple houses, tools, ornaments and even jewellery. A lot of this really old stuff, mostly made out of stone, was either just dumped or lost, or buried with the dead owners in pits. That is why one generations' rubbish is often another generations' archaeological treasures, because they provide the only clues to what our ancestors were really like all those years ago. Hot desert countries where there was a lot of really dry sand, like Egypt, is where a lot of these treasures have been uncovered, because they did not rot and decompose as they would have done in damper climates. It's not just the big stuff like pyramids that stirs the archaeologists: small beads and bits of broken pottery , especially if they are decorated or illustrated, often cause great excitement.

It may have been sometime around about 100,000 years ago that man started getting clever and began to use tools. The first tools were probably used when someone picked up a stone and threw it at an animal and hit it, so that it fell over and could be captured and eaten. Probably they started doing this even before they discovered how to use fire to keep warm. Before this, fire used to scare these simple, uneducated and superstitious people. Well, what would you think would happen when some men brought home a big animal to eat? They'd have to eat it raw and would have trouble cutting it up. A big problem would have been when there wasn't enough to go round, or when the neighbours were starving and didn't have any of their own. Then there would be big fights, much like today and, maybe, the cleverer of the tribes would throw stones at the others and end up winning. They probably would have used sharp bits of stone to cut the meat up. But the really exciting thing would have been when there was too much to eat. What if they just left the excess by the side of their tame fire? In the morning they could have had the first ever cooked breakfast. Other men could learn fast and copy and so the great secret of cookery slowly spread throughout the land and they started trying various recipes and cooking other foods like vegetables, nuts and maybe even leaves in water, to drink, like tea. One thing they certainly started doing was grinding seeds between stones and cooking them up. This made a sort of porridge or gruel, which they could add other foods to. They never had sugar as we know it, but they did find honey sometimes and that must have been a real treat.

This use of grinding stones was a major advance for our ancestors and you may well agree that a good name for us to give to an age where man was using stone would be the 'Stone Age', which is exactly the name we give to it now. They didn't call it that then though, probably just "now" in their language.

All this seems to have been going on in Africa and a lot of scientists will tell you that is where we all originated from, a long time before the stone age. By the time of the stone age, man had spread through much of the world; just wandering round and finding good places to stay, settling down, having children who eventually wandered off somewhere else. Of course they never had any maps and didn't know where they were headed and it may have often happened that they found someone else had got there first and blocked their way, so they would have to either stop still, go back, or have a fight. That is probably why a lot decided to stop where they were even though it might not have been the best place to be. So there were men all over Africa, Asia, Europe and even America, although they never called those places those names. In fact we only invented most of those names a few hundred years ago.

One of the most interesting of the ancient races were the Egyptians. We are very lucky, because Egypt was one of those dry sandy places, so a lot of bits and pieces have been found that give us an idea of what was going on. In those days, before 5000BC, Egypt was populated by a very basic, simple people, who lived in tribes, up and down the river Nile, doing their farming, having their little squabbles. It appears that some ten to twenty thousand years ago the desert was growing rapidly, forcing other tribes of nomadic hunters to head towards the fertile region of the Nile.

These ancient people buried their dead in round or oval pits in the sand. Some of these bodies have been excavated and examined and we can see that a lot of them died young and a lot were very sick with all sorts of problems from arthritis to the worst toothaches you can get, so bad it even killed them. Another problem was getting eaten by wild animals like lions and crocodiles. Bearing this in mind and the fear of being attacked by other groups of men, it certainly was a good idea to live close together; so small villages and farms were built, mostly out of mud with thatched roofs. It's reasonably certain these simple people kept cattle and goats and grew vegetables, and grains, ate honey and even made a type of beer, probably by accident after leaving food so long so that it fermented.

Each tribe had its own special god, usually representing some aspect of nature and embodied in the form of an animal, such as a baboon or ibis or lion. Each tribe probably had its own stories about where they came from or how the world was made and, like today, many probably believed they were the special 'chosen' ones, favoured by their god whom they continually tried to please. There were also gods who ruled over certain aspects of nature and the environment, such as river gods, gods of childbirth, gods of happiness or strength. In fact after the rulers, who were later to be called the Pharaohs, arrived along the Nile, nobody is sure from where, many of these local gods were accepted by them and became the gods of the individual Nome districts of Egypt – there were forty-two of them, twenty in the valley and twenty-two in the Delta.

About 3500BC, we know that men and women were living on land above the Nile, in Egypt, from the Delta at least as far South as Aswan. Settlers had come to Egypt from Palestine, Syria and Libya. Traders were arriving from Southern Iraq by boat and bringing new goods, crafts and skills. Most Egyptians were living in villages of thatched mud huts, domesticating cattle, catching game and fish to eat and growing crops such as barley and wheat. There were a lot of battles over territory and kingships and Egypt was very much a divided country, ready to be invaded by any more advanced, organised and ambitious people. Life expectancy in Egypt was not high; the dead were buried in brick lined oval shaped graves, together with small articles which they had possessed. All this has been learnt from archaeological finds. But, things were about to change.....

2

FACT, THEORY AND FICTION

Bearing in mind the huge range of years which the title 'From Dot to Cleopatra' suggests – billions of years – it may be surprising that the first chapter consists of only a few pages yet covers all the time up to about 3000BC, yet the remainder of the book covers only the Ancient Egyptians over about 3000 years. Now that you have read Chapter One you may be wondering "Well, what is true?", which is really the reason why I have included it. My intention was not, however, to confuse you or make you feel any pointlessness in studying history; on the contrary it is designed to give you a taste of forming your own conclusions, establishing your own beliefs and starting you off on the fascinating journey of unravelling the fact from the fiction. There are certainly a lot of gaps in our knowledge of our past and the past of our planet and the universe, a lot of 'dark' times about which we have little or no knowledge and have to rely largely on guess work and theory. In addition there are very many theories and beliefs and different interpretations of the solid discoveries that have been made.

History and Egyptology are both subjects which, like science, rely on observation, but in these cases the observations are of 'items' left either purposefully or accidentally, from the past. What these things mean is a different matter. Like scientists we must look at what we have before us and form a theory; then we must look at whatever else we know for sure and check the theory out for consistency. If the facts don't fit we have to change the theory. Remember it was not so long ago that mankind believed the Earth was flat and that we could fall off the end. That was a theory based on observation. But there came a time when someone sailed round the world and never did fall off and then we had to get rid of the idea and believe the Earth was round.

There are two types of past which I am talking about, the Prehistoric and the Historic. History is the study of the past based on records kept, of particular interest to us now; records of people, places, events, activities and changes in society, the people and the rulers. In a perfect world, history would be an unbroken record of what actually happened. Unfortunately the world of man is never perfect: there are plenty of gaps in our knowledge. For a start, before we could have records we had to have some sort of writing or drawing in symbols. Then we had to feel the need to record events for posterity. Then those records had to survive until today, or at least until someone else could find and rewrite them, in which case that person's interpretation would come into play.

Prehistory, then, is the study of the time before records were kept. On a world scale this time finished on different dates in different places. The Ancient Egyptians started writing about 3000BC, whereas in Britain and Europe it came much later. Prehistory becomes history when we reach the stage in the development of the civilisation where they considered dates important. Before that we have to rely on what we can see now and on what is recorded as having been seen in the past. Scientists such as astronomers, cosmologists, cosmogonists, archaeologists and geologists base their theories on what is seen to happen, what it looks like has happened and what they postulate will happen, making the best guess possible. These guesses may be reasonable inferences or vague ideas. Sometimes there are so many observations which confirm the ideas that the theories become accepted as facts.

Consider, for instance, dinosaurs. We know that they existed, because plenty of bones have been found. We can infer their appearances by imagining how the bones fitted together and how they would be covered by muscle and skin. We can guess at what they ate by looking at fossils found from the same periods and looking at their teeth and comparing them with teeth of other creatures. We can guess that they were not very clever from the size of their brains, supposing that their brains were in their heads! But do we know what colours they were? Do we know what they did each day? Do we know why, after surviving for millions of years before any recognisable form of man came along, they suddenly died out? When dinosaurs roamed the world the ancestors of the creatures which would one day walk and talk, write and sing and cook and use tools and so on, that is us, were little more than clever little rodents living off leftovers. We can only guess at the answers.

History, being based on written records, should produce a more reliable picture of the past, but, you will see, that is not always so. We have a lot of modern day techniques such as radiocarbon dating, which enables us to date organic materials by measuring the percentages of a particular radio isotope of carbon, carbon 14 and we have computers to tabulate and analyse finds. We have stone stele and papyrus scrolls to study, often fragmented and needing rebuilding like a jigsaw puzzle. We have literally thousands of finds to ponder on. We have the tombs with their wall paintings and huge pyramids and temples with hieroglyphic carvings. From all this we can get a fairly good picture of what was happening.

The discovery of a stone tablet which you will read about, now called the Rosetta stone, which was found in Egypt at a place called Rosetta and, after about 20 years hard work deciphering it, we have been able to start to read the thousands of inscriptions and papyri. So we are able to create a picture of what happened all those years ago. But there will always be questions unanswered. For instance, imagine a stone tablet found out in the desert; it may hold script including the name of the writer and information from which we can date it – we cannot use radiocarbon dating on stone. Do we know this was the name of the person who wrote it? Well we do know that certain Pharaohs wrote their names – or rather got workmen to carve them – on their predecessors' monuments, thus making them appear to be their's instead. Sometimes even a royal name was chiselled out and a new name put in, or left blank. Another occurrence could have been when someone came along later and carved a name where there had been none, the name he may have thought should have been there. Would we know whether the name was the right one, carved at the time of building, or even a thousand years later? There was a particular Egyptian historian who became interested in the 'Ancient Monuments' some 2000 years after they were built and he is known to have visited the Step Pyramid at Saqqara. Upon seeing the absence of the king's name on one of the other pyramids, he chiselled it out – Unas, or Wenis.

Imagine another situation where a tomb or a hole in the ground is discovered and in this is found a corpse together with some everyday objects such as a comb, a doll, or a piece of jewellery. On one of these items there is a name. Is this the name of the owner? Was this the name of the living person whose body is in the grave? Often there is no way of knowing. Certainly there have been finds in places where such items would not normally be expected to occur. Maybe the item was transported, lost or robbed, and buried or sold on. This type of discovery was made in Giza near Cairo, at the site of the Great Pyramid. The Great Pyramid did not seem to bear the name of the builder, which would seem rather strange if it had been built as a monument to the Pharaoh of the time. Many people have thought that the Great Pyramid was built as the result of an egotistical urge of the Pharaoh to proclaim his greatness. This argument has serious flaws; for a start they say that the Pharaoh's successor also built a pyramid, but if it also was a result of ego then we may well ask why this Pharaoh built one slightly smaller and why the next Pharaoh built his one smaller. But how do we know who these Pharaohs were? Well, not far from the outside of the Great Pyramid, deep within an underground shaft, was found a very small statuette of the Pharaoh Cheops (now in Cairo Museum). In fact this is the only representation of Cheops so far ever found and it was upside down as if dropped. Based on this find it is generally accepted that Cheops was the builder of the Great Pyramid, although the reasoning is hardly reliable.

What about stories handed down generation after generation before being written down? How reliable are those? If you have ever played 'Chinese whispers' with about seven or so people, you will have seen how repeated words can change. Over hundreds or thousands of years the stories would certainly be subjected to colourful embellishments and exaggerations. Even if an event was recorded at the time, was that how it happened or simply how the writer or his superior wanted it to look? Did Adam walk on Earth?

What about *Osiris*? Was there a great flood? If there was, did the people who survived know what caused it, or only guess? Who selected what to record and what to miss out?

In the Bible the name Egypt is mentioned hundreds of times, yet in Egyptian history the name Israel is hardly mentioned at all. In the Bible, Moses is mentioned and the king is simply referred to as Pharaoh, so we do not know for sure which one it was. Whoever it was, the Exodus of the Israelites from Egyptian slavery must have been a momentous event, yet there is no record of it at all in Egypt's records and no mention of Moses. Maybe the defeated Pharaoh, like most people, preferred to record his winnings to his losses!

So Egyptology is vague. In this book I am trying to show you the difference between what I know, what I am reasonably sure of and what I can only guess at and leave the decision of what to believe up to you. As you go on to read more you can always change your mind and opinions without shame. There is not always a clear cut right and wrong. For a moment think about the fantastic discoveries from the Tomb of Tutankhamun in The Valley of the Kings. There was huge wealth inside. We can reasonably believe that the items were put there due to religious beliefs and stayed there because it was not found earlier! Other Pharonic tombs, when rediscovered in modern times, mostly contained nothing save a damaged mummy. We can surmise that this was because they were robbed and we know that this was a big problem in the time of Ramesses X. Since many of the Pharaohs were a lot richer than Tutankhamun it is reasonable to say that their tombs would have contained a lot more than his. So where did all that stuff go? Who were the robbers? Poor men, workers maybe, corrupt officials, later Pharaohs, foreign invaders? Nobody knows.

If you decide to scratch a little deeper into the mysteries of Ancient Egypt you will find every section an ever deepening intrigue before you; you will realise the contradictions between authors both in opinion and so-called fact. You will see whole dynasties moved about through hundreds of years and anomalies such as tombs apparently built before the owner's birth. Many are the remaining mysteries. Yet sacred

Egyptian writings promise that one day all will be revealed.

Next I want to mention the names of the Pharaohs and how we know them. Firstly consider that we know the hieroglyphs were all consonants; there were no real vowels. So if we get a name like, Rmsss, it could be Ramesses, Romassis, Remosses and so on. So we are not entirely sure we are pronouncing the name as it was pronounced in those days, but that really is not very important since a name is merely a means of reference and providing we keep to the same name for the same person, we should not get too confused. Think of them as nicknames.

A lot of the information we rely on was written by historians of the past; in particular, we rely on them for lists of Pharaohs' names. The first person who wrote history was a son of the famous Ramesses II, called Khaemwese, who lived about 1250BC By this time the pyramids were ancient and the Valley of the Kings old. Khaemwese was actually a Magician and a High Priest of *Ptah*. He visited many tombs at Saqqara and studied books in the Royal Library. He was the one who chiselled the name of Unas on the pyramid at Saqqara and he also carved a message saying that it was he who carved the name, "since it was not found on the face of the pyramid, because the priest Khaemwese loved to restore the monuments of Upper and Lower Egypt".

In about 450BC a Greek writer called Herodotus visited Egypt and tried to sort out the fact from the fiction, basing his work on the results of discussions with people, in particular the priests. Herodotus had been born in Halicarnassus and travelled a lot and in his later life wrote a book called 'The Histories'. He is now considered the 'Father of History' and we rely upon his reports, although he was sometimes inaccurate, relying so much on hearsay. Some of his information, such as the time when the Pharaoh Cheops was said to have closed the temples, has since proved inaccurate, but his information on certain other Pharaohs, such as Amasis, is all we have. In fact we know very little about Herodotus himself. The lives of the writers were not recorded in great detail, or at least none have been found. We know that Herodotus was the son of Lyxes called Carian and Dryo. He seems to have been very much influenced by the Inonian culture of Greece and, in fact, Ionic was the language in which he wrote. His large volumes contained information on the geography, history and ethnography of Egypt. His observations in Egypt, at the time after the invasion by Cambyses, are invaluable. Herodotus wrote of Egypt "Such animals as there are in Egypt, both wild and tame, are held to be sacred".

During the reign of Ptolemy II, there lived a priest called Manetho (305–285BC) and it is to him we owe the division of the Pharonic times into 31 dynasties. Manetho wrote in Greek and took his information from surviving documents, now lost. He gave the ancient Pharaohs Greek names. Some of the dynasties he listed were contemporaneous with each other, there being one ruler in Upper Egypt and another in Lower Egypt. These were competing dynasties.

As well as dividing the large time span into dynasties modern day historians have divided it into periods. These are the approximate dates of the different periods:-

Archaic Period	3100–2686BC
Old Kingdom	2686–2181BC
First Intermediate Period	2181–2133BC
Middle Kingdom	2133–1633BC
Second Intermediate Period	1633–1567BC
New Kingdom	1567–1085BC
Third Intermediate Period	1085– 750BC
Late Period	750– 323BC
Ptolemaic Period	323– 30BC

As with most dates from ancient Egypt these are subjective.

During Roman times tourists were able to move around and visit many of the monuments, including the Pyramids and the Valley of the Kings and they often left graffiti to commemorate their interest. What were in those days simply uncalled-for scribbles on the monuments have become, to us, historic inscriptions in themselves!

In 25BC a Greek called Strabo wrote 17 books called 'Geographia'and although mainly about geography, the last book provides some interesting information. Strabo mentions the two huge statues of Amenophis III, on the West Bank at Thebes, known as the 'Colossi of Memnon'. They once flanked a large mortuary temple. In 27BC there was an earthquake which cracked the monuments and led to a very strange and eerie sound in the mornings. By the time Strabo arrived there were tales of the singing colossi! However, it is now known that it was caused by the morning temperature rise which made the insides of the statues vibrate as the warm air passed through the cracks. Strabo listed the names of towns, pyramids, tombs, temples and also made notes on the Nilometer at Elephantine, near Aswan. A very useful 2000 years old list.

In the years of the Roman occupation of Egypt there lived another historian, Pleny the Elder (27 -79AD) who wrote his 'Historia Naturalis', drawing from many older sources which have since disappeared. He described the Sphinx and obelisks (one of which was transported to Rome and stands there to this day) and mentions some of the techniques of preparation of mummies.

A few years later Plutarch (50–120AD) wrote an account of the myth of *Osiris* and *Isis*. This is very fortunate for us, since no original Egyptian version has survived until today.

At the same time a Roman historian, Flavius Josephus, wrote his own work using extracts from Manetho and making comments on Moses, the Exodus and the Hyksos invasion.

In the following few centuries AD, Egypt became a Christian country for a while. The Christians held no respect whatsoever for the monuments, destroying many of the inscriptions on temples and even scraping the paint off the walls of tombs. The Christians considered the ancient religions of Egypt to be evil. Monks who adapted tombs as their living quarters often defaced or obliterated the wall paintings.

By the time the Arabs arrived in Egypt in the 7th century AD, the population had forgotten all about the early civilisations and lost the ability to read the hieroglyphs. The Arabs, like the Christians, considered the monuments evil, thinking that the huge pyramids and statues had been built by giants or magicians. They ignored them, except when they wanted to destroy one, or take it apart for the materials for their new buildings and mosques.

In more recent times, especially since Napoleon Bonaparte's visit to Egypt in 1798AD, interest in the old cultures has regrown. There were several major explorers and discoverers who have contributed a tremendous amount to our knowledge. Belzoni (1778–1823AD) discovered the tomb of Aye, the magnificent tomb of Seti I and four others. He was also responsible for opening the Pyramid of Khephren and the discovery of the colossal statues of Ramesses II at Abu Simbel. His competitors, John Lewis Burckhart (1784–181AD), Bernardino Drovetti (1775–1852AD) and Henry Salt (1780–1827AD) were also very active in Egypt, often bringing items back to European museums. Drovetti, an Italian, made a major find, the Turin Canon of Kings.

Various people had tried to understand the hieroglyphs over the years. It was one William Warburton (1698–1779AD), who became the Bishop of Gloucester, who recognised that hieroglyphics was in fact a written language and not just symbolic. But none of his contemporaries liked his ideas much, sticking to the notion that it was a symbolic script which would be impossible to understand.

In 1741 William Stukely, a doctor and famous antiquarian who was active at Avebury and Salisbury (in England), founded the Egyptian Society in London. Interest in ancient Egypt became more widespread. Stukely had examined the hieroglyphs on a statue in Turin and concluded that they were completely different from Chinese characters, which 'experts' were claiming had been derived from the hieroglyphs. He claimed that it was a symbolic script and that the hieroglyphics were beyond understanding.

Napoleon's troops discovered the Rosetta Stone in Egypt. Wax impressions of the scripts (there were three on the stone – Hieroglyphs, Greek and Hieratic, which was an easier and quicker everyday form of hieroglyphs for everyday documents), were circulated amongst historians in Europe. The Stone itself was brought to Britain after the British troops had ousted Napoleon's men from Egypt in 1801, following Nelson's victory at the Battle of Aboukir.

Thomas Young (1773–1824) became fascinated by hieroglyphics and discovered the other written languages of Ancient Egypt. He realised that hieroglyphs were in fact alphabetical as well as ideogrammatic. He also suggested that the oval shaped Cartouche contained Royal Names, which we now know is true.

A major advance in our knowledge resulted from the decision made by Jean François Champollion to try to decipher the hieroglyphs. He spent his early years learning many languages and scripts, including Hebrew, Sanskrit, Arabic, Parsi, Persian, Zend, Pali, Chaldean and Coptic. He realised that the hieroglyphs were phonetic. When he eventually started to understand the inscriptions they were able to find out more about who owned what. In 1768 another great discoverer, James Bruce, had found a tomb in the Valley of the Kings but was not able to discover which Pharaoh it had belonged to. It turned out to have been Ramesses III's.

Robert Hay (1799–1863) constructed 49 volumes of beautiful and detailed drawings of the monuments. This is now housed in the British Museum. It was about this time that another keen investigator of antiquity founded 'Egyptology' in England. This was John Gardner Wilkinson, 1797–1875. Wilkinson excavated many tombs at Thebes, adding much to knowledge of the Pharaohs.

Egypt was now becoming a popular tourist attraction for the wealthy. Florence Nightingale visited the monuments of Luxor in 1849. When she saw the Colossus of Memnon on the west bank, she exclaimed that it did not look so big after all, and that it was consistent with its surroundings stating that she thought it is us who were the dwarves. Another who visited to Egypt was Mark Twain in 1869.

A Frenchman called Auguste Mariette (1821–1881AD) became interested in Egyptology after his son, Nestor l'Hôte, had been to Egypt with Champollion. He studied Egyptian writing and started building catalogues of items in the museum in Boulogne. He was then sent to Egypt himself, to collect rare manuscripts. He visited Saqqara and noticed the head of a sphinx sticking out of the sand and, having read Strabo's descriptions of an avenue of Sphinxes, decided to start digging. This resulted in the discovery of the avenue, several tombs and the Serapeum where the Sacred Bulls had been buried. These were sensational finds at the time, especially the finding of the mummified bulls. Mariette decided he would love to open a museum in Egypt itself and, after some political changes in Egypt, Mariette was offered the post of Director of Ancient Monuments. This was the start of the first Egyptian museum. He then initiated excavations all over Egypt, at thirty-five different locations, including Dier el-Bahari, Karnak, Thebes, Abydos, Esna and Elephantine. His work led to an international exhibition including the precious jewellery of Queen Ahhotep, which was found at Thebes. Unfortunately though, it may be that Mariette's enthusiasm for artefacts left a trail of damage and debris; seldom did explorers take care with how they worked, often using explosives instead of slower methods, to force entry, destroying untold valuable evidence of the past.

Until 1870 nobody (in the modern world) knew that Royal Mummies had been moved in the time of Ramesses X and XI, in the Valley of the Kings. The mummies were simply assumed to be missing or destroyed. It was Gaston Maspero (1846–1916AD) who rescued them after they had been discovered in a cache in 1871 by a local villager called Ahmed Abd er-Rasul, accidentally, while he was searching for a lost goat!

Since then there have been many Egyptologists working all over the country. People like Sir W. M. Flinders Petrie (1853–1942AD) and Howard Carter (1874–1939AD), a student of Petrie, have made monumental discoveries and filled museums in Egypt and around the world. There are 120,000 objects in the National Museum in Cairo. One could spend weeks roaming the corridors looking at statues, stele, small items, mummies, sarcophagi, papyri and so on. But without a very good guide book and, at least some ideas of who was who, one would probably be becoming more and more confused.

Petrie discovered tombs at Abydos, information on the Pharaoh Akhenaten and royal treasures from near the pyramid at Lahun. He also discovered over two thousand predynastic graves at a very ancient site, Nagada and the old city which had been given for the Greeks to live in, Naucratis. Howard Carter discovered, of course, the incredible tomb of Tutankhamun, amongst others, in the Valley of the Kings.

An American, George Reisner (1867–1942) was responsible for finding the tomb of the IVth dynasty Queen Hetepheres at Giza and the Valley temple of Menkaure and mastaba graves of nobles on the same site.

Mummies had become a valuable commodity in Europe and Asia, because people believed they had medicinal properties, which led to the exportation of mummies on a massive scale. One wonders which of the ancient Pharaohs and nobles were eaten in Europe, to cure a wide range of ailments such as coughs, nausea, ulcers, concussion and abscesses! The word mummy, derived from the Persian for bitumen, was often confused with bitumen itself. Even the King Francis I of France carried some ground up mummy, mixed with rhubarb, to cure his aches and pains. In 1809 Queen Victoria was given a gift of a mummy from the King of Persia. By the 18th century trade in mummies was so huge that it had to be made illegal.

As for the names of the Pharaohs, we rely on several sources, which together still do not give us a complete list. These are:-

(a) Manetho, who wrote Greek versions of the names.
(b) The Turin Canon of Kings, also known as the Turin Papyrus, now in the Museum of Turin. This is a Hieratic papyrus from the time of Ramesses II, which, although ruined gave us eighty to ninety Kings' names.
(c) The Gallery of Lists in the Temple of Seti I at Abydos shows seventy-six ancestors of the Pharaoh Seti.
(d) The Table of Karnak from the time of Tuthmosis III, discovered in 1825, originally held sixty-one names but not all have survived to be read.
(e) The Table at Saqqara originally had fifty-seven names but only fifty are legible now.
(f) The Palermo Stone, badly broken, held the names of the first five dynasties and went back into pre-dynastic times, listing also the lengths of the Pharaoh's reigns. It was originally compiled in the fifth dynasty. There are only five surviving pieces, now housed in museums in Cairo, the Palermo Museum and in the private collection of Petrie in the University College London.

Having several lists to refer to has both enabled Egyptologists to try to make a complete list and complicated matters further! This is because the Pharaohs each had more than one name and different lists refer to different names. In fact some finds previously attributed to two different Pharaohs are now known to be the work of one with two different names. Added to that is the fact that the ancient historians used other different names, even Greek versions and it is names like these that are often recognised today, like Cheops who was probably called Khufu. The works of the ancient historians such as Manetho have not survived, but were copied by later historians and not always copied well. It is particularly confusing for the first and second dynasties – dates are uncertain, names are changed, lengths of reigns are different in different lists. The first few Pharaohs offer a very small amount of evidence as to who they were exactly. We call the first Pharaoh Menes, but his hieroglyphs reveal the name Narmer. We do not know whether these names belonged to the same man or not. Before Narmer or Menes we believe there was a great pre-dynastic conqueror called Scorpion and after Narmer there was a Pharaoh now known as Hor-Aha. These names may apply to one, two, three or four different Kings, or for that matter even whole tribes. Apart from these names we actually know very little about the individual Pharaohs. We know some were great warriors and conquered other lands, whilst some seemed to have been peacemakers. Yet others were weak and under the thumbs of noblemen. One or two were very different, such as Akhenaten, who changed the religion and was later regarded as a heretic. There are a few stories which have come down to us from ancient times, which tell us that so-and-so was a cruel king or a kind king. It seems that the Pharaohs of dynasty four were quite cruel men, at the time of the building of the massive pyramids of Giza, although there were very few slaves. Mostly it seems that the local peoples worshipped the Pharaohs as gods, at least in the very early periods. As I have said we know very little and have to guess a lot.

Pharaohs of the first dynasty by the publications of the twentieth century show the comparisons and the different orders:

Reisner	Smoith	Hall	Weigall	Petrie	Hayes
Hor-Aha*	Narmer*	Scorpion*	Hor-Aha*	Narmer	Narmer*
Narmer	= Menes	= Hor-Aha		Narmer	Hor-Aha*
Zer	Zer	Zer	Zer	Zer	Zer
Uadji	Uadji	Uadji	Uadji	Uadji	Uadji
Udimu	Udimu	Udimu	Udimu	Udimu	Udimu
Enezib	Enezib	Enezib	Enezib	Enezib	Enezib
Semerkhet	Semerkhet	Semerkhet	Semerkhet	Semerkhet	Semerkhet
Ka'a	Ka'a	Ka'a	Ka'a	Ka'a	Ka'a

* called Menes

Despite the vagueness and fuzziness of Egyptology and the large lists of strange names, it is this uncertainty which can lead to the fascination of unravelling it all. We are talking of a period of time longer than we are since Jesus and, apart from the Bible, there is little evidence of Him either. It can sometimes be far more enjoyable than knowing for sure, just like the fun of the jigsaw puzzle is in putting it all together.

Over the years the tombs and monuments of Ancient Egypt have continually suffered from tourists and explorers alike. From olden times finds have been exported from Egypt, both for museums and private collections. As well as removing and destroying mummies, deliberate damage was done to tombs and monuments by Christians and Moslems. In more modern times damage has been done accidentally by tourists. The fantastic tomb wall paintings of Nefertari, for instance, has suffered terribly form the results of thousands of tourists simply breathing! The salts in their breath have started to crystallise on top of the paint and chemicals in the rocks have crystallised under the paint, due to humidity. So the beautiful images have started falling apart, which, fortunately in this case, led to the closing of the tomb to the public and reparation work by experts. Other problems are solved far less easily, or maybe not at all, being caused by atmospheric pollution from 20th century factories. What little rain falls around Giza today is acid rain. Bits have been falling off the Sphinx, no longer hidden by sands, and have to be stuck back on. Another point of interest here is the face of the Sphinx. In all honesty it's very ugly! It was actually badly damaged by invading Mameluks who decided to use it to test their canons! It is amazing it still stands at all, this 'Father of Time' as the Arabs call it.

If you visit Egypt and pay entrance fees to museums or tombs and pyramids, you can do so with the awareness that your money is going towards saving these precious monuments from the ancient past. Once they have gone they will never be built again!

3

THE ANCIENT EGYPTIANS

The Ancient Egyptians believed that the world was once ruled by gods in the 'The first time', which they called 'Zep Tepi'. They believed that this was when the waters of the abyss receded, the primordial darkness grew light and the human race learned cultivation. They believed there had been intermediaries between the gods and men, called Urshu, or watchers, who had supernatural powers and, although mortal, they could appear as man, woman, child, animal, bird, plant or tree. The first divine Pharaohs were considered to have been *Ra, Shu, Geb, Osiris, Horus* and *Thoth*. The historian Manetho wrote "After the gods, demigods reigned for 1255 years, then another line of kings for 1817 years, then came thirty more kings reigning for 1790 years, then again ten kings ruling for 350 years. There followed the rule of the Spirits of the Dead for 5813 years". The kings who ruled after the gods have been called the 'Followers of *Horus*'.

Egyptian legends told that the area had been governed by a very great King, called *Osiris*, who eventually became deified, which means people started regarding him as a living god. He was said to have taught men to grow corn and applied himself to civilising his subjects, taking them from their barbarous ways. The pre-dynastic Egyptians – those are the ones before the Pharaohs – were farmers. The very dry desert sand where the dead were buried enabled the bodies to be preserved and over recent years examinations have been performed on them. Professor G. Elliot Smith has examined stomachs to see if he could find out what the people of those days used to eat. Not particularly a pleasant job that, looking in someone's stomach 5000 or 6000 years after they were dead, but scientists do very strange and unpleasant things in their search for knowledge and it's often a good job they do, or we wouldn't know half of what we do about our past. Anyway, the Prof' found barley husks and some millet, so we know man ate these and that he cultivated them. The strange part is that it is considered unlikely that mankind would ever have started doing this by instinct alone, or by accident, as unlikely as it would be for an ape to get some seeds, clear a patch and plant a banana tree! So who told him how to do it? *Osiris?* Maybe.

Being able to grow food meant that mankind became able to move about more and settle in places where there was otherwise little to eat. Equally, people could stay in their favourite place without having to worry so much about food or water running out. Not to say that there weren't good years of plenty and bad years of famine, natural disasters and all the dangers from wild animals and human enemies, diseases and all sorts of things to make a family want to move. But, being able to stay in one place and stay about the village more often, meant a growth in the population.

Society and villages always need something to hold them together and this is often religion, which in this case was *Osiris,* the life principle, who also controlled the Nile and thus was responsible for flooding and the fertile silt left behind afterwards and thus the crops and thus the life of the village. Egyptian religion also told that *Osiris* travelled around a lot, teaching the whole world. The cult of *Osiris* worship lasted throughout the times of the Pharaohs until the Greeks adopted and renamed him as their god *Dionysus.*

Larger quantities of food also meant trade with other peoples and other countries. Even before 3000BC the Egyptians had boats, first just reed rafts, then papyrus boats with oars, which enabled them to cross the seas. From a few small seeds mighty empires can grow.

To help them decide when it was best to plant, when the Nile was due to flood (which meant moving up onto high ground) and when to harvest best, the Egyptians learned to measure the flow of time and account the seasons. They developed a calendar which was used for thousands of years, until changed slightly by Julius Caesar. It is this same calendar, changed again by Pope Gregory, which is used around the world today.

The farmers also needed to measure how far the Nile would rise and invented a measuring device, which was a series of marks, called a Nilometer. They were placed at various points on the Nile and used to record the height each year to see if there was any regularity. Nilometers were used throughout Egyptian history, right up until the 20th century Aswan Dam project and several can still be seen in Egypt. There is one in Cairo where you can go down steps and see the whole measure and just how high the Nile would flood. It was marked so the lower level meant a poor flood and hence a poor crop, the middle was good, but the high level would have meant people down river running for their lives.

What little information we have about pre-dynastic Egypt comes from fragments of pottery and items found in the basic graves. In Lower Egypt, Neolithic sites around the Fayum Lake and at Merimba near the South-Western edge of the Delta have revealed remains of houses and signs of farming with crops and domesticated animals. In Upper Egypt, some metal objects from what we call the Badarian culture, have been unearthed, along with beads made from malachite.

Research and digging at other pre-dynastic sites such as Maadi (near Cairo) and Minshat Abu Omar in the Delta and southern sites, possibly contemporaneous, such as Naqada I and Naqada II, has produced important finds, now mostly in museums around the globe. Finds at Maadi indicate there was contact with the South and trading with people from what is now Palestine and Syria. At Minshat Abu Omar finds similar to items found at Naqada II have suggested a somewhat peaceful co-existence between Upper and Lower Egypt, which conflicts with the general belief that Egypt became united as a result of warfare.

Pottery found at all these sites has been dated using the modern carbon 14 dating technique. This is the only non-archaeological method of dating remains. There was nothing written down, at the time, to be found. There were also, however, many bits of pottery and ornaments and figurines with representations of animals, fish and birds. These include hippopotami, crocodiles, lions, cows, bulls, snakes, dogs, hares and the *Seth* animal (which I will mention again later); in fact the oldest found representation of the *Seth* animal was found at El Mahasna. Pottery models of boats have also been found.

In Upper Egypt many of the sites investigated were burial sites, although recently more burial sites in the Delta have been examined. Many northern sites were remains of settlements. It is apparent that at Merimba the people lived in oval houses with mud walls, the house often being partly below ground level. Thompson and Gardner found remains of grain silos and hearths in villages in the Fayum Oasis area. At El Omari there were round huts and burial pits. At Maadi there seem to have been underground storage cellars, along with oval huts.

The Ancient Egyptians developed their round and oval house structures into rectangular shapes, in particular at El Tarif and at Hierakonpolis and the shapes of the graves changed accordingly. An important find from the Naqada II period, now in the British Museum, is a model of a rectangular house. The original house is estimated to have been about 26 feet by 18 feet.

The shapes of the burial pits seem to have matched the shapes of the houses. Bodies were buried with consistent orientation within each area and period. The bodies were covered, often in a foetal position and accompanied by pottery and jewellery such as combs, figurines, hairpins and slate palettes for cosmetics. Pieces of leather have also been unearthed.

Over the years there seems to have developed a variation in the size and quality of graves within the villages, suggesting the development of some sort of class division. At Hierakonpolis there is a tomb with walls painted with men, animals and boats.

Many of the bodies found were quite well preserved, due to the natural dryness of the desert, a fore-runner to mummification. From examinations of the bodies it is thought that constipation was a major problem for people and that circumcision was common. Some of the bodies found still have hair, such as the remains of a man now known as 'Ginger' mentioned elsewhere.

It is from these remains that Egyptologists get their limited information and then guess the rest. I cannot emphasise enough just how little knowledge we really have and just how much is theory and mystery. That is the fun of the subject at hand, that is the unravelling of the mystery

At about 3400BC Egypt changed from a conglomeration of separate and often feuding tribes living along the Nile and in the Delta, to two well organised monarchies, that is Upper Egypt (the Nile river) and Lower Egypt, each with its own King, crown, customs and gods, although some gods were worshipped by both.

Then, around about 3000BC, a very strong tribe arrived in Egypt, led by a powerful warrior called King Scorpion, who subjugated both Upper and Lower Egypt. Egypt, now united under one King instead of being two distinct kingdoms, advanced very rapidly indeed. All of a sudden the Egyptians used writing and studied astronomy, medicine, architecture and what we can only refer to as magic.

Nobody knows for sure where these people came from. Some believe they came from Libya, from outer space, or were gods and others even say they came from Atlantis, although there's no proof that Atlantis ever existed at all. Atlantis is said to have been a very ancient island or continent inhabited by an advanced (possibly technologically) civilisation, of which there is no definite trace. It has been suggested that ruins of Atlantis may lie beneath the ice at one of the poles and that the city may have been destroyed due to a massive movement of the Earth in its orbit around the sun or on its axis. This, it is claimed, caused ice at the poles to melt, a world-wide flood and the covering of Atlantis (then at the new pole) with ice. It is certain that there has been severe changes in the Earth's climate. Marine fossils have been found in deserts and fossil fuel in Siberia (suggesting that Siberia had once been covered with forests – now it is barren). But wherever the invaders came from they were a lot more clever than the simple natives in Egypt and it didn't take long to beat the natives down and take over Egypt for themselves.

The earliest Kings of Egypt were referred to as the 'Followers of *Horus*'. Remains have been found in predynastic graves, of a larger and maybe superior type of man to the natives, with a larger body and larger head, quite distinct from the majority of the locals and from the people who previously inhabited the area. This is thought to suggest two distinct races, the invaders and the natives, who seemed to merge racially. But where exactly those larger men came from remains a mystery. Evidence suggests they were an external invader, as paintings found in tombs at Hieraconpolis and the style of work on an ivory knife handle found at Gebel-el-Arak, with depiction of a sea battle with invaders, shows. There are, for instance, two distinct type of ship shown, the Egyptian type and a strange type not seen before.

All in all this was not such a bad thing for the development of the human race. Egypt was united into one land with one King, Aha or Narmer, who may have been the same person, or the same person as Scorpion! Narmer's people brought with them writing and reading abilities, mathematics, medicine, weapons and a lot more. Narmer advanced from his city in the south, Abydos or Thinis, and subdued the Lord of the Delta. There is an old stone tablet in Cairo Museum, called the Narmer Palette, depicting Narmer beating down his enemies. On it he claims to have captured 126,000 men, 400,000 oxen and 1442 goats. He was the first King of the whole of Egypt, the founder of the first dynasty and recognised as all powerful Pharaoh of Upper Egypt in the South and Lower Egypt in the North. There had been two different crowns, the Red Crown and the White Crown, but Narmer

THE NARMER PALETTE

THE RED CROWN THE WHITE CROWN

wore a Crown which, for the first time, was a combination of the two. The king of Upper Egypt had worn the white crown with a vulture as the emblem, whereas the king of Lower Egypt wore the red crown with the head of a cobra. The vulture and the cobra were ancient gods. Later Pharaohs wore either of the three different Crowns.

Narmer and a whole line of successors stretching over thousands of years called themselves Pharaohs, or in the Egyptian language something like *"Per aa"*, which means 'Great House'. Narmer made a special crown to signify his rule, combining the 2 crowns of Lower and Upper Egypt and also wore the URAEUS, the symbol of divinity, on his head. The White Crown was like a sort of high conical hat, whereas the Red Crown was like a flat topped cap with a tall piece projecting from the back and a long curved feather coming forwards. The combination of these produced the Great Double Crown, which bore both cobra and vulture. Often the Pharaoh would wear a different crown depending on whether he was in Upper or Lower Egypt.

The Uraeus was in the form of a cobra which was worn around the crown and symbolised the goddess *Buto*, who was sometimes identified with the goddess *Hathor*. The name *Hathor* is composed of Hat and *Horus* and the Pharaoh was considered to be the manifestation of *Horus* on earth. The king was represented in the Uraeus by the sun disk, sustained by the wings of the vulture goddess *Nekhebet* and protected by the fire-spitting tongue of *Buto*. The two main gods worshipped by the two parts of Egypt were *Seth* and *Horus* and the battle between these two (maybe representing the unification of Egypt), was retold on monuments throughout the three thousand years of ancient history in Egypt.

One important aspect of the Pharaohs was that succession was matrilineal. It was the eldest daughter who would pass on the crown. In order to keep the throne in the family this often meant a brother marrying his mother, sister or even his own daughter and often successive Pharaohs took the same queen. For example, Amenophis III married his daughter, Situmun.

The name Narmer, when translated, means 'Catfish-Chisel', although nobody knows why he was called this. Maybe he had whiskers like a catfish. Or maybe he was as hard as a chisel. The Pharaohs of this, the first dynasty, often had meaningful names, such as Djer which means 'Stockade' and Den, which means 'Killer'. They all wanted to sound strong, like all military men and warriors.

Actually the Pharaohs had five parts to their name, the whole of which together is called the 'titular name'. The first part of the name was the *Horus* name and was usually written in a rectangle, possible representing the palace, surmounted by the falcon *Horus*; several Pharaohs such as Peribsen replaced the falcon by the *Seth* animal and some, such as Khasekhemui, used both. The second name was the 'Nebty' or 'Nebti' name or 'Two Ladies' name, representing the vulture goddess *Nekhebet* of Upper Egypt and the cobra goddess *Buto* of Lower Egypt, which was a constant reminder of the unity and interdependence of the two lands. The third part of the titular name was the Golden *Horus* name, the significance of which is not truly understood today. Between this and the fourth name was a title which read "He who belongs to the Sedge and the Bee", again symbolising the two lands of Upper and Lower Egypt. The fourth name was the 'prenomen', the Pharaoh's principal name; after the time of Cheops this was often joined with the name of the sun god *Re*. The fifth name was the 'nomen', preceded by "Son of *Re*", usually a family name of the dynasty or a personal name of the King before he ascended the throne. The prenomen and nomen were normally enclosed in separate cartouches, or ovals.

Here is an example of the full titular name of Tuthmosis III, as it would appear if in English: 'Strong-Bull-arising-in-

Thebes (Horus); Enduring-of-Kingship-like-*Re*-in-heaven (Two Ladies); Powerful-of-Valour-and-Holy-of-Diadems (Golden Horus); King of Upper and Lower Egypt (Sedge and Bee); Menkheper-*Re* (prenomen); Son of *Re*, Tuthmosis-Beautiful-of-Appearance, Beloved of Hathor, Lady of Turquoise (nomen).'

In addition to all these names we have the added confusion today of being faced with the Greek versions of many names used by the ancient historian Manetho, such as Cheops, Cheophren, Sethos, Amophis etc. Different authors use different names, or even spell the same name differently. It is really a matter of choice which name to use, provided we all know who we are talking about! I have chosen to use the most popular names in this work.

The Pharaoh's people also brought with them their own religion, which proclaimed the Pharaoh as a sort of living god, to overshadow the simple religious beliefs of the natives, who mostly worshipped animals and birds. In many ways Narmer's gods were not that different from the locals' gods in the early days However, the new rulers believed that most of the gods could manifest or appear either as an animal or as a humanoid with an animal or bird head. Some gods could also appear as a man or woman. They believed that thousands of years before themselves, the earth was populated by gods, who were called names like *Osiris*, *Isis*, *Seth*, *Horus*, *Hathor* and *Ptah* and lots of others. You will read a few interesting and very old stories about some of the gods.

Egyptian religion and mythology are actually very complicated topics because the ancient Egyptians believed in a whole range of gods and several distinct systems existed at various times. Egyptian religion and magic came from pre-dynastic times. They believed that the sky, earth, air and underworld were populated by a whole range of gods, both visible and invisible, which possessed many human characteristics, passions, emotions and weaknesses. They thought that it was possible to get magical powers transferred from the gods to themselves, so that they could compel the gods to do their wishes.

When Dynasty 1 was established at a place called Memphis, just outside modern Cairo, to the South, the priesthood decided that their creator god, *Ptah*, should be made the highest. Unlike the other beliefs which we will come to, these priests believed that the world had been created out of the mind of *Ptah* and His Word. In the British Museum in London there is a very old basalt stone, called the *Shabaka Stone*, which comes from the reign of Shabaka, 716–702BC, but which had actually been copied from a much older text.

Unfortunately, as has happened with so many ancient artefacts, the block has been used for other purposes and partially ruined, but archaeologists have been able to decipher the gist of this story of creation. The story starts with struggle between the two gods, *Horus* and *Seth*, for control of the whole of Egypt and the struggle finally ended in the 'Balance of the Two Lands', represented in a Temple of *Ptah* at Memphis. *Ptah* then created the other gods, including Atum from his heart and tongue. *Ptah* himself remained supreme and gave life and soul – *Kha* – to all the gods. *Ptah* then created the earth and everything in it, built cities, divided Egypt into districts and placed the gods in their shrines. *Ptah* is represented in ancient drawings as a mummified man holding a staff in his hand, with an amulet around his neck.

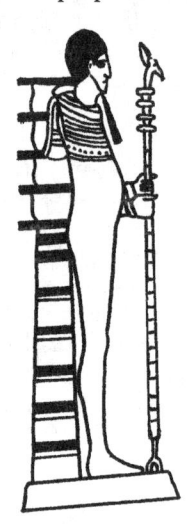

PTAH

Another system of belief regarding the creation was that adopted by the priests of the ancient city of Heliopolis. Heliopolis was called Innu or Innu Mehret and in the Bible it is called the City of On. In this theology gods are grouped together in what is called an *Ennead*. There is a record of this, on papyrus, in the British Museum, translation of which reveals the following story.

In the beginning there was nothing but the watery waste of *Nun*; no light, no darkness and no earth. Then, within this waste, something moved. It was the god Atum who took the form of *Khephre*, the rising sun. In order to have something to rest on he made a piece of solid land, which was like a small island rising out of the waters. *Atum* then created two more lesser gods to help him, *Shu* and *Tefnut* the God of Air and the Goddess of Moisture. They, in turn, created *Geb* the Earth God and *Nut* the Sky Goddess. These two created the world and had four children, *Osiris*, *Seth*, *Isis* and Nephthys. *Nut*, however, had been cursed by the god *Re* so that her children were not to be born on any day of the year, which must have made it very difficult for *Nut*, but the god *Thoth*, the reckoner of time, got together with Aah the Moon god and managed to create five days that were outside of the year and so did not count. The children were born on these days.

Each of these gods had responsibilities and were all extremely important to the Pharaohs. The names are often incorporated into the name of the Pharaoh, such as Ramesses (*Ra* or *Re*), Tuthmosis (*Thoth*), Seti (*Seth*), Amenophis (*Amun*) and so on. As you read this and come across the names of Pharaohs, see if you can pick out the parts which are names of gods.

Without wishing to confuse you with too many names and beliefs I cannot avoid mentioning the Creation according to

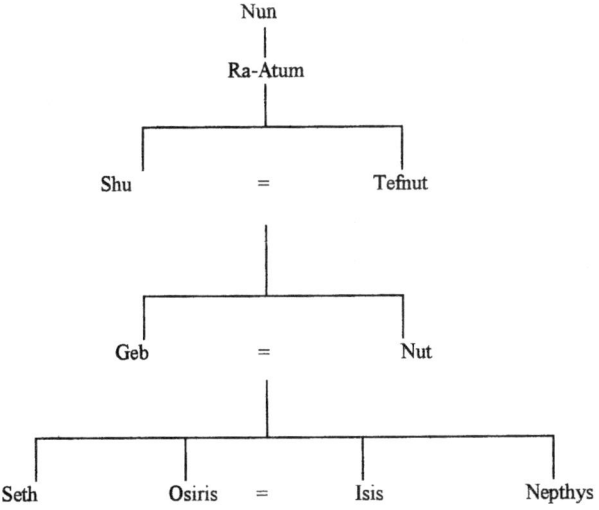

the people of Hermopolis, a city of Middle Egypt. Here there were no less than eight gods worshipped, known as the *Ogdoad of Hermopolis*. These were *Nu, Nunet, Amun, Amunet, Heh, Hehut, Ke* and *Kekut*. Notice how the names are in pairs, representing male and female aspects. These are amongst the oldest of the Egyptian gods. It was believed that the original mound of earth appeared at Hermopolis and this was where the Sun god first stood, having been created by the Ogdoad. Associated with them was *Thoth*, the God of Wisdom, called in Egyptian *Djhuti*, who was said to have invented writing. In the judgement scene on the walls of tombs, where the dead Pharaoh is having his soul weighed against a feather, to test for purity, it is *Thoth* who checks the scales. There is no creation story for *Thoth*.

Of course there must have been a lot of arguments between the priests of Hermopolis and those of Heliopolis who had a much more complete story and, at some point, the priests of Heliopolis seem to have won and their religion became the more widespread.

Much later the Pharaoh called Akhenaten, who ruled with his wife Nefertiti from BC 1352 to 1344, changed the state religion. He adopted his god *Aten* as the god of Egypt, which didn't please the priests of the old religion (themselves politically very powerful men) and he forced them to close down their temples of *Amun*. Akhenaten believed that there was only one god, *Aten*, the Sun and even today, in Cairo museum and on walls in tombs, we can see pictures of the great sun god beaming down on Akhenaten and Nefertiti. Akhenaten had his name changed from Amenophis IV (Amenhotep IV). One very interesting point is that Akhenaten also changed the style of art for the first time. Throughout all the dynasties of Egypt art stayed remarkably consistent and the Pharaoh was always represented as a perfect being. Akhenaten, however, had himself represented in a

THOTH

much different way and , whether true to life or not, the several statues and paintings of him in the Museum of Egyptian Antiquities in Cairo reveal a very grotesque and deformed Pharaoh. However, these changes did not last long and within thirty years of his death the priests of the old religion of *Amun* managed to persuade his successor, Tutankhaten, to change the state religion back again, re-open the temples and reinstate the priests and even to change his own name to the one we now recognise as Tutankhamun. There are paintings of Tutankhaten with *Aten* in the museum too.

Because the Ancient Egyptians were so preoccupied with death and the afterlife they always buried a whole lot of goods, including food and drink, trinkets, furniture, boats and in the early days even slaves, with the dead Pharaoh for him to use in the afterlife. Some of the Pharaohs lived quite a long time but others died of natural causes when still young. Others were killed by their enemies. They were all buried in tombs near their religious centres and many of these tombs can be seen in Egypt even today. The first dynasty Pharaohs were buried at a great religious centre that they established at Abydos and their tombs can be seen there today, although in poor condition. There was sometimes a second tomb built, somewhere else, to house the soul or *Kha* of the Pharaoh. The *Kha* was like a spirit-double and it was necessary to make offerings to this spirit too.

There were thousands of tombs built, not only for the Pharaohs, but for their wives (they often had more than one each) and daughters, noblemen, scribes etc. The earliest tombs of the Pharaohs were underground, with a raised mud-brick surround and are now called 'Mastabas', which is an Arabic word for bench.

For convenience Egyptian history has been divided into a number of dynasties. It is a largely arbitrary way of dividing up the several thousand years that the Egyptian Pharaohs spanned and the very first Pharaohs were in dynasty 1. When a Pharaoh died his successor was chosen from amongst his surviving male relatives. The throne was actually passed down through the female side of the family to the eldest daughter, so the eldest son or desired heir would have to legitimise his claim by marriage. Dynasties often contain members of the same families. The Pharaohs' families were very strange in themselves as the Pharaoh often took his dead father's wife as his own wife (married his mother) and sometimes even his sisters or his aunts. It must have been very confusing when his mother, sister and aunt were also his wives. Sometimes a Vizier or a General of the army would succeed to the throne.

These ancient but advanced Egyptian people were also very good at writing and mathematics. They wrote mostly in little pictures of men, animals, birds and wavy lines – some of them a bit strange looking, but it worked well for thousands of years until they were defeated by foreign invaders and their writing was unfortunately no longer understood. These little pictures we now call Hieroglyphics. Many have been found in Egypt on stone tablets and on the walls in tombs. Some have even been found on a type of paper, called Papyrus, which was made by criss-crossing and pressing flat a type of grass – called papyrus – which grew by the Nile. This was probably the first paper in the world. Before papyrus was invented people carved on wood, on clay tablets and on stone. It seems quite remarkable but this same plant which enabled them to make paper also provided material to make boats. These boats were sailed up and down the Nile and into the Mediterranean enabling the Egyptians to trade with other ancient races like the Greeks.

Here you can see the names of two famous rulers of Egypt, written in hieroglyphics.

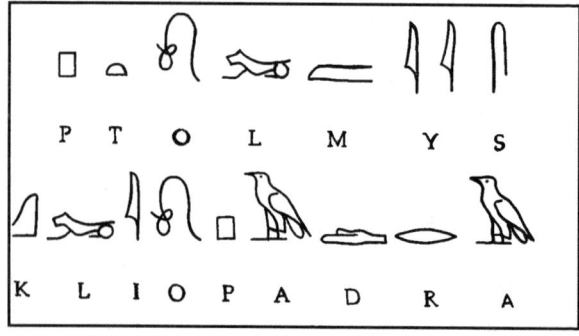

HIEROGLYPHICS OF PTOLEMY AND CLEOPATRA

The hieroglyphics are read either forwards or backwards from the direction in which the birds or animals face.

Hieroglyphics were translated to reveal religious works, essays on morality, letters, hymns, poems, stories, deeds of sale, magical and medical treatises, geographical and astronomical records and even romance stories. Before we understood them there were huge gaps in our knowledge of the ancient past. Now we know a little more – or at least we think we do.

4

GODS AND GODDESSES

The Ancient Egyptians were very preoccupied with death and spent much of their lives preparing for it by learning spells and prayers to utter at the right times, building their tombs in readiness and learning to recognise all the gods and goddesses, who, you will see, there were plenty of. It seems that the people were very attached to the green fertile land and lived in dread of having nothing in the afterlife and so spent a lot of time trying to ensure that they had supplies of all of life's luxuries. They believed in every god but different people had different favourites, as did the Pharaohs. Most Pharaohs actually took the names of gods to include as part of their own names : Tuthmosis took the name *Thoth*, Ramesses took the name *Ra* and so on. Certain gods were worshipped by priests who were sometimes so politically powerful that they could select the next Pharaoh and see their religion as the state religion. They wanted extra money to build and run their temples and probably to make themselves very rich.

The people believed that at one time, about 10,000 years earlier, some of the gods and goddesses walked and ruled on earth. There were stories told about how the gods behaved, took wives and/or consorts, had children by various supernatural means and had arguments and battles. Many of the gods could manifest in human form, with or without the head of a bird or animal, or in the form of the bird or animal. Amongst the animal and bird heads appearing on Egyptian gods and goddesses are the bull, cat, cow, crocodile, dog-faced ape, donkey, falcon, frog, hippopotamus, ibis, jackal, lion, lioness, ram, scarab beetle, scorpion, serpent, vulture, wolf and an unknown but evil creature representing *Seth*.

The gods which seemed to have appeared earliest in the prehistoric period were *Horus*, who seemed to have arrived with the early conquering Pharaohs and *Seth* who seemed to have been indigenous to the already present population. In the eastern delta the god *Osiris* supplanted the local god *Andjti*, inheriting his double plume and crook. Each main part of Ancient Egypt adopted their favourite god, as did individual localities. Many gods were fused together and even mixed up. In the many capitals of prehistoric Egypt there were several major gods worshipped by the local populations. In Heliopolis they worshipped *Re* or *Ra,* in Memphis it was *Ptah* the creator, in Busiris it was *Osiris*, whilst in Coptos they worshipped *Min* the fertility god. During the second dynasty the gods *Re* and *Horus*, the son of *Osiris* and *Isis*, were amalgamated into a god who was to remain important throughout Ancient Egyptian history – *Re-Harakhte*. The Pharaohs were regarded as divine sons of *Re*, the living form of *Horus*.

Certain gods had special responsibilities, such as *Thoth* who was concerned with writing and learning and presided over the weighing of the dead Pharaoh's soul. He was the God of Wisdom and is depicted as wearing on his head the crescent moon and disk, often carrying the writing reed and palette of the scribes. *Thoth* was one of the Moon Gods and the Reckoner of Time. At Hermopolis he was considered the head of an *'Ennead'* of eight gods who were the primordial deities. The name *Thoth* was probably derived from the early name for the ibis, *tehu*, which is the bird head which *Thoth* uses, although it may have been the other way round. He was also associated with baboons. He was also known as 'Lord of the Sacred Words' and often acted as a messenger of the gods. In fact thousands of years later he became *Hermes* to the Ptolemies. He was regarded as either having been created from the heart of *Re* or even to have created himself. He was an extremely important god because it was believed that he supervised the weighing of the soul of the dead Pharaoh against a feather and the judgement of the Pharaoh's deeds.

There were two other gods associated with writing but to a lesser extent. *Sheshat* was believed to have recorded tales of the Pharaohs' campaigns and jubilees and to have kept count of the cattle. She also kept count of how long the Pharaoh had reigned and she was represented on earth by a priestess who did her jobs and acted as a librarian at the temples. The other goddess connected with writing was *Sefkhet-Abwy*, who came along in the 18th dynasty and was represented as a woman with a seven pointed star on her head, usually under an inverted bow. She was believed to encourage writing and concerned herself with 'Stretching the Cord' which was a ceremony in which the king measured the ground ready for building a temple.

As you will see from the list of gods and goddesses to follow, there are a lot, in fact over 2000 of them, although many are representations of the same gods in different forms.

AMON-RE

RE

The gods, male and female, were not generally thought of as good or bad and had quarrels amongst themselves and faults of their own. It was some comfort, apparently, to the Ancient Egyptians, to know the gods had human characteristics. There were celestial gods, terrestrial gods and infernal gods, as well as inferior gods.

The Pharaohs incorporated the names of three goddesses into yet another of their names, the three ladies name.

Here is a long list of most of the important gods and goddesses:

LIST OF MAIN EGYPTIAN GODS

AKER	A cosmic god with the fore parts of a lion joined together facing each other.
AMEN	See Amun.
AMUN/AMUN-RE	Amun-Re : 2 plumes, sometimes ithyphallic. King of the Gods. Sometimes blue skinned. Main deity of Thebes.
AMAUNET	Female counterpart of Amun.
ANAT	Canaanite goddess.
ANDJTI	God of the eastern delta, with double plume and shepherds' crook, supplanted by Osiris.
ANUBIS	Recumbent dog or jackal, or dog headed; white crown with gazelle horns. God of mummification.
APIS	Sacred bull of Memphis, with markings and sun-disk. Regarded as incarnation of Ptah.
ASTARTE	Canaanite goddess (like Aphrodite of the Greeks).
ATUM	Primeval Creator.
BASTET	Lioness/Cat headed war goddess; = Sekhemet; worshipped at Bubastis.
BES	Dwarf with mask-like face, often with a crown of feathers and lion's mane; protector of pregnant women and of children.
BA-NEB-TETET	Ram God of Mendes/ Memphis.
BUCHIS	Bull incarnation of Ptah.
DUAMUTEF	Son of Horus; jackal-headed.

GEB	God of Earth.
HARISHAF	Ram or ram headed.
HARSAPHERES	Ram or ram headed.
HAPI	Son of Horus; ape-headed.
HAPI	God of the Nile, seldom portrayed, thought to live in a grotto above the first cataract. Both male and female
HATHOR	Sun disk, cows horns and head; goddess of women,
	sky goddess, tree goddess; deity of Amenti.
	Necropolis goddess of Thebes, Dendera and Abu Simbel.
HARPOKRATES	Naked child with finger in mouth, side lock of hair, Son of Isis and Osiris.
HEKET	Frog-headed goddess of birth.
HORUS	Hawk headed, double crown; appears in various forms
	sky God; son of Isis and Osiris. Local deity of Edfu.
HORUS OF BEHEDITE	The winged disk form of Horus.
IMHOTEP	Deified architect of Djoser's pyramid; Patron of scribes; healer, sage & magician. Regarded as son of Ptah and woman KHREDU'ANKH.
IMSETY	Son of Horus; human headed.
ISIS	Woman crowned with sun-disk surmounted by throne, sometimes enclosed between horns; wife of Osiris. guardian & magician. Her soul resided in Sothis, the Dog-Star. Adored at Abydos and Philae.

KA/KHA	The human soul.
KHENTAMENTI	Wolf or jackal, protector of the dead, at Abydos.
KHEM	Mummified human form, wearing head-dress of Amun-Re; right hand hold up flail; god of productiveness and generation. Chief deity of Khemnis. Later identified with Amun as Amen-Khem.
KHEPERA	A scarab god also signifying "he who becomes". In Helioplolis represented the rising sun.
KHNUM	Ram or ram headed god who created man on his potter's wheel.
	Also called Kneph, or Knouphis. The soul of the gods.
	Worshipped at Elephantine and the cataracts.
KHONSU	Moon god. Child's side-lock of hair, moon crescent, mummiform.
	Hawk-headed, crowned with sun disk. Stands on crocodile.
MATIT/MEHIT	Lioness goddess of Hieraconpolis and Thinis, with three or four bent bars projecting from her back.
MEFDET	A cat goddess, later a female figure clad in a cat's skin; protectress against snake bites.
MESKHEMET	Goddess presiding at childbirth.
MIN	Cap with 2 plumes & ribbon, mummiform & ithyphallic,
	right arm raised. Originally at Akhmin and Coptos.
MNEVIS	Bull incarnation of Ptah.

MONTU	Hawk headed, sun disk & 2 plumes..
MUT	Vulture's head-dress or crowns; also lioness-headed. Adored at Thebes.
NEFERTEM	Lotus Flower on head, sometimes with 2 plumes.
NIT	Goddess of Sais; with shield and crossed arrows, a huntress and war deity.
NUN	God personifying the primeval waters.
NEITH	'The Lady of the West'. Female with Red Crown of lower Egypt, or 2 crossed arrows on shield on head, sometimes bow and arrows. she presided over war and the loom. Worshipped at Thebes. Protectress of Sais.
NEPHTHYS	Woman with hieroglyphics on head dress.
	Sister of Isis; guardian deity.
NUT	God of air and light. A woman with body curved so as to touch the ground with her fingers. The vault of heaven, mother of gods.
ONURIS	Thinite god of war; local god of This.
OSIRIS	Mummiform, spectre & flagellum, white crown with plumes and horns; god of dying vegetation, ruler of the Netherworld; the 'Good Being'; consort of Isis; brother of Seth; father of Horus and Harpokrates. Adored throughout Egypt, in particular at Abydos.
QEBHSNUF	Son of Horus; hawk-headed.

PTAH	Mummiform human headed, 3 sceptres; creator god, "The Father of the Beginning"; patron of craftsmen.. Chief deity of Memphis.
RE-HARAKHTY	Sun disk on head, hawk headed Sun God. Horus of the Horizon
SATIS	Feather head-dress.
SED	A god of the dead, same as WEPWAWET; a wolf standing on a Nome standard.
SEKHMET	Lioness goddess; consort of Ptah.
SEFKHET-ABWY	Eighteenth dynasty goddess of writing. Woman with 7 pointed star under bow, on head, holding writing materials.
SELKIT	Scorpion god.
SETH	Unidentified animal, muzzle and ears of jackal, body of an ass, upright tail like a lion, or as a man, god of disorder, deserts, storms and war. Enemy and brother of Osiris.
SHESHAT	Goddess of writing and learning, a librarian and counter of cattle who recorded the deeds of men and of gods on the leaves of the Tree of Heaven. Woman wearing plain dress covered by panther skin with tail hanging to her feet, with star or rosette in a headband with papyrus tucked in .
SHU	God of sky and air, shown with arms raised.
SOBEK	Crocodile headed, or crocodile.
SOPDU	Bearded man, protector of the Delta.

TAWERET	Hippopotamus & woman combined with lions paws, crocodile tail. Protector of pregnant women.
TEFNUT	Primeval goddess personifying moisture.
THOTH	Ibis headed, often with moon or crescent; God of writing and counting. Often has pen and palette. local deity of Hermopolis.
WADJET	Cobra goddess of Buto, guardian of Lower Egypt.
WEPWAWET	A god of the dead, same as SED; a wolf standing on a Nome standard.

In addition to all these gods and goddesses there were many more, sometimes the same ones but with different or variations on these names, sometimes combinations of gods. *Horus* was closely associated with *Re,* or *Ra,* as were *Khephre, Re-Harakhty, Aten* and *Min.*

The popularity of these gods waxed and waned with the power of the priests. The ordinary folk tended to have very simple ideas of who these gods were, often keeping one or two statuettes in their homes, but tending to regard them as magical rather than divine. There was no problem in their minds regarding the unions between the gods; stories revealing the more human sides of the gods' behaviour were very popular and easily understood. The most surprising change throughout the whole of Egypt's history was brought about by the Pharaoh Akhenaten, who saw no god other than *Aten*, which was represented as a Sun Disk, having no physical manifestation. Akhenaten ordered the closure of many temples, diverting funds and sacking priests. With his new concept he was far ahead of any of the other Pharaohs. Akhenaten himself was seen as the direct manifestation of the god on earth.

5

DIVINE PLAY

Osiris and *Isis* were supposed to have been like husband and wife (as well as brother and sister!) and *Horus* was their son. *Horus*' uncle was *Seth*. It was believed that one day, before *Horus* was born, *Seth*, who hated and decided to kill *Osiris*, gathered together a group of seventy-two conspirators.. What *Seth* is said to have done was to organise a banquet and make a special coffin. So, after everyone at the banquet had feasted, it was suggested that *Osiris* each guest try out the coffin. For some it was too large, for others too small, but when *Osiris* tried it , it fitted perfectly, like Cinderella's slipper. Then *Seth* and the others quickly sealed it and poured in molten metal so *Osiris* could not breathe and died. Then they took the coffin and put it in the Nile, so that it floated away into the sea and eventually landed at Byblos (near modern Beirut), by a tamarisk tree. The tree knew who was in this coffin and grew fantastically, so that the King of Byblos, who did not know anything about the coffin, was so impressed he cut it down and used it to build part of his palace. When *Isis* found out that her beloved husband was dead she decided she would have to travel all round Egypt and look for the body. You might think that was a very hard thing for a woman to do 10,000 years ago, but remember she was a Goddess and could do heaps of powerful magic. She left her child, *Horus*, with the cobra goddess Wadjet, to protect him from *Seth*. Eventually, by asking a lot of children, she managed to trace the coffin to Byblos and after curing a sick prince, she was able to get the pillar which had been made from the tamarisk tree, split it right down the middle and

OSIRIS

revealed the coffin of *Osiris*. *Isis* took the coffin back to the Delta and hid it while she went to get her son the baby *Horus*. Unfortunately for *Isis* this was not the end, for poor *Horus* had been bitten by a scorpion so *Isis* had to wait for him to recover. Meanwhile wicked *Seth*, who was hunting wild boar in the marshes, came upon the coffin accidentally (she obviously hadn't hid it very well, had she?). So *Seth* tore open the coffin and chopped the body of *Osiris* into many pieces (some say 8, 14 or 16) and scattered them throughout the lands. After that *Seth* laughed and said "It is impossible to destroy a God's body, but I have done it!" When *Isis* found the empty coffin she started her search all over again and every time she found a piece she kept it and built a shrine there, using her magic powers. In fact her magic was so strong that she was able to conceive a child by her dead husband, but even she couldn't keep him alive on earth for ever, so he went to the great-distant-beyond that the Pharaohs believed in, called 'Duat', the 'Underworld', where he became 'Judge' and 'Ruler of the Dead'. *Horus* stayed on the Earth. They believed that the Pharaoh was an embodiment of *Horus* and when he died, he had to have his soul weighed against a feather of Maat to make sure he was pure and then he would go to live in the underworld and *Horus* would be reborn again as the new Pharaoh.

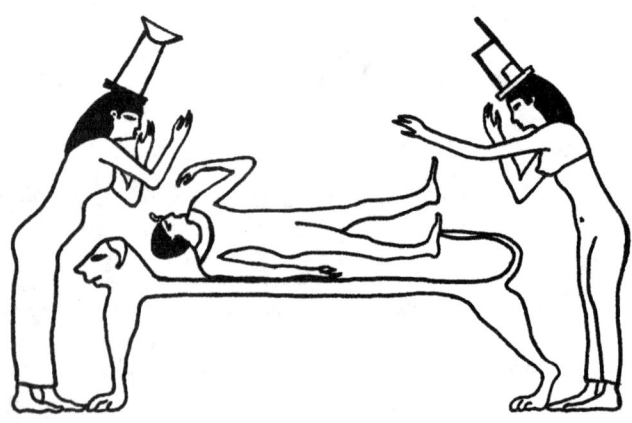

ISIS AND NEPTHYS WITH OSIRIS' BODY

It is said that the body of *Osiris* was eventually buried at Abydos, which became the traditional resting place of the god.

Isis

Here is an interesting inscription which was found in two identical texts, one on the Greek island of Ios and the other from Andros, which concern the goddess *Isis*, 'Mistress of Magic', sister and wife of *Osiris* and mother of *Horus*. Of course it is highly unlikely that *Isis* wrote this poem herself.

> I am *Isis*, Mistress of Every Land
> I was taught by *Thoth* and by his help
> I found out demotic script,
> that all things should not be written with the same letter
> I laid down laws for mankind and I ordained things
> which no one has the power to change (like the goddess Sheshet)
> I am the eldest daughter of *Geb*
> I am wife and sister of *Osiris* the King
> I am she who governs Sothis
> I am she who is called divine among Egyptian women
> For me was built the city of Bubastis
> I divided the earth from the sky
> I marked out the path of the stars
> I prescribed the course of the sun and the moon...
> *(Inscriptionese Graecae, Vol XII, fasc. V, pt 1)*

Horus and *Seth*.

After the death of *Osiris* and his journey to the underworld, an argument apparently developed between *Horus* and *Seth*, over who should inherit the throne of Egypt. This story has been translated by Alan Gardiner from the Chester Beatty Papyrus No. 1. The scene opens in the courtroom of the gods where the boy *Horus* is making claim to the throne. He is wearing the White Crown of Upper Egypt and starting to make his cartouche. At this point *Thoth*, who supported *Horus*, then announces the presentation of the *Eye*, of religious importance, to *Amun*, the leader of the Ennead of Heliopolis and *Shu*, the God of the Air, chooses this time to propose that *Horus'* application be granted. This motion is seconded by *Thoth*. Atum, however, is not yet satisfied and prevents the vote. Then *Seth* arose and demanded that *Horus* be evicted so that he, *Seth*, could demonstrate his power. *Thoth*, however, then stated that fighting would be no way to settle the dispute and that it would not be right to give the throne to *Seth* whilst the descendant of *Osiris*, *Horus*, was still alive.

This annoyed *Ra-Harakhte*, who supported *Seth*, and Atum suggested that they send for the Ram-God *Ba-neb-tetet* and that the gods should abide by his decision. He came along to the court and brought with him *Ptah-tatenen*, the earth form of the god *Ptah*. Ba-neb-tetet refused to make a decision because he said he was not fully aware of all the facts in the case and he advised that they write to *Neith*, the goddess of Sais and mother of *Re* and ask her decision. So *Thoth* was instructed to write to *Neith* who replied declaring that the kingdom should be given to *Horus*. She also threatened that if this was not done she would cause the sky to fall down on the earth, a danger the Ancient Egyptians were always afraid of; but that if it was done then *Seth* should be rewarded with two Syrian goddesses, *Anat* and *Astarte*. Most of the gods in the court agreed to this, but not mighty *Amun* who disliked *Horus* for being so young! The only god to give voice against this was the god *Baba*, who said " Your shrine is empty", meaning he had no ground to stand on and that his argument was no good, which caused *Amun* to leave the court sulking and *Hathor* had to chase after him, cheer him up and bring him back. By this time the gods were getting tired and impatient, because the trial had been going on for eighty years already, before our piece of the story had even started. *Horus* and *Seth* were called to state their cases. *Seth* claimed that he was the strongest of the gods and travelled daily in the Boat of *Re,* fighting back the sun god's enemies and nobody else could do that, which was enough to entitle him to the throne. Surprisingly the gods agreed, but

ISIS AND BABY HORUS

HORUS THE ELDER

Horus cried out that he was being defrauded in front of the Nine Gods and *Isis* lost her temper.

To calm *Isis* the Nine Gods changed their minds, which in turn annoyed *Seth* who threatened to kill them all one at a time. Now it was *Re-Harakte's* turn to became impatient with *Isis'* interference and suggested that they all cross to an island, have lunch and make their decision there. She told Anti, the ferryman not to take *Isis* across. *Isis* disguised herself as an old woman and bribed Anti and so got across, where she transformed herself into a beautiful young girl. When *Seth* saw the girl he fell deeply in love. She told *Seth* a story that she was the widow of a farmer who had kept cattle and that she had a son. A stranger had come to attack her son and taken the cattle. So she asked the infatuated *Seth* whether he would help her. *Seth* replied that "Shall the cattle be given to a stranger while the farmer's son is alive?", thus condemning himself out of his own mouth. When *Seth* found out it was only a trick, he told the court the whole story, but *Re-Harakhte* now ruled against him saying "You have passed judgement on yourself, what is there for you to do next?". Tired of the long court session the Nine Gods had meanwhile adjourned to a hillside in the Delta. *Re-Harakhte* sent for them and told them that they must want *Seth* and *Horus* in and out of court for ever that they should come back and put the White Crown

SETH

back on to the head of *Horus*. *Seth* was not happy with that and challenged *Horus* to an underwater fight in the form of hippopotami. *Isis*, in a panic, made a harpoon in order to help her son and threw it into the water, but it hit her son *Horus* by accident, so she used her magic to withdraw it and threw it once again, hitting *Seth* this time.

Seth was, as we know, *Isis'* brother and she felt sorry for him when he cried out so set him free, which made *Horus* very angry so he came out of the river and cut off *Isis'* head with his axe and took the head to the mountain top. *Isis* magically turned herself into a headless flint statue and *Horus* ran away to stop the gods punishing him. *Horus* tried to hide under a bush, but *Seth* found him and gouged out his eyes, which he set up to light the desert. Meanwhile the blind *Horus* was found by *Hathor*, the cow goddess, who poured milk into his eyes to restore his sight and told the other gods what had happened. So they were called back in front of the Nine Gods and told to stop misbehaving and make friends. They agreed to this and *Seth* organised a feast, but when *Horus* got drunk he was attacked by *Seth*. It was decided to write to *Osiris* who was in the underworld to ask his opinion, but *Osiris* replied that he was sick and tired of all this to-ing and fro-ing and that where he was there were a lot of dog-headed messengers who he would send to destroy the gods if the dispute was not settled! The gods then immediately confirmed *Horus* as King and imprisoned *Seth*.

The Battle of Horus and Seth

Before going to the Court of the Gods about their dispute, *Horus* and *Seth* had spent a great deal of time arguing over the throne. Presumably Egypt was without a King for this time, but time for the gods must flow differently than for us mortals. The two gods had a physical war as well as the court case. The following account originates from texts on the walls of a Ptolemaic temple to *Horus* the Behedet at Edfu on the Nile, south of Thebes.

In this tale the war began in the sixty-third year of the earthly reign of *Re-Harakhte*. *Re-Harakhte* had accumulated some enemies, and one time, when *Re* had sailed down the Nile with *Horus* to Edfu, *Horus*, had flown up to heaven in the form of a great winged sun-disk and attacked the enemies. Then *Thoth* named him 'Great Protector'. But more fighting was to occur.

The enemies of *Re* turned themselves into hippopotami and crocodiles and attacked the boat. *Horus* saw what was happening and immediately returned to the boat with his men, armed with harpoons, which is why he was called '*Horus* the Harpooner'. The story tells that 651 of these creatures were slain near Edfu. But more was to follow. *Horus* chased the remaining enemies southwards and then northwards , killing many with his axes and spears of iron. (Remember the story was written a few hundred yearsBC, when they knew about metals, whereas the time we are hearing about was some many thousand years earlier, before the Stone Age!).

The enemies rose up to meet *Horus* on a lake and *Re* said to *Horus* "Behold these enemies have assembled on the Western Water of the Nome of Mert, to band themselves together with the enemies who serve *Seth* who are in this place". *Horus* begged his lord to let him go and fight them, which he did and killed many and captured 381 enemies and gave them to his followers. Then *Seth* raged against *Horus* like a 'cheetah of the south', because *Horus* had killed so many of his followers. Roaring like thunder, he turned himself into a snake and went underground. The surviving followers of *Seth*, knowing he was still alive, banded back together, so *Horus* changed into the winged sun-disk and attacked and routed them.

THE WINGED DISC OF HORUS

This day was celebrated throughout the times of the Pharaohs, on the first day of the inundation and on the seventh day of the first appearing of mounds after the inundation.

Horus sent out his men to capture the remaining enemies and they caught 160 from the East and 160 from the West and sacrificed them to *Re*.

Yet again the enemies amassed against *Horus* and attacked him, so he changed into a fierce lion and killed and captured yet more. *Thoth*, who was in the boat, then rose up and did a

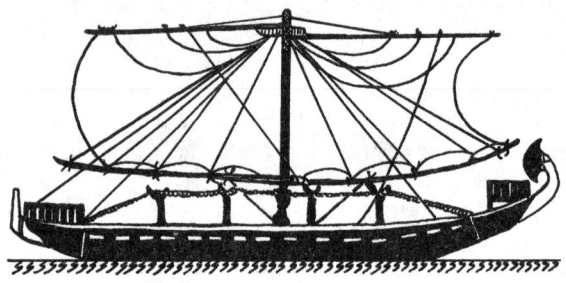

AN ANCIENT EGYPTIAN SHIP

spell which caused the wind to cease and the waters to become quiet, so they could see no more sign of enemies. *Re* and *Horus* then sailed down the Nile to Ta-Kens, the Land of the Bow, later called Nubia. *Horus* changed into the winged disk and was accompanied by two goddesses from the North and South, in the form of cobras with crowns on their heads and again he fought and defeated his enemies.

Now, some said the war was over and *Horus* the victor and that *Osiris* would return to rule on earth. But others said that the war was not yet over and that even if *Seth* was trapped underground, there would not be peace until he could be killed. By this time *Horus* had become a young man and *Seth* returned and challenged him before *Re,* so there was yet another battle. *Horus* had weapons of iron and *Isis* decorated his boat with gold, saying "You will be victorious for you are fighting for the throne of your father and I am with you". *Seth* transformed himself into a hippopotamus and went South with his men and cursed *Horus*, causing a terrible tempest. *Seth* roared like thunder and a heavy storm broke out over the boats, the wind raising the waves and tossing the boats like straws and, to this day, that part of the river is the most dangerous. *Horus* changed his shape into that of a young man, eight cubits high and threw his harpoon at a red hippopotamus he could see by the reflected light from his gold boat. At the first throw the weapon sank into the head of the hippopotamus and into the brain and *Seth* was killed.

The destruction of mankind by *Re* and Sekhmet

This story has been translated from inscriptions in the tomb of Seti I, in the Valley of the Kings. In the beginning mankind was grateful to *Re* for the benefits he gave to them and worshipped him, but after a while they stopped and said *Re* had grown old and so they left the temples. *Re* secretly consulted with the other gods in the Council, asking for advice. First he asked *Nun* because he was one of the oldest and *Nun* advised him to send his *Eye* against mankind. *Eye* was his daughter, also called *Sekhmet* and *Hathor*. *Eye*, as *Sekhmet*, in the form of a fierce lioness, went out and killed many men both in the valley and the desert where they ran and she enjoyed it so much that she could not be stopped, even when *Re* had a change of heart; she said "I swore by my life that when I gained mastery over men it was very satisfying to my heart." *Re* again turned to the gods for advice and they suggested he give *Sekhmet* some beer, of which she was very fond and mix it with a red dye called Kharkady so that it looked like blood and pour it on the fields. Next morning when *Sekhmet* saw the fields full of blood she admired herself in the reflection and drank the beer and got so drunk she did not know where she was and fell asleep. So the human race was saved. *Re* said "I will protect men with this beer I have made" and he welcomed back *Sekhmet*, saying "Come in Peace".

From that day until the end of the Pharaohs, jugs of beer have been made and celebrated at the festivals of *Sekhmet-Hathor* and at Dendera where there was a 'Festival of Drunkenness'.

Sekhmet was a very popular goddess in Ancient Egypt and, although she is represented in this tale as a very fierce feline, she also had her good side and was worshipped by many. You will find her name in Pharaohs' names if you study the list at the back of this book.

Ra, *Re*, Amon-*Re*, *Kephri* and Ra-*Harakhte*.

By now you may be feeling slightly confused by these three

names, at least, but fear not! They are all basically the same god. For a start *Ra* and *Re* are the same. In the writing of Ancient Egypt there were no vowels and so when we read the names in hieroglyphs which consist of consonants only and insert the vowels we think most likely, some people may chose an 'a' and others an 'e'. Doesn't help much eh? All these names are names of the same god, the Sun God. At dawn this god was called *Kephri* by the ancients. *Kephri* was pictured in the form of a scarab beetle which made the sun rise and cross the sky. *Ra-Harakhte* was portrayed as a great and powerful hawk. *Amun Re* was the form of the sun god which acted as patron for the Pharaohs and was the king of all the gods.

These gods should not be confused with *Aten*, the god worshipped as the One and Only Sun God by Akhenaten.

In Ancient Egypt, when we look back, it looks like there were so many gods, but remember, just like in modern Hinduism, that all the gods and goddesses were aspects of the One and Only Supreme Being, who could be worshipped in many ways and who could take many forms. The interplay between all these forms, both the good and the evil forms, was really seen as some sort of divine play.

The Journey and the Weighing of the Soul

As has been said the Egyptians were preoccupied with death and spent their lives preparing for it. This involved not only building their tombs, but also learning many magic spells to recite on their journey through and by tests, which the soul had to pass in the underworld of *Osiris*, called 'Duat'. Sometimes the spells were painted on tomb walls, or written on papyrus and left in the tombs, to help the dead. These spells were concerned with purification, proclamation of purity and the naming of the gods. The deceased person's soul was believed to have to pass through seven halls, one of which was the Hall of Judgement, where the soul would be weighed against a feather, the ceremony witnessed by many gods, presided over by *Thoth*, with a crocodile ready to devour any soul that failed! There is, however, no tale of any Pharaoh failing.

According to the ancient papyri the deceased should have

learned a declaration which goes "Hail ye Seven Beings who make decrees, who support the Balance on the Night of Judgement of the UTCHAT, who cut off heads, who hack necks to pieces, who take possession of hearts by violence and rend places where hearts are fixed, who make slaughtering in the Lake of Fire, I know you and I know your names; therefore know me, even as I know your names." After reciting this the deceased would hold no more apprehension of evil befalling him. When he comes to the Hall of Judgement he says "Homage to Thee, O Great God, Thou Lord of Maāti, I have come to Thee, O my Lord and I have brought

THE JUDGMENT SCENE AS SEEN ON TOMB WALLS

myself hither that I may behold Thy beauties. I know Thee and I know Thy name and the names of the two and forty gods who exist with Thee in the Hall of Maāti." After the seven halls the soul had to pass through twenty-one hidden pylons of the House of *Osiris* in the Elysian Fields, declaring the names of each pylon and the doorkeeper of each. Then, if he had a boat, he could carry on his journey, on the underworld river; but first had to know the secret mystical names of the river and the river banks. After this he could sail around in the Elysian Fields at will. He still had to avoid beings who 'lay snares and work the nets and who are fishers' and needed yet more spells for this.

The Priests and Sacred Ceremonies

All the gods were worshipped in temples throughout the land and the priests were responsible for conducting the many rites and festivals. Ordinary folk never went into the temples; that privilege was reserved for priests and Pharaohs.

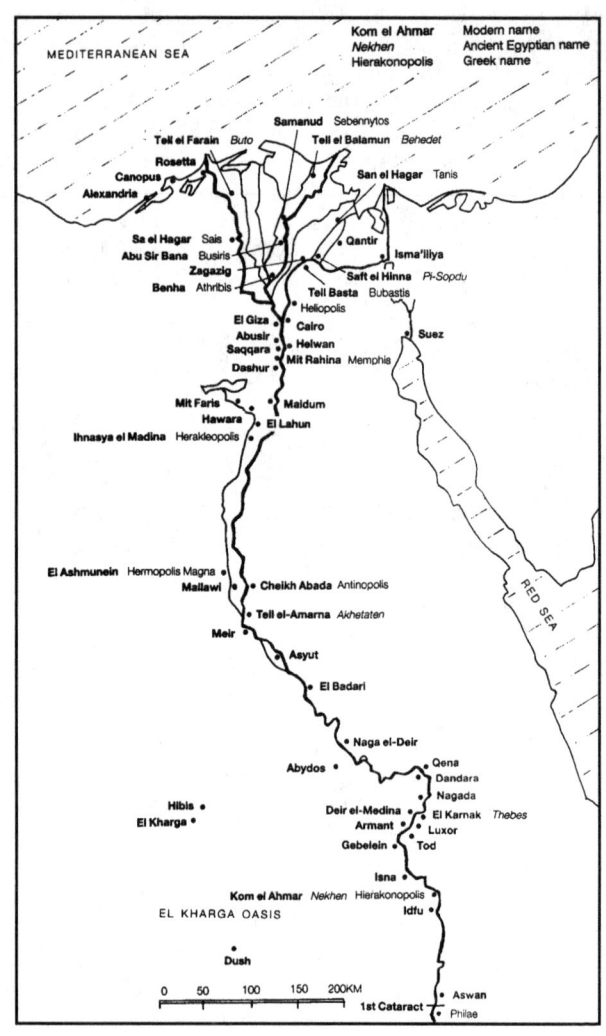

THE NILE VALLEY, SHOWING EGYPTIAN, GREEK AND
MODERN PLACE NAMES

The ceremonies performed with the Pharaoh were passed down from original aged rituals of *Re* and *Osiris*. A standard daily service was held, which the Pharaoh had to attend. Sometimes he would be in a different part of the country and the ceremony would be performed there. From the Middle Kingdom on, the day started, for the Pharaoh, with the 'Rite of the House of the Morning', in which the Pharaoh was first purified by washing him with water from the sacred lake within the temple grounds, symbolising the primordial waters of *Nun*, causing the Pharaoh to be symbolically born again. He was then anointed with sacred oils, robed and invested with the Royal Insignia, by two priests wearing masks of *Thoth* and *Horus*. This was all done before the next ritual, the daily service, started. In this the Pharaoh was led around the sanctuary. After breaking a special door seal he approached the statue of the god. The breaking of the seal represented the 'opening of the two doors of the sky'. The Pharaoh prostrated himself before the god and recited a hymn of the morning "Wake in Peace, as the goddess of the two crowns. Wake in Peace!". The Pharaoh then purified the statue, took it in his arms, robed it and symbolically fed it. He then replaced it and left the shrine, resealing the door, until the next day.

The two major ceremonies during the Pharaoh's reign were his coronation and the Heb-Sed feast. On his coronation, the King was first purified by two priests, again wearing the masks of *Thoth* and *Horus* (or *Horus* and *Seth*)and the new King was then presented to his people, having his titles proclaimed. He was crowned twice, once with the White Crown and once with the Red Crown, symbolising his authority over both parts of the country.

The Heb-Sed feast originated in pre-dynastic times and represented the rejuvenation of the Pharaoh. It seemed to have happened whenever it was felt necessary to reaffirm the Pharaoh's divine authority and not at regular intervals. Ramesses II took part in five Heb-Sed festivals. In this the Pharaoh re-enacted the life and death of *Osiris*, symbolically rising from the dead to reclaim his throne and re-proclaiming his powers.

There were other less important ceremonies such as the

'Stretching of the Cord', which was the Pharaoh symbolically measuring and consecrating the ground before a temple or pyramid was built. He would often lay the first cornerstone, or cut the first turf before walking around the proposed site.

Each god also had his or her own particular feast and each Nome which had its own god organised their own festivals. Some of the most spectacular were the Feast of Amon-*Re* at Thebes and the Feast of *Horus* at *Buto*. The Feast of Amon-*Re* was held at the beginning of each year and lasted for 24 days. At Abydos they performed an annual 'Mysteries of *Osiris*' which represented the cycle of life, death, mummification, resurrection and enthronement of *Osiris*. In this the local population would often join in as extras, forming the two armies of *Horus* and *Seth* and re-enacting a mock battle which often resulted in injuries to both sides.

The priests within the temples formed a hierarchy and had titles such as Chief prophet, Deputy Prophet, Priest, Deputy Priest, but of course in Egyptian. They were all exempt from taxes and all manual work. Although they wore special costumes when in the temples and shaved their heads, they often wore everyday clothes outside and carried a special staff or wand of office. They generally had a monopoly on reading and writing skills, and often worked as scribes with responsibility for educating the nobility. Hence they were very powerful men, sometimes powerful enough to overthrow a Pharaoh. They even had sacred concubines and, in the cult of the fertility god *Min* at Karnak, sacred prostitutes.

6

TOMBS, PYRAMIDS AND MUMMIES

Before going into the various type of tombs (mastabas, pyramids and rock cut tombs) in Egypt, it is worth mentioning a very peculiar practice which the Egyptians developed, that of mummification. The word 'mummy' originated from the Persian word 'Mumia', which meant pitch, or bitumen. To tell you the truth it is not the nicest of subjects and not for the squeamish. What they wanted to do was preserve their dead bodies for ever, because they believed that they would need them again at the end of time. You might think that's a bit crazy but remember that these were a very superstitious people and that it was not that different from some modern day religions that believe the dead will raise on the last day. So these Pharaohs were prepared to hire a lot of experts to try to develop some means of preserving their bodies. These bodies are still about today in museums. Tutankhamun's is still in his tomb in the Valley of the Kings, which is on the West Bank of the Nile near the modern city of Luxor, a capital city for many of the Pharaohs and, in those days, called Thebes. Most of them have been damaged or rotted away though, or lost or destroyed, so they weren't very successful, although they did well to make them last thousands of years. The hot and dry climate of Egypt helped once again. What they did to produce the mummies was, basically, this: first they dried out the dead body (bodies are composed of about 70% water) by immersing it for two to three months in a chemical called natron or native sodium carbonate; then they disembowelled it and removed the brain by drawing it out through the nose; they left the heart in the body as they believed it would be needed for weighing against the life's deeds in the judgement ceremony in *Duat,* the underworld. Then they stuffed mud or sand under the skin to reform the body shape and the limbs and packed the insides with sawdust; then they completely wrapped the body in lots of linen bandages soaked in resin, sometimes putting pieces of jewellery or amulets between the layers for good luck in the afterlife. They then put the vital organs which they had extracted into four jars, called Canopic Jars, each associated with one of the four sons of the God *Horus*, although later in time the process was changed and the organs were wrapped in linen and returned to the body.

This was the basic process which they used for several thousands of years, not only on Pharaohs, but also on noblemen and even poorer ordinary people who probably had a cheaper and less efficient mummification done and even on cats, oxen, crocodiles and the other creatures that they considered holy. The Ancient Egyptians worshipped their animals and it was actually a capital offence to hurt a cat. Today it may seem a bit gruesome, but these peoples were very preoccupied with death and wanted to ensure that their loved ones would be OK in the underworld; remember the underworld to them was heaven rather than our modern day beliefs of hell. In fact the process was quite successful considering some mummies three to four thousand years old are still about today in museums throughout the world and very many of them in Egypt. There is, though, an even more extraordinary fact about mummies which you probably wouldn't guess. They made very good fuel. This meant that over the thousands of years many that were found were used to make fires by the poor people, because of the great shortage of wood in the desert. This was probably a great shame but we can't blame the living for wanting to survive.

The Ancients believed that each person not only had a physical body which would be mummified, but also a spirit double, called *Ka* or *Kha*, which survived death and that the soul, called the *Ba*, would also survive and would visit the mummy in the tomb, being able to pass through the rock in the form of a hawk with the head of the human. Sometimes the Pharaohs had two tombs built, one for the body and one for the Ka, where offerings were made. This is yet another confusing legacy which they left us, since two tombs have sometimes been discovered, both belonging to the same King, both with a sarcophagus and neither with a mummy! The Great Pyramid contained a sarcophagus, as did many others, but no body was ever found, as far as our history tells us.

Although it may appear that the ancients were preoccupied with death, it was rather their love of life that encouraged them to build such elaborate tombs and pyramids. They believed that human death was only a transition, and that the afterlife was very similar to the earthly life. Tombs were considered as gateways to eternity. Everything that had been useful in this life may be needed in the next. In other words they took their wealth and possessions with them. It was also thought that faithful service to the Pharaoh would mean his help in the underworld, and being buried close to him was considered auspicious. Early Pharaohs even had servants killed to accompany them, although later the bodies were replaced by models. Whilst Pharaohs covered their tomb walls with prayers and spells, lesser nobles had paintings of their homes and families and of everyday scenes. Wealthy landowners even had models of their farms. Such elaborate paintings and models which have survived have provided valuable insight into life in the days of the Pharaohs.

One of the major problems which developed during the New Kingdom, was tomb robbery. When you consider that most of the Pharaohs were very, very, rich men and that the religious beliefs of the time dictated that they would need all sorts of items and wealth for the afterlife which were always buried with them, it was just too tempting for certain people, despite the death penalty on anyone caught thieving. Some of the less than honest administrators of the Pharaoh's kingdom wanted some of that wealth for themselves and they were the ones who knew exactly where the tombs were. So they often employed people to go and break in to steal the gold and jewels. As time went on and more and more tombs were desecrated and robbed, later Pharaohs went to extreme lengths to hide their future tombs, even to the extent of executing some of the builders and sometimes even an architect or two.

Despite all the guards and precautions, nothing could be done to stop the robberies and thousands of years later, in the nineteenth and twentieth centuries of our time, many tombs were empty when rediscovered. We will come to the different types of tombs in a while, but first it is worth mentioning Tutankhamun, a name which is now known worldwide. Tutankhamun's tomb was discovered in 1922 by an archaeologist called Howard Carter who came from Norfolk and worked for the 5th Earl of Carnarvon (1866-1923). Mr Carter managed to discover a tomb which even the robbers had missed, because the entrance had become covered and hidden by rubble from a later tomb excavated higher up the valley side. When he eventually managed to gain entry to the tomb, on 17 February 1923 and looked into the inner chambers he found an incredible wealth including several gold coffins, two of which contained the small mummified bodies of Princesses, possibly Tutankhamun's daughters, as well as a sarcophagus, or inner coffin, actually containing the mummy of Tutankhamun. There was also a lock of hair labelled as belonging to the boy Tutankhamun's grandmother, the Great Queen Tiye. Carter did realise though, that the tomb had previously been disturbed and items seemed disarranged, as if they had been put back in a hurry; it may have been that the tomb had been robbed thousands of years ago, the robbers caught and probably killed and the treasures put back. This had been in the time of Ramesses IX, several hundred years after Tutankhamun. The treasures Carter found inside have been taken around the world for displays and made the study of Ancient Egypt or 'Egyptology' very popular in our time.

Although the treasure found in Tutankhamun's tomb is extremely beautiful, valuable and impressive, it is interesting to realise that Tutankhamun was really a relatively minor Pharaoh who died (in a hunting accident but he may have been murdered) as a teenager. He had once been called Tutankhaten after a different God (*Aten* had been the state God for some years before, established by a Pharaoh called Akhenaten, but the priests of the older religion of *Amun* managed to persuade Tutankhaten to change the state religion, the capital city and his own name). Tutankhamun was alive in 1336BC. His tomb is one of sixty-two in the Valley of the Kings. The nearby Valley of the Queens and the Valley of the Nobles contain hundreds more, including the lovely

Queen of Ramesses II, Nefatari. These are names we give to these valleys nowadays.

Over the thousands of years that Egypt was a great empire the shape of the tombs of the Pharaohs changed. As stated, the really ancient ones, those of the first two dynasties, with names like Narmer, Aha, Den, Djet, Peribsen, and Kha'sekhemwy, built their tombs in the mastaba shape. The mastabas were shaped like wide benches, rectangular with a flat top. There were often structures built underneath the mastaba, with corridors and chambers. Some of these Pharaohs actually seem to have had two tombs, one at Abydos and one at Saqqara, suggesting that some tombs and, later, maybe the pyramids were built for reasons other than housing the mummified corpses. The names which Manetho gave to these first dynasty Pharaohs were Athosis, Kenkenes, Kenephes, Usaphaidos, Miebidos, Semempses (Semerkhet) and Bieneches.

After some few hundred years a Vizier (a man who helped run the country) who was also a brilliant mathematician and architect, called Imhotep, came up with the idea of building mastabas on top of each other, but with successive ones decreasing in size. What do you think it would look like? Imagine pieces of square wood six inches thick; put one about a foot square on the ground, then one about eight inches square on top of it in the middle, then a smaller one on top of that and so on, so it would look like a series of steps and the overall shape would be that of a PYRAMID. That is exactly what it was, the first ever BIG pyramid. It was built for a Pharaoh called Hosar or Djosar and is today called the Step Pyramid of Hosar. It is still standing not far from the modern city of Cairo, at a site in the desert called Saqqara.

Although it is generally believed amongst Egyptologists that the Step Pyramid was the first pyramid, it is nevertheless possible that it was a copy of an earlier pyramid in Egypt; where, I hear you ask, is the first pyramid then? Well, as I have already mentioned, according to evidence of weathering at Giza, it is conceivable that the Great Pyramid, the Second and Third pyramids, the Sphinx and the Sphinx temples, had all been built by an unknown civilisation of master builders and astronomers before the floods which followed the last ice age, some ten thousand years earlier. Tradition from at least the third century BC, found in the Book of Sothis (which may have been written by Manetho), claims that a great Hall of Records from a lost civilisation exists hidden below the Pyramids and Sphinx of Giza. This may mean that Imhotep simply tried to reproduce the Great Pyramid in his stepped work. It would certainly seem strange that after Imhotep's stepped structure made of comparatively small blocks, the Egyptians had suddenly acquired the knowledge to build almost impossibly precise structures at Giza, only to forget how to do it within a few hundred years. Although there is a beautiful tomb painting depicting 160 slaves pulling one single statue along rollers, the generally accepted opinion that this was how the pyramid of Cheops had been built, is, I feel, nonsense. The logistics of such a venture, using muscle alone, without wheel or pulley, suggests that it would have taken hundreds if not thousands of years. I will explain this in more detail soon, but the my point here is that we do not know whether the Giza complex was already in existence, at the time of Hosar, or not.

Hosar ruled in Egypt from 2630 to 2611BC, which was in the IIIrd dynasty. This building was a truly remarkable feat; it was sixty two metres high, built by a civilisation that was still in the Stone Age. Around the pyramid there were chapels and small buildings and other tombs built underground, but this big pyramid, it is believed, was built to house the body of the Pharaoh, although it was never found inside it.

By now you will have realised that many of the Pharaohs had names that sound strange to us, with the same name spelt differently by various experts. In fact these were probably not the names they were called by their close families, which is much the same as amongst royalty today. These names were their official names, or something close to them, but many that we know of were changed later by Greek historians. In addition to this they also had Cartouche names. A Cartouche is a sort of oval shape containing hieroglyphics which was often carved on stone monuments and painted on coffins or tomb walls. These are even more difficult to pronounce so I will stick to the simpler names, although sometimes the Cartouche name is the only one we know. To make matters worse, as mentioned before, some of the less scrupulous Pharaohs ordered their predecessor's Cartouche wiped clean and had their own name carved out, so that people would think they had built the monument! Not exactly fair but it happened. If you want to try to get your tongue round a Cartouche name try "Userma'atre'setepenre" who was Ramesses the Great!

Hosar's IIIrd dynasty successors must have been very impressed with Imhotep's big pile of stones in the desert, because they often decided to build pyramids of their own, or rather have them built by workers and slaves for them. Over the next fifty years there were at least six more built at Saqqara and at Meidum, some of which were never even finished. These are amongst the eighty odd pyramids that are still to be seen in Egypt today, some built out of mud-brick and now collapsed and some out of stone and in remarkable condition and extremely impressive. At Saqqara there are the IIIrd dynasty unfinished pyramids of Sekhemkhet and Kha'ba and, at Meidum, that of the Pharaoh Huni.

Before continuing with the development of pyramids it is time to tell you a story about Hosar that was told to the Egyptian children some two thousand years after him. It was discovered in 1889 AD carved in thirty-two columns on the face of a granite bolder, on the island of Sehal in the First Cataract on the Nile, by a man called Wilbour. It turned out to be a very important discovery, because when it was translated it revealed Hosar as the builder of the step pyramid.

The story runs like this :

Year eighteen of the *Horus* Neterkhet (Hosar), the King of Upper and Lower Egypt. Hosar (called Zosar) was mourning in his palace because the Nile had not risen for seven years and there was famine in all the land. There was no grain in the royal stores. All kinds of food had become scarce and men had become weak so that they could not go about searching for sustenance. Everyone was in distress. There were no offerings to give to the temples. Young and old suffered alike.

Hosar enquired of his chief of works, Imhotep, as to where Hapi rose. (Hapi was a god). Imhotep was unable to say so he consulted with the priests of the 'Temple of the Net', which was one of the names for the Temple of *Thoth* at Hermopolis. Imhotep's lector priest quickly went to Hermopolis and consulted the sacred books, from which he learnt that the headwaters of the river rose at Elephantine, the first Nome of Upper Egypt, bordering on Nubia (Wawat) to the South. The river was said traditionally to rise in two caverns where dwelt Hapi, but *Khnum*, the ram-headed god of the cataract, controlled its flow as he held the bolt of the door in his hand. He was known as the Lord of the Fields because he supplied the water for the crops, controlled the fowl and fish of the river. He controlled not only the Nubians to the South, but the quarries that lay round the first cataract. It is here that the stone was obtained for the temples of Egypt and the statues of the gods and the kings. Hosar, having learnt that *Khnum* was the god who controlled the waters of the Nile, made the god an offering and slept in the temple. There he had a dream wherein *Khnum* appeared to him in a kindly fashion. The god addressed him, saying "I am *Khnum* your maker. My arms are around you to steady you and to save you. I give you the rock to build your temples and rebuild those which have fallen into disrepair. I am the Creator God who fashioned mankind on my wheel, but of recent years my shrines have fallen into decay and no offerings have been made to me. If this it remedies, the Nile will rise again.".

Hosar was delighted to find the cause of the trouble and he hurried to make a decree in favour of *Khnum*. He offered him control of all the land on both sides of the river as far as Takompso, a region extending twelve stadia, a Greek measure, South of Elephantine. He gave him control of all the fishermen and hunters of the region, possession of all the land and the tenant farmers who were working there, as well as all mineral rights and one-tenth of gold, ivory, ebony, wood, carnelian and all precious stones that were found there. As

Elephantine was the trading post with Wawat and the South, this gave *Khnum* a very large revenue. The temple was also to have one-tenth of the dues from the royal quarries and all that was necessary to be supplied to the temple.

This would have made the Priests of *Khnum* amongst the richest people in the land and the temple would have become very powerful.

Pyramid building became better in the IVth dynasty, although in fact the evidence to show that the greatest of all pyramids was built during this dynasty is very weak; personally I wonder why the Egyptians suddenly became so skilled at building only to lose the skill within a hundred or so years. Could it be that the Pyramids of Cheops and Cheophren, which I will mention in more detail soon, were built long before the Pharaohs ever controlled Egypt, back in an age, maybe eight or ten thousand years earlier, at the time of the building of that other mysterious wonder, the Sphinx? For the time being though, let us accept the classical Egyptologists view of history.

The first Pharaoh of the fourth dynasty was called Snorfu and finished off his father, Huni's, pyramid at Saqqara, before having two of his own built at a place called Dahshur and at Meidum, which we now call the 'Bent pyramid' and the 'Stone Pyramid'.

Snorfu was the father of the most famous pyramid builder in the world from the year 'dot' until today. Cheops – also called Khufu – the builder of the Great Pyramid of Giza, one of the Seven Wonders of the Ancient World. Cheops ruled Egypt from 2551 to 2528BC, only twenty-three years, but his pyramid is the biggest of all, an absolutely massive 479 feet tall, with a base measuring area of 2,475 square feet and containing 91,000,000 cubic feet of rock! The stones that were used were cut from quarries in the South and floated up the Nile. It is said that if you took all the churches, chapels and cathedrals built in England since the time of Jesus, then the Great Pyramid contains even more stone work. In fact it was so big that the original outer white limestone coating was removed by orders of a 'modern-day' (a few hundred years ago) ruler of Egypt to rebuild parts of his city and to raise a huge mosque, the Mosque of the Sultan Hassan, which can still be seen in Cairo. Inside the pyramid there were corridors leading up and down, some leading apparently nowhere and some leading to huge chambers called by us the 'King's Chamber' and the 'Queen's Chamber', made out of blocks of red granite some weighing 20 tons each. The names of these chambers are modern names and nobody really knows what they were for. Although a stone sarcophagus (coffin) was found and can still be seen today, no body was ever found. Some people believe the pyramid was a symbolic burial place for the Pharaoh's soul or *Kha*, with his body buried elsewhere. Others believe it was some sort of religious initiation centre. Others even think it was magical or built by aliens to teach the Egyptians. However and why ever it was built, it remains very impressive and illustrates the incredible stone technology they had. It is unlikely that any construction company in the world today could build such a structure with such accuracy – the angles are near perfect – to last over 4500 years.

Outside of the Great Pyramid is an awe inspiring collection of ruins. Next to the pyramid, a few years ago, excavations revealed two massive pits in the ground and inside these pits were two huge dismantled wooden boats, presumably put there for Cheops in his afterlife. One of these was painstakingly reconstructed and now stands on public display in a special covered museum next to Cheop's pyramid. The other has been left underground for later research.

Now it is storytime again, this time a story found in the Westcar papyrus, now in Berlin. These stories were supposedly told to Cheops while he was watching the building of his Great Pyramid. The first was told to him by Prince Khephren and is about one of his predecessors, the now familiar Pharaoh Hosar, builder of the Step Pyramid at Saqqara.

King Hosar has decided to visit the Temple of *Ptah* and took with him his priest, Ubaoner. Now Ubaoner had a wife who was in love with a townsman, who cannot be named and this townsman said to the wife of Ubaoner "Let's go and enjoy ourselves in the pavilion by the lake in the garden of

Ubaoner". In the evening the townsman went for a swim in the lake and was seen by the house steward. When Ubaoner returned the steward reported what he had seen. Now Ubaoner was a powerful magician and so sent for his staff of office of ebony and gold and made a wax crocodile and put a spell on it and said "Whoever comes to bathe in my lake do you seize and hold him". Then Ubaoner told the loyal steward that if the townsman came to bathe in the lake again, to throw the wax crocodile, which was life-size, in behind him. When Ubaoner was away and the townsman came again for fun and games with the wife and, in the evening, went to bathe, the steward threw in the wax crocodile which became alive and it seized the townsman in its jaws and went down to the bottom of the lake. Now Ubaoner was away with the Pharaoh for a whole week and the townsman remained at the bottom of the lake, without air. Ubaoner told the King what had happened and they both went to the lake where Ubaoner called up the crocodile. When it came up the King was afraid of it because it was so big, but the magician took it up in his arms and it turned back into wax. Ubaoner then asked the Pharaoh to pass judgement on the wife and townsman. The Pharaoh told the crocodile "Take what belongs to you", which it did and disappeared and ordered that the wife be taken away and burned and her ashes scattered in the Nile. When Cheops heard this story he immediately ordered offerings to Hosar, of flesh and fowl and bread and beer and a small offering to Ubaoner.

Also around the Great Pyramid stand two more impressive pyramids, those of Khephren (Khafre, over 470 feet high – this was Cheop's son and maybe he didn't want to overshadow the achievement of his father, so built his three metres shorter) and Menkaure (Mycerinus 215 feet high) and several smaller pyramids associated with each and called Queens' Pyramids. There are several remarkable facts about these pyramids as a group, as well as being individually impressive. Firstly they were built so that the shadow of one never falls on the other! Secondly, they are said to be very special and their sizes and relative positions are astronomically significant. It is claimed that they pointed to a certain star in the constellation of Orion, (in the belt) and some people claim this really means that the pyramid builders originally came from the stars! Thirdly, there are certain special mathematical ratios, like Π as in Πr^2, the area of a circle with radius r and Π is always equal to 22/7), I and ε. Don't worry, I'm not going into complicated mathematics, you can read about this in books dealing specifically with the Great Pyramid. The measurements were of such accuracy that the ratio of the height of the pyramid to the length of the perimeter of the base reveals Π, the exact ration of the radius or the earth to its circumference. Lastly, there were tombs dug deep into the ground, around the pyramids and, in fact, more interesting archaeological treasures have been recovered from these than from the pyramids themselves.

There is, of course, yet another phenomenal construction near the pyramids at Giza (which is just outside Cairo), that is the Sphinx. The Sphinx was part of a chapel from which a causeway ran up to the second pyramid of Giza, that of Khafre. It has been believed for some time that this huge monument was built for Khafre. A stele, excavated by Gion Battista Caviglia in 1817, at the site, contained the syllable *Khaf*. The stele commemorated the work of Thuthmosis IV in clearing away the sand. The stele was badly damaged even when it was found, now it has entirely flaked away. It is only an assumption that this syllable was part of the name Khafre and that Khafre was the builder of the Sphinx. It is also plausible that Khafre rebuilt, changed or painted the Sphinx many years after it had been built. You will remember that recently examinations of the stone and the water wear shown, compared with the wear on stones on nearby walls, carried out by John Anthony West, have led to speculations that it was actually built 10,000 years before, that is longer before Khaphren than we are since. If this is true it certainly poses some questions and will please those who advocate that we were visited by aliens more than once. It would definitely not fit in with modern theories of mankind's development.

After the immense and perfect pyramids of the IVth dynasty they seemed to have lost the knack somewhat. Although there were numerous attempts at building equally big and lasting structures, the Pharaohs of the following dynasties were not nearly as successful as even Hosar. Today most stand in ruins. Nevertheless they would be very magnificent considering how long ago they were built.

In the XIIth dynasty several powerful Pharaohs built pyramids, the remains of which can still be seen in Egypt but not in good condition. Senusert I, called Sesostris I by the Greeks, built a pyramid at a place called Khenemsut, later called Lisht and Amenemhat III (Ammenemes III) built a couple of pyramids the remains of which can be seen today, at Dahshur and at Hawara., But by this time the skills of perfect construction had been lost.

Pyramids were constructed in the Vth, VIth, IXth, XIIth and XVIIIth dynasties, which is a time span of over 1000 years and many can be seen in Egypt today at places with modern day names like Meidum, Dahshur, Abu Ghurab, Abu Sir and Saqqara.

There is a story which comes from the Middle Kingdom, which was very popular at the time and we have a version which comes from two papyri that are in the British Museum. It is about Sinhue, who was an attendant of Nefru, the wife of the Pharaoh Senusert I and daughter of Amenemhat I. When Amenemhat died Sinhue was at Khenemsut at the pyramid of Senusert. Senusert himself was returning from a successful campaign against the Libyans. When he was told that his father-in-law had died, he rode on ahead without telling anyone. However, Amenemhat I had other sons who arrived at the court first and Sinhue thought there would be trouble and fights over who should take the throne and that he would get drawn into it. Instead he ran away into the desert, passed the quarries at Gebel Ahmah, crossed the 'Walls of the Ruler' and entered the Sinai Desert where he nearly died of thirst. Fortunately a tribe of Bedouin, who were wandering desert nomads, came along and saved him. He went with them and soon the ruler of Syria, who had heard who he was, sent for Sinhue and asked why he had fled from the court of the Pharaoh. Sinhue told some of the truth, as far as the death of Amenemhat I, but never said he was scared. Sinhue stayed with the ruler of Syria, the Prince of Retinu and married his daughter. Sinhue was given a nice piece of land in Yaa, where he could keep cattle, grow figs, grapes and barley, make oil and collect honey. He could also hunt plenty of wild game in the desert, so he lived well on meat, fowl, wine and beer. Sinhue had children of his own who grew up and became tribal leaders and opened up his house to receive envoys from Egypt. But the local people started to become jealous and eventually the toughest challenged Sinhue to a fight. Sinhue disposed of him with an arrow in his neck and chopped off his head, thus receiving the challenger's land and property and becoming very rich.

However, as he was getting older, Sinhue was not happy, because he was homesick for Egypt. So Sinhue decided to write to Pharaoh Senusert I and ask if he could come home. The Pharaoh replied with gifts and a Royal Decree, saying there were no charges against him and that he should come home and think of his death and burial. "You shall not die abroad. Nor shall the Asiatics bury you. You shall not be wrapped in sheep's hide as a coffin. Too long have you been wandering the world away from Egypt. Come home, think of your dead body", was the message. So Sinhue became overjoyed and wrote back saying he had fled in fear, of what he did not say, but that he would sell everything and return, which is what he did. After travelling some time he was met by an overseer of the Pharaoh and escorted safely back to the court of the king, where he prostrated himself saying "I did not know myself, my *Ba* was gone, my limbs trembled, when this god addressed me". The Pharaoh made Sinhue a 'Companion among the Nobles', a very good position. Pharaoh sent him to be bathed and dressed finely as an Egyptian (since he was still dressed as an Asiatic), shaved and have his hair combed, with his body anointed with oil. He was given a house and land and a place prepared for his burial. "I was in favour with the King until the day of my departing".

The pyramid structure was very important in the Egyptian religions, because the ancients believed that when the world was created out of the waters of nothingness, the first bit of land which rose up out of the waters was shaped like the top of a pyramid (a smaller pyramid in itself). In fact, when the Pharaohs of later years gave up pyramid building and decided to cut their tombs out of rock, they selected an area on the West Bank of the Nile, opposite the ancient and then capital city of Thebes, which I have already told you is now called the Valley of the Kings, in Arabic *Biban-el-Muluk*. The ancients must have noticed this natural feature – you can hardly miss the view of the mountain of Qum as you approach the valley. It looks just like the top of the Great Pyramid. In this particular case the gods seemed to have done some of the work for them!

LIST OF EGYPTIAN PYRAMIDS

Dynasty	*Pharaoh*	*Site*
3	Hosar	Saqqara
3	Sekhemkhet	Saqqara (unfinished)
3	Kha'ba	Saqqara (unfinished)
3	Huni	Meidum
4	Snorfu	Dahshur
4	Cheops	Giza
4	Ra'djedef	Abu Roash
4	Khephren	Giza
4	Menkaure	Giza
5	Userkef	Saqqara
5	Sahure	Abu Ghurab
5	Neferirkare	Abu Ghurab
5	Niuserre	Abu Sir
5	Djedkare	Saqqara
5	Unas (Wenis)	Saqqara
6	Teti	Saqqara
6	Pepy I	Saqqara
6	Merenre	Saqqara
6	Pepy II	Saqqara
12	Senusert I (Sesostris I)	Lisht
12	Amenemhat III	Dahshur
12	Amenemhat III	Hawara

7

The Great Pyramid of Cheops: Facts

"The Pyramid which is the Place of Sunrise and Sunset"
Fourth dynasty; approx. 2575BC ?

As the reader will know the pyramids at Giza are amongst the greatest and most mysterious structures ever built. I hesitate before saying "ever built by man". We do not know who really built them, when or why!

Although it is generally believed that these massive structures were built over about 70 years, anyone with any knowledge of even the most up-to-date engineering technology available today will know that this would be an impossible task now, let alone thousands of years ago before they had even invented the wheel or the pulley. Classic Egyptologists tend to rely on their readers ignorance or lack of imagination when they state figures like 100,000 men taking 20 years to build the Great Pyramid. A quick calculation reveals the impossibility of such a feat, using ropes and rollers and dragging stones up to 70 tons up ramps, placing them in incredibly accurate positions which aligned perfectly with the stars. They seldom consider how these ancient workers could have dragged and lifted the stones weighing 200 tons used to build the temples and causeways around the pyramids and Sphinx.

Although it is often stated that the Pharaohs Khufu, Khafre and Menkaure ordered the building of these wonders in the fourth dynasty, there is no actual evidence of this. Quarry marks inside the Great Pyramid may be forgeries; the tiny statue of Khufu found, upside down as if dropped, in a crack in the ground outside the pyramid no more suggests that he was the builder than would the finding of Nelson's Column in Trafalgar Square suggest that Nelson engineered the Square.

Not only are these impressive structures surrounded by mystery, but it appears that even the Egyptian authorities are keen to suppress any new discoveries and many explorers have in recent days been stopped from continuing their work on the point of possibly momentous discoveries. This is precisely what happened to the work of scientist Rudolf Gantenbrink who, using a robot, examined the so-called ventilation shafts leading from the so-called Queen's Chamber in 1993. Having found evidence of a small door at the end of one shaft and seen (through the robot eye) a piece of wood which could be dated to reveal the true age of the pyramid, his work was halted and he has not been allowed to continue since. Others, like John West and the geologist Robert Schoch of Boston University, have been ignored, because the results of their work would seriously effect the classic Egyptologists view of the past; their work on the weathering of the Sphinx would suggest it is much older than Egyptologists want it to be. It certainly appears that either there is some hidden knowledge which us common folk are not privilege to, or else there is some sort of anti-intelligence conspiracy.

There are hundreds of books written on the Great Pyramid. Authors approach the monuments from a variety of angles. For some it is evidence of extra-terrestrial life or of an advanced civilisation from the past. Others see the Pyramid as a cosmic message, either warning us of some great disaster or promising us the coming of a Messiah. Measurements, undeniably precise, can be interpreted as magical, astronomical or numerological. Some claim the Pyramid was a tomb, others an observatory of the stars and yet others believe it was a centre for mysterious initiation ceremonies. Whatever its true purpose, it is now certain that a great number of inscriptions, paintings and papyri refer to Giza in terms we are only just beginning to understand.

As the author of this presentation, I would have thought the whole thing was no more than science fantasy, if I had not myself been able to walk around, enter and climb upon the Great Pyramid.

Items found within the Great Pyramid of Giza

Iron Plate 2.6 cms x 8.6 cms, discovered by J.R.Hill (1837) stuck inside joint inside southern shaft from King's Chamber. Purpose and origin unknown. Now in British Museum.

Three items found in northern 'ventilation' shaft from Queen's Chamber: *

1. Piece of cedar wood: may have been a measure
2. Bronze forked hook-like item, believed to have been used for Opening of the Mouth ceremony, with part of wooden handle.
3. Green granite ball, 0.850 kg (1lb 3oz)

All discovered by Wayman Dixon and Grant in 1872.

These so-called 'ventilation' shafts where these objects were found do not appear to have run as far as the outside of the pyramid.

Size and comparison of size

Height	418.9 feet (146.0 m)
North side	755 feet 4.9818 inches
West side	755 feet 9.1551 inches
East side	755 feet 10.4937 inches
South side	756 feet 0.09739 inches

Corner Angles : SE 89° 56'27"; NE 90° 3'2"; SW 90° 0'33"; NW 89° 59' 58"

Area 53,000 square metres

Estimated number of rocks = 2,500,000; average weight 2.6 tons

91,000,000 cubic feet

Estimate of tonnage of rock = 6,300,000 tons

The following size comparisons have been made:

The pyramid contains more solid masonry than all the cathedrals, churches and chapels built in Britain since the time of Christ.

The Great Pyramid could contain the cathedrals of Florence, Milan, St. Peter's, Westminster Abbey and St. Paul's.

The base of the pyramid occupies 13 acres, equivalent to 7 New York city blocks!

The casing blocks were removed by Arabs to build the

mosques of Cairo; the mosques contain less material than than the outer casing of the pyramids.

Early entries:
It seems likely that the Great Pyramid was open through most of the New Kingdom and then sealed up, maybe due to local superstitions that it housed powerful magic or a powerful and frightening magician.

Within the period of fairly 'modern' history there was a report by the historian Strabo in 24BC, that the entrance to the Great Pyramid was through a hinged stone door, which, once replaced, was indistinguishable from the rest of the outside of the pyramid. There is no evidence of this, although one of the pyramids at Dahshur does have such a doorway. At this time it must have been an even more magnificent building since the outer layer of polished limestone was still intact. Remember that the pyramid was, to Strabo, as ancient as Strabo is to us today.

The first major attempt to re-find or create an entrance after the original entrance was lost, was in 820AD by the young caliph Abdullah Al Mamun. Convinced that the pyramid contained much treasure the caliph used the services of many men to try to burrow in through the side. Hammers and chisels failing they then tried cracking the stones by throwing cold vinegar onto the stones heated by red hot fires, knocking out the pieces. This process enabled them to tunnel in one hundred feet. They met up with a passageway 3 feet wide by nearly 4 feet high, sloping at an angle of 26°. They discovered a large stone on the floor, which seemed to have been dislodged from the roof. They then discovered the original secret entrance ninety feet to the North and some forty-nine feet above the base of the pyramid. Following this tunnel, the 'Descending Passage' as it became known later, they came upon the empty 'pit'. Returning to the fallen stone they attempted to dislodge further stones from the ceiling but were unable to do so.

They decided to dig in along side this huge 'plug'. After six feet they found another plug, then a third. Eventually they came to limestone so hard that they could go no further so they forced there way into the 'Ascending Passage', again

4 feet high, at a slope of 26° again. They crawled 150 feet along this slippery passageway, reaching a horizontal passage which itself led to a rectangular limestone chamber with a gabled limestone ceiling, which later became known as the 'Queen's Chamber', although there was no evidence that it related to any ancient queen; in fact it was the Arabs who buried their women in tombs with gabled ceilings. There was an empty niche in one of the walls, which attracted Mamun's attention further, which could have once housed a statue or hidden another passage or chamber. Mamun decided to get his men to burrow into this niche, but they gave up after 3 feet.

Returning to the Ascending Passage they discovered they were in a narrow gallery, some 28 feet high, stretching up at a slope of 28°. This became known as the 'Grand Gallery'. With great difficulty they climbed 150 feet to find a huge stone which they had to climb over. Beyond this stone the passage levelled out, the ceiling now only 41 inches high. The explorers found another chamber (the 'Antechamber') and a larger chamber made from massive polished granite blocks, 34 feet long, 17 feet wide and 19 feet high. Notice the ratio of the length to breadth of this chamber is 2 : 1. The roof here was level and the chamber became known as the 'King's Chamber' because that was the type of ceiling used in Arab tombs for the men. Unfortunately this chamber was empty except for a sarcophagus without a lid, although this in itself became fascinating to later explorers because it is slightly too big to pass through the chamber door. There were reports that a stone statue had been found in the sarcophagus although there is no other evidence of this. Mamun and his men had become so frustrated with the lack of treasure that they attacked the floor!

Years later, after an earthquake had destroyed much of the Arab city El Kaherah, the Arabs removed 22 acres of outside covering from the pyramid, to rebuild the city, as well as two bridges! In 1356AD Sultan Hassan removed stone to build his mosque which still stands in modern Cairo. There was much rubble left piled up and this eventually covered Al Mamun's entrance Although the removal of the outer layer had uncovered another two possible entrances, there were now rumours of black magic and nobody wanted to enter the pyramid.

The next entry of interest was made by John Greaves, a mathematician and astronomer. He climbed the rubble and followed Mamun's route to the Queen's Chamber which now stank so bad he had to abandon it. He visited the King's Chamber and collected much data and measurements. Greaves also discovered the 'Well' in the Grand Gallery. He descended 60 feet into this well (there was no water in it) finding that it widened into a rough chamber later called the 'Grotto'. Unfortunately the stench and the large volume of bat dung forced his retreat. He then climbed the outside of the pyramid counting the courses and estimating the height to be 481 feet without the missing top layers.

The Well was entered again in 1765 by Nathaniel Davison, an explorer, only to find the bottom blocked in. Davison also made another remarkable discovery, the area above the roof of the King's Chamber, by climbing the Grand Gallery and crawling down a hole only 2 foot wide. The chamber he found had been made from rough granite slabs, weighing each some 70 tons. How these slabs could ever have been lifted and placed so perfectly is yet another mystery. The chamber is now known as 'Davison's Chamber'. The ceiling of this low crawl space is also made from 70 ton slabs.

In 1798 Napoleon arrived in Egypt and visited the Pyramid with a unique group of scientists and soldiers, to search for knowledge of the ancient past. Napoleon was a man convinced of supernatural powers and fascinated by magic, but they found nothing more except even more bat dung. On August 12 1799 Napoleon himself entered the King's Chamber and asked to be left alone. Upon exiting he was asked what he had found as he looked shocked and pale. He answered nothing and never spoke about his experience, until his dying day when he started to speak but then said "What's the use, you'd never believe me" (in French, of course).

The next discovery was made by an Italian, Caviglia, who cleared the bat dung from Davison's Chamber and dug a tunnel off it, finding nothing. Then Caviglia descended the

Well and tried to clear the rubble that had collected since Mamun's men had burrowed up into the ceiling. He struggled 150 feet down a stifling passage, the Ascending Passage and, despite sickness from heat and smell, he pressed on another 50 feet, finding a low doorway leading into a hole. Digging into this they emerged into the bottom of the Well.

About this time an Englishman, Colonel Howard-Hyse, arrived on the scene at Giza. His team dug up the floor of the Queen's Chamber but found nothing there, so thoughtfully refilled the holes! Discovering a crack in the roof of Davison's Chamber they tried to dig into the roof, but were unable to do and so blasted their way up. Here Hyse discovered another chamber, the floor of which was the roof of Davison's Chamber. The ceiling was made of 50 ton blocks. Continuing upwards they found another similar chamber made of 8 granite blocks. Over the next four moths they found three more chambers, all empty, except for a fine black dust originating from decayed insects. Howard-Hyse named these chambers after Nelson, Lady Ann Arbuthnot and Colonel Campbell. They are now seen to be a means of relieving the immense pressure that would otherwise be directly on the roof of the King's Chamber; the topmost chamber also had a gabled roof. Red painted cartouches (upside down so probably quarry marks rather that decoration), were found on some of the stones up here and proved to be of a fourth dynasty Pharoah called Khufu. Khufu was believed to be the Cheops whom the historian Herodotus had heard of and reported. It was therefore concluded that Khufu built the Great Pyramid, although there is very little direct evidence to support this conclusion. Howard-Hyse also found two shafts running from the King's Chamber through 200 feet of solid masonry to the outside of the pyramid; there is no knowing whether they ever went through the original outer layer, although it is now widely accepted that these were ventilation shafts – air poured through when they were unblocked. Incidentally Howard-Hyse also took the sarcophagus from the third pyramid at Giza, that of Menkaure, but this was lost off the coast of Spain in a shipwreck and now lies deep in Davy Jones' Locker.

The Subterranean Chamber

A passage only 3 feet 6 inches (1.1 m) wide and 3 feet 11 inches (1.2 m) high, at an angle of 26°, descends 345 feet (105 m) from the true entrance, into the bedrock. It ends in a roughly hewn pit measuring 46' x 27'1" x 11' 6" (14 m x 8.3 m x 3.5 m), 600 feet (183 m) below the apex of the pyramid. There is a hole sunk into the floor, leading nowhere. In the western side there is a squared, polished, passage, cut horizontally, 100 feet (30 m) long, leading nowhere. In 1992 Professor Jean Kerisel used radar to examine the walls and floor of the subterranean chamber and reported that he found evidence of an undiscovered system of corridors within the Great Pyramid. Unfortunately the Egyptian Government has not allowed this to be further investigated. Strangely Herodotus had reported being told of an underground chamber at Giza.

The Ascending Passage

This passage leads up into the pyramid, at an angle of 26°, matching the Descending Passage. It is 129 feet (39 m) long, but too low to stand up in. Where the passage levels out, it forks, one way to the Queen's Chamber, the other down steps to the Grand Gallery.

The Grand Gallery

Height 28 feet (8.52 metres); Length 157 feet (48 m); Angle of ascent 26°

Seven courses of limestone, each course corbelled in 3 inches over the lower course.. The gallery is 62" wide (1.6 m) at the bottom but only 41" (1 m) at the top.

In present times the gallery is fitted with a wooden ramp.

The King's Chamber

Size : 34'4" (10.45 m) E-W; 17'2" (5.23 m) N-S; height 19'1" (5.81 m)= 20 x 10 Egyptian Cubits

Reached by a passageway from the top of the Grand Gallery, it is empty, apart from a broken sarcophagus which is too wide to have been carried through the passageway. The passage leads to an antechamber with three deeply cut grooves, which may have been to house a portcullis. A pair of granite leaves are set above the portcullis entrance, with a small protuberance or seal on the granite face, on the lower leaf. The meaning of this is unknown, it is not hieroglyphic. The antechamber becomes a restricted passage for a few feet, then opens up to the King's Chamber.

The floor is made from 15 massive granite paving stones. The floor plan of the chamber is the ratio 2:1; the height is in the ratio of the diagonal of the floor, representing the Golden Section, or Phi, the formula $\Omega(1+(5)$.

The walls are formed from 5 courses of stone containing exactly 100 blocks, each about 70 tons. The ceiling is formed from nine immense red granite stones, some of which weigh over 50 tons.

The sarcophagus is still inside the King's Chamber. As mentioned already it is bigger than the doorway so it could not be moved out. The sarcophagus has inside measurements of 6 foot 6.6 inches long, 2 foot 2.81 inches wide and 2 foot 10.42 inches deep, whilst its outside measurements are 7 foot 5.63 inches long, 3 foot 2.5 inches wide and 3 foot 5.31 inches deep. This makes it about an inch wider than the doorway, so it could not have been carried through the lower entrance (now plugged). The sarcophagus is made of chocolate coloured granite with hard granules of feldspar, quartz and mica. It is wondrous how such a piece could ever have been cut in the Stone Age. It would require saws 8 feet long, made of some material such as bronze and jewels – diamond was extremely rare in those days. How on earth such a block could be hollowed out remains a mystery, as no saws or drills have ever been found.

There are small 'ventilation holes' on the North and South walls, although these may have been wrongly named.

The Queen's Chamber

A horizontal passage, 127 feet (39 m) long, from the Grand gallery leads to the Queen's Chamber; the floor of this passage drops two feet towards its end. There is a stepped niche cut into the chamber's southern wall. The floor of the chamber has been left rough. Two 'ventilation shafts', left sealed at the outer extremity, run from the walls.

Davison's Chamber

Above the roofing slabs of the King's Chamber, closed to the public, a series of rough hewn blocks set in 4 layers, rise to a roofed compartment. This causes an echo in the King's Chamber. It was discovered by Davison in the eighteenth century and it is believed to be a device for relieving the pressure on the roof of the King's Chamber. On one of the upper levels were found quarry marks containing the cartouche of Cheops – Khufu.

The Well or Grotto

At the junction of the Ascending Passage and the passage to the Queen's Chamber is a sealed entrance to a narrow, roughly hewn, shaft, running partly perpendicular, partly obliquely, to the Descending Passage, near its lowest point in the bedrock.

How Did They Build IT?

Bearing in mind the huge size of the pyramids, classical Egyptologists have kindly calculated that it must have taken something like twenty years and 100, 000 men to build the Great Pyramid of Giza. I think this statement must require some quantitative analysis.

Firstly we must not, of course, forget that this building was achieved (we think) in the Stone Age, before (we think) the invention of the pulley or the wheel. However the work was done it would involve (as far as we know) only the power of human and animal muscles, along with basic rollers, ramps and levers. We do not know whether such human muscle would have been provided by reluctant slaves or devoted servants, but one thing is sure, it would take several highly experienced generals of the calibre of Napoleon or Caesar to organise such a work-force in one place. Then there is the question of the number of highly trained engineers needed constantly on site, supervisors for lifting and dragging the stones weighing from 1 to 25 tons each. We must not, of course, forget the huge task force required to feed the workers.

Next consider how the stones were actually lifted and moved. "Dragged up ramps", the Egyptologists explain. But here we are considering dragging huge stones along rollers, probably wooden and constantly in need of replacement, up a ramp from river level to an eventual height of hundreds of feet, to be then placed perfectly. Such a ramp would in fact involve something like three times the material involved in the pyramid itself – some 8 million cubic metres – and would need to be something like 4800 feet long. This material would need to be very strong and hard and would itself require a huge task force to transport it (and, presumably move it away afterwards, since it doesn't seem to be around any more). Now for a little mathematics. It is estimated that the Great Pyramid contains some 2,5000,000 stones, a total weight of about 6,300,000 tons (an average of about 2.6 tons each). The 23rd course alone consists of several hundred 5 ton limestone blocks. Now we are told that the workers built only during the time of the annual inundation, when they were not required on the land. But let's be generous and assume that the work force worked 365 days a year for the twenty years and each day they worked 16 hours. This gives us a total of about 116,800 hours. So they had to cut, transport, drag, lift and place some two and a half million 2.6 ton (average – a lot weighed over 20 tons) stones in 116,800 hours. That is one stone every 3 minutes! Quite a feat trying to imagine the large numbers of men crowded into the available places, pulling and pushing to the shouts of their supervisors "Left a bit, up a bit, back a bit, down – no, up and forward a bit – now down again – oh sand, we'll have to move that one again!". I very much doubt that any construction company in the world today, with all the technology and power available, would take on the task. 54 tons of solid stones moved each hour, 16 hours a day, 365 days a year, for 20 years. Obviously, we cannot sensibly accept these figures based on what we know today, let alone in Stone Age times.

Now here we have a problem. How can we cook the books? How can we adjust the figures to make this construction more feasible. To increase the work force would be difficult, since only so many men can occupy the space. We do not know any way of making the stones smaller or lighter. We cannot increase the hours worked per day, or the number of days in a year, so the number of years must be changed. So far we calculated the time taken to lift and place a stone to be 3 minutes. This in itself cannot be possible given our technological knowledge. Safely lifting huge stones takes a lot longer. But if we estimate 30 minutes the overall time factor is increased tenfold, that is it will take 200 years. This is all being on the generous side; it would, of course, have taken longer still. This means workers and bosses alike dying off, as well as the Pharaoh himself. Then there would be the Second Pyramid of Giza, as huge as Cheop's, to build – another few hundred years. We are now faced with the prospect of a huge organisation spanning over several hundreds or a thousand years and many successive Pharaohs (many of whose names we seem to have lost). Do you believe it?

Personally I can only conclude that such a feat as the building of three pyramids at Giza is physically impossible given our technological knowledge (hardly considering the other 70 odd pyramids in Egypt). The problem is that the pyramids are not science fiction, but real, I have been inside them, like millions of tourists over the last few hundred years. Sure, there must be some explanation, it was done. But how? Alien technology, lost magic, the will of the gods? I'll leave you to think about that one!

The Valley Temple
Almost as fascinating as the pyramid is the nearby so-called Valley Temple, composed of hundreds of limestone blocks as large as 30 feet by 12 feet by 10 feet and weighing up to 200 tons each (yes 200!). How could these blocks be lifted 40 feet into the air and placed so precisely. In 1997 AD there are only two cranes in the world capable of lifting such a massive stone and these require 6 weeks preparation by a team of 20 specialised men, as well as a huge counter-weight. Egyptologists seem to ignore these questions.

The Ground Plan of Giza
There are a remarkable number of coincidences in the way in which the three main pyramids at Giza are laid out. As well as the representation of mathematical concepts such as (

and the alignment of the pyramids with the poles, it has now been suggested that the ground plan may be a representation of part of the sky at night. Certainly an aerial photograph of the pyramid plateau reveals a great similarity with the shape of the stars in the belt of the constellation of Orion, with the third pyramid slightly out of line with the other two. Recently, with the aid of computer generated images of the sky thousand of years ago, it seems that at least one of the so-called ventilation shafts pointed directly at Orion. What is even more incredible is that if you look at the situation of the other pyramids in that part of Egypt, they represent even more stars of Orion, with the Nile representing the Milky Way. Maybe there is some significance in this, because we know the Ancient Egyptians were fascinated by the night sky. Why Orion? Could it have been the home of *Osiris*?

8

A MILLENNIUM AND A HALF

One thousand five hundred years or so – a long time? If you look up in history books you will be able to see the stage we had reached in Britain 1500 years ago and you will sense just how big a time span it has been. But we are talking of the 1500 years before the New Kingdom was established in Egypt. In the times of Tutankhamun and Ramesses II, the period we are talking about was already ancient history, indeed the New Kingdom people regarded the pyramids as ancient monuments! Not only is it a very long time, but so much must have happened about which we know nothing. We do know so many snippets of information, that it is not an easy matter to know what to include and what to miss out, since I don't want to give you a mere list of people, events and dates. But we have to start somewhere, so how about 3150BC? Before the Pharaohs, before the pyramids and before the tombs. Just about the time when people were starting to use symbols as writing with some consistency, rather than simply painting and carving pictures.

Around about 3150BC there was a semi-mythical king in Egypt, called Menes. He is sometimes thought to have been the same person as the first Pharaoh, Narmer, and is considered to have been the founder of Egypt as a nation. King Menes built his capital city at Memphis (just outside modern day Cairo), close to the border between Upper Egypt and Lower Egypt. Heliopolis, nearby, became an important religious centre.

The Egyptians already had boats and could sail easily up and down the Nile and out into the Mediterranean. People had originally started using reeds to build rafts, then added sails and eventually developed them into simple boats capable of carrying men and goods. It was often far easier travelling by river rather than roads, which didn't yet exist. The huge stones used for building the pyramids were transported by river after being hewn out of quarries near the Nile.

The new united Egypt was governed by an administration consisting of sixty two 'Nome's, each one with it's own patron god and each with its own ruler, often a very powerful man. The Pharaoh ruled as almighty over these and was considered to be a divine embodiment of *Horus* at first, although over the years not everyone agreed and there were revolts amongst the local governors who wanted more power for themselves. The priests were also very powerful men and would sometimes cause great difficulties and even overthrow a Pharaoh if he was too weak or not ruthless enough. On the other hand certain Pharaohs would cause problems for the priests, closing down temples and destroying statues, if they chose to believe and worship a god other than a state god, or if they were foreigners taking control. One thing can be sure though, the ordinary folk experienced none of the wealth and glory of the Pharaohs, Priests or Nomarchs (rulers of the Nome's).

The throne would pass down, after the death of the Pharaoh, to the husband of the eldest female offspring. This meant that a son, or uncle, would often marry the girl so that he could legitimately gain the throne. Sometimes a Pharaoh would appoint his son as co-regent during his own reign, to ensure the dynasty continued.

In the second dynasty, 2890 – 2686BC, Egypt continued to be run as an united country. In about 2646BC there seems to have been some disruption caused when the new Pharaoh, Peribsen (2646 -2629) came to power. He seems to have preferred the god *Seth* as the patron of the Pharaohs, either alongside *Horus*, or displacing him. This must have caused a lot of bad feeling with the priests. Peribsen's successor may have solved the problem by incorporating the name of both gods into his own, *Horus*-and-*Seth* Khasekhemwy (2629–2600BC).

The third dynasty (2649–2575BC) saw the beginnings of massive monuments in Egypt. By this time the Pharaohs must have become rich and powerful enough to pay their workers and almost certainly used slaves. The country was governed by an efficient civil service which acknowledged the absolute power of the king. The Step Pyramid at Saqqara was built by the Pharaoh Hosar. He is also called Zosar, or

Djosar in other works. His full name was *Horus* Netjerykhet. Pyramid building was an almost continuous Pharonic occupation for the next 400 years.

It was about this time that a great invention was introduced to Memphis – the potter's wheel.

By the fourth dynasty (2575–2464BC) the Egyptians were building ships 170 feet long, sending them off on expeditions to the Phoenician coast to bring back cedar wood. It was Snorfu (Snerfu) 2575–2551BC who brought Nubia under control (the far South). After Snorfu built his pyramid, his son Cheops (also called Khufu) started his own huge pyramid at Giza, which was to become the Great Pyramid and one of the seven wonders of the Ancient World.

Just next to Cheop's Great Pyramid at Giza, two large pits were discovered, each pit containing an incredible boat, put there to aid the Pharaoh's journey on the underworld river. Both boats were dismantled, but one has now been put back together and is on display to the public under cover next to the pyramid. When you walk into the building housing the boat, you see a boat, well designed but not very impressive in size. That is a model. When you look up, you see the real thing towering above you! You can then climb a staircase to see the full-size boat and it is impressive! Consider the age that it was built in – the stone age. Several boats have been found near pyramids. Although these paticular ones were not built for sailing in this world, they were capable and did sail.

The huge cost of building the pyramid must have caused a lot of problems. Cheop's son and immediate successor, Ra'djedef (or Djedefre, as he is often called) ruled for only eight years, 2528–2520 BC and built his own pyramid at Abu Roash, North of Giza and weakened the empire enough to lead to the eventual collapse of the dynasty about 50 years later. In the meantime, more huge pyramids were built at Giza, those of Khephren (2520–2494BC) also known as Khafre and Menkaure (2490–2472BC), who was later called 'Mycerinus', by Greek historians. The last Pharaoh of the fourth dynasty was Shepseskaf (2472–2467BC).

During the fifth dynasty (2465–2323BC) the sun god *Re* of Heliopolis grew in dominance and a solar cult was established. Not so much effort was spent on pyramids but several

Pharaohs built Sun Temples that we know of, near Saqqara and Abu Sir. The monarchy owed its survival to the support of the Priests of *Re*, so had to spend a lot of money on temples! The Royal Tombs became far less grandiose, but the tombs of nobles and their families were better built, still using the mastaba shape. This makes us think that the Pharaoh's powers decreased whilst those of the nobles and Nomarchs strengthened. Local governors started placing their tombs in other sites, rather than just close to the King's. The Pharaoh's Divine Status was disappearing, although Khephren was still worshipped as a god two thousand years later. The Pharaohs quite often married into families of local rulers to re-establish themselves. Previously the high officials had usually been members of the Pharaohs own family, but now lifetime appointments were being replaced by hereditary governorships.

The sixth dynasty (2323–2152BC) saw the continuation of pyramid building at Saqqara. There were economic problems throughout the dynasty and the authority of the Pharaoh was collapsing, as control over Nubia was being lost. The sixty-two Nome's were struggling for individual powers. Pepy I (2289–2255BC) tried to rescue the situation by marrying into powerful provincial families and several stories tell of the woes of the times, which were to last for another 150 years. In 2246BC Pepy II came to the throne at the age of six. Maybe he ruled far too long, sitting on the throne for ninety-four years, until 2152BC. By the end of his reign Egypt was again divided.

Egypt's internal problems were exasperated by hoards of Asiatics trying to invade. During this time there were many squabbles and fights between district rulers and the throne. The internal society of Egypt was collapsing, irrigation systems became abandoned resulting in famine, the dead remained unburied and the land became disease ridden. Pepy II, who had become a feeble old man, was unaware of these conditions, so they got worse and worse, although a wise man called Ipuwer tried to improve matters without success. The wealthy times of the Pharaohs and the law and order of the land finally disappeared, to be replaced by the chaos of the First Intermediate Period. The poor actually rose up and overthrew the monarchy for the first time ever. Strangely enough these changes had been prophesied and warned against at the end of the VIth dynasty and there is a papyrus in the Leiden Museum called the 'Admonitions of the Prophet' which tell something of those days. Another interesting piece of writing which has survived is the 'Dispute with his Soul of One who is tired of life'. This is a story of a man who is so fed up with living conditions that he wants to kill himself, but his soul, as a separate being, persuades him to carry on, prepare his tomb and live for the glory of the afterlife to come. Fortunately for the man, his soul wins the debate.

With all these troubles and the overthrow and consequent fall from divinity of the Pharaoh, there were obviously going to be great changes to religious beliefs. Everybody, not just the royalty, wanted their own tombs and wanted to pass the tests in the afterlife, gaining eternal life. *Osiris* was accepted as the most powerful and worthy of the gods, since he offered resurrection.

The First Intermediate Period covers dynasties VII to XI. Feeble kings ruled from Memphis. These were overthrown by more powerful rulers from Heracleopolis, but it was not long before fighting started with the strong families in Thebes, the first four of whose Kings were called Imyotef. By the XIth dynasty the anti-Theban coalition of monarchs was finally overthrown and Egypt was reunited yet again under the leadership of Mentuhotep I Nebhepetre. He brought an end to the feudal system and is recognised as the founder of the Middle Kingdom, fighting off Asiatics, Libyans and Nubians. At the same time he increased foreign trade. Mentuhotep I decided to put his tomb in Dier el-Bahari, on the West Bank at Thebes. Thebes had been his capital city and now it became the religious centre. The tomb contained aspects of pyramid structure as well as new features. This unique and glorious tomb and mortuary temple was largely destroyed when in the XVIIIth dynasty Hatshepsut decide to build her mortuary temple next to it. There were also several tombs of royal ladies.

Some historians consider Mentuhotep's dynasty as part of the First Intermediate Period, whilst others put it in the

Middle Kingdom, but whichever you chose, good old Mentuhotep I was able to leave a peaceful of prosperous kingdom for his successors, Mentuhotep II and III.

The twelfth dynasty (1937–1872BC) was founded by a man who may have been a vizier under Mentuhotep III, called Amenemhat I or Ammenemes I (1937–1908BC). Once again, these times had been prophesied, by a priest called Neferti in the reign of Snorfu, who said that the troubles and strife (of the First Intermediate Period) would be overcome by a commoner whose mother came from Elephantine. This too has survived and is in the Museum of Leningrad, called 'The Prophecy of Neferti'. Amongst the major changes made by Amenemhat I was a change suggested by his name; can you guess? Yes, it was the introduction of the god *Amun* as patron to the throne, replacing Montu, the god of war, who had been adopted during the previous two hundred years. *Amun* was also associated with *Min*, the god of fertility. Amenemhat I also moved the capital from Thebes to It-towy, near the Delta. A new royal burial site was started at Lisht and pyramids were built there.

Despite the prosperity of the dynasty, there was still a lot of internal strife and in fact Amenemhat's position on the throne was questionable since he had been a commoner; he had to treat the local Nomarchs with care. Amenemhat tried to secure his dynasty by introducing a system of co-regency, putting his son Senwosret I (Sesostris I as he was called thousands of years later, by Greek historians), on the throne beside himself. Although this secured the throne, troubles with the Nomarchs continued; they had their own armies and built their own tombs. Finally Senwosret III (1836–1817BC) took control over these Nomarchs by reorganising the country into large administrative districts, each governed by loyal officers appointed by the Pharaoh and his vizier.

There were still attempts to invade by Asiatics. Amenemhat I had built the 'Wall of the Ruler' in the desert, exactly where we do not know, to keep the foreigners out of Egypt. However, Egyptian influence in Syria, Mesopotamia and the Aegean and sovereignty over Nubia was re-established with some difficulty. A new people, who we know only as the C-group, had entered Nubia and proved to be difficult opponents. A series of forts were built to keep the population under the Pharonic thumb.

Trade expeditions were sent out to Punt and Sinai and Crete, to get turquoise, gold and incense. Amenemhat also started land reclamation projects in the Fayoum, where he enlarged the natural lake (Lake Moeris) and built a Temple of Sobek (the crocodile god). It is not certain how Amenemhat I died, he may have been murdered by conspirators.

Senwosret (Sesostris) II (1842 -1836BC) became known as one of the greatest of the Pharaohs and was actually worshipped as divine during his lifetime. He is said to have done great deeds and to have been a peaceful king. He built a pyramid at Lahun, including a few new designs to try to confuse tomb robbers. Of course this didn't do much good and when the pyramid was opened by Petrie in 1889 AD, nothing was left except the sarcophagus. However, nearby there were other royal tombs, one of which was found to contain the jewellery of Princess Sit-*Hathor*-Iunut. Petrie also unearthed remains of a town, called Kahun, which had been built for the pyramid workers near the pyramid. The original name of this town meant 'Senwosret is content'. Petrie found traces of workers' houses, villas which belonged to the bosses as well as a palace. Strangely, the town, which thrived for a 100 years, was suddenly deserted and everything left behind, from tools to toys, jewellery and furniture. Petrie found documents such as wills and a medical document dealing with woman's' ailments, child birth, pregnancy testing and even contraception. These finds have provided good insights into everyday life.

The wealth of the times is also visible from the greatness of tombs built by nobles. This was, however, stopped by Senwosret III(1836–1817BC). The non-royal tomb building had increased due to the popularity of *Osiris*. The design of coffins had become much more elaborate, it becoming popular to have two coffins, one inside the other, and a 'soul house' had been included in the tomb structure. Food supplies for the dead and written spells, known as 'Coffin Texts', were painted on the coffins. The Pharaohs were not keen on the idea of rich nobles having big tombs and put a stop to it.

Senwosret III seems to have been the antithesis of Senwosret II: he was a warrior king and made expeditions and military campaigns to Nubia and to Syria. He also cut a channel 260 feet long and 34 feet wide, through the cliffs at the first cataract of the Nile, to enable his ships to travel South.

The next Pharaoh was Amenemhat III, described in his time as 'the good god', who did much to benefit the people of Egypt. He helped control the annual flood by sending his engineers to the Fayum Oasis to continue to build the artificial lake called Moeris.

The dynasty seems to have faded away with Amenemhat IV, who seems to have been something of a non-entity.

Dynasty XIII (1783–1635BC) and dynasty XIV, which were contemporaneous, are also a bit vague in history. Times were certainly turbulent and reigns usually short. The real power of dynasty XIII was held by court officials and was based at Thebes and, according to the historian Manetho, there were sixty kings. The fourteenth dynasty had seventy-six kings! They ruled from Xois in the Delta. This is over a period of about a hundred and thirty years, so you can imagine there were a lot of changes. The internal conflict in Egypt meant weakened borders and again the country was invaded from the North. Foreign kings, the 'Hyksos', ruled in the XVth and XVIth dynasties. It is uncertain from where the Hyksos originated. The Hyksos set themselves up as traditional Pharaohs. It was the Hyksos Kings who introduced the horse drawn chariot to Egypt, as well as a new form of dagger, swords and bows. They also introduced the hump-backed cattle, the vertical loom, the lyre and lute and new building and metal work techniques. Egypt was now in the iron age; economically and artistically, though, they were decadent. They worshipped *Seth*, the god of strength and confusion, although they never considered him to be an evil god. They established their capital city at Avaris.

Native Egyptians returned to the throne yet again with the ousting of the Hyksos by princes from Thebes. Dynasty XVII was established by Mentuhotep IV, claiming descendancy from the thirteenth dynasty and re-uniting Egypt. It is not entirely clear how this happened, but one story tells that the Pharaoh Apophis, ruling from Avaris, made complaints about the ruler at Thebes, Seqenenre Tao I (c 1625BC), claiming that hippopotami at Thebes were keeping him awake at night. They must have been very loud brutes, since Avaris was 1200 kilometres away! The 'tolerance' of the Hyksos towards these southern princes finally ran out and they attacked, determined to expand their power. They fought Seqenenre Tao II (1565–1555BC) and his battered skull is now a prize exhibit in Cairo museum. His successor, Kamose (1555–1550BC) marched successfully against the Hyksos and the Hyksos were driven back. The final phases of the ousting of the Hyksos was achieved by Ahmose, who was to establish the New Kingdom and the XVIIIth dynasty. A new empire was born.

Ahmose would later become the centre of a funerary cult at Abydos. He was a mighty warrior and said to have been personally brave.

9

MOSES, MAGIC AND WRITING

One of the peoples who were around at the time, actually little more than desert nomads living in tents and herding goats, were the original Israelites. A lot of our knowledge of the Israelites comes from the Holy Bible, in the Old Testament which makes mention of the Egyptians and the Pharaoh. There is no mention of any specific Pharaoh, except one (I Kings 14) called King Shishak, whomay have been the Pharaoh Sheshonq III (835–783BC), but this is almost one thousand years after the time I am talking about now. In fact, as recorded in the Bible, the Israelites were enslaved by the Egyptians and, for generation after generation, were treated cruelly and used to build cities and monuments. There is no mention of the Israelites in the few contemporary Egyptian stories that we have discovered and no mention in the Bible of any pyramid building (although there is a reference to a capstone). The only building task named in the Bible is connected to the city of Pi-Ramesse, which was somewhere in the Nile Delta and long destroyed.

Reading and writing had been around in Egypt for at least 1500 years by this time, but was reserved for royalty, scientists, doctors, astrologers, military commanders and courtiers. The 'ordinary' people and certainly the slaves, had very little education outside the family group or community and lived very basic lives, working hard from a very early age. They were involved with farming, goat-herding, construction, service to the rich, army duties and worshipping their various gods. A papyrus has been found that lists the cost of feeding one large group of pyramid construction workers; it seems that they mostly had to survive on things like unleavened bread, onions and garlic! The rich, no doubt, enjoyed a wide range of fish, birds, meat, vegetables and fruit and almost certainly drank wine and beer from very early times. Many of the tomb paintings in Egypt show scenes of life for the Pharaohs and their courtiers, including scenes of hunting, fishing and even making wine.

There is, however, a very interesting and relevant story in the Bible, about an Israelite who became very powerful and went against the Pharaoh and eventually won, enabling the slaves to escape Egypt. The story is called Exodus and the hero was Moses.

The Bible story tells that the Pharaoh strongly believed in astrology and when his Royal Astrologer predicted that an Israelite boy would be born and grow to overthrow the Pharaoh, he hit back and cruelly ordered that all the newest born Israelite boys should be slaughtered. So Moses' mother decided to hide him in a basket in the bulrushes which grew along the Nile. Well, the story goes, the Pharaoh's daughter, or one of them, happened to be bathing in the river and spotted the basket and , after sending her maids to bring it back, looked inside and saw the beautiful boy baby whom she named Moses. If you think about the name Moses and realise some of the Pharaohs had names like Amenophis, Tuthmosis and Dudimose, you may see some similarity. Pharaoh's daughter was so in love with this baby that she decided to keep him for herself and educated him in reading and writing, which the Israelite slaves could not do. She brought him up into the Egyptian way of life, keeping him in ignorance of his true origins. This was a big mistake for the Pharaoh, because eventually Moses grew up and discovered he was really an Israelite and turned against the Pharaoh.

Moses adopted a different religion to the Pharaoh and worshipped the Hebrew god *Yahweh*. Moses also became very sensitive to the suffering of the slaves, his own people, and the scripture tells us he received instruction from his god to end the bondage of the slaves. Moses went to the Pharaoh and said "Let my people go!", or words to that effect. Of course the Pharaoh wasn't too happy about letting all this cheap labour go, so he refused and Moses had to resort to threats of violence and destruction, claiming that his god, *Yahweh*, was much more powerful than the Pharaohs' gods all put together.

It is uncertain who the Pharaoh was when Moses was born, or when Exodus happened. Maybe it was Merneptah in the XIX dynasty, 1213–1203BC as some claim, but other historians think differently. In his book 'A Test of Time', David Rohl presents a good argument that the Pharaoh of the Exodus was probably Dudimose, the last Pharaoh of the thirteenth dynasty, about 450 years earlier. Rohl also reconsiders the dating of the dynasties based on lists of Israel's Kings. The Bible tells us that the Exodus was 480 years before the founding of the Temple of Jerusalem by Solomon. An early Christian historian Eusebius, referring to the work of an earlier Jewish historian, Artapanus, tells us about a Pharaoh called Palmanothes, who was cruel to the Hebrews He had a daughter called Merris who adopted a Hebrew boy called Mousos. Merris then married a Pharaoh called Khenephres who eventually became jealous of Mousos, causing Mousos to flee. Rohl argues that Khenephres was in fact the Greek version of the name Khaneferre, meaning 'the perfection of *Re* shines in the horizon', the twenty-third ruler of the thirteenth dynasty, Sobekhotep IV. Sobehhotep IV was a great and powerful ruler. Moses was 80 years old at the time of the Exodus and this was when Dudimose ruled. According to the historian Manetho the reign of this Pharaoh witnessed a 'blast of God'. Other writers place Moses in the eighteenth dynasty and some even claim he was the same person as the Pharaoh Akhenaten. The truth is that nobody knows who the Pharaoh of Exodus really was.

Although there had been magicians in Egypt for many years, Moses' magic was said – in the Bible – to be a different sort of 'magic'. The difference was that Moses prayed to his God *Yahweh* for the miracles, whereas the Egyptian magicians were said to have performed their feats through powers which they had learned.

Moses, whether through prayer or magic, was able to do some very magical and wonderfully nasty things to the Pharaoh and his people, eventually starting plagues, turning the river to blood and causing the death of the new-born. The Pharaoh had to let them go. But that was not the end of the story because the Pharaoh cheated and went back on his word, leading his armies to bring his slaves back. This was really the worst thing he could have done, because somehow Moses was able to pray and part the waters of the sea, just long enough to let the Israelites through, but, when the Pharaoh and his army went through to chase them, the waters fell back together, drowning them all. Moses, with his brother Aaron, led the people on and on through the deserts, performing many miracles, causing 'manna' to fall from heaven, which they could eat when they were starving, as well as getting water out of a rock when they were thirsty. Moses had been taught how to read by the Egyptians and wrote down the stories that had been passed down through the generations, about how the world was made, Adam and Eve, Noah and his ark and who was whose son. In fact Moses wrote the first 5 books of the Old Testament.

As I said, there were many stories of magicians in Egypt long before Moses and in fact documents have been found with stories of similar miracles or magic being performed even as long as 1200 years earlier. For instance, the parting of the waters story can be seen in an old papyrus document, called the Westcar Papyrus, which was written in the early part of the XVIIIth dynasty, about 1550BC, but it is clear that it has been copied from stories dating from the time of the Great Pyramid of Cheops, 2550BC. The story is told to King Cheops by a person called Baiuf-Ra and is said to have happened in the time of the King's father, Snorfu. It is about a powerful magician called Tchatcha-em-ankh (sorry about that, but I didn't name him!). Well, apparently, one day old Snorfu was feeling a little miserable so called to his nobles to do something to cheer him up. After a while they brought in Tchatcha-em-ankh and he suggested that the king go out on the lake. "For", said the magician, "the heart of Your Majesty will rejoice and be happy when you sail about and see the beautiful thickets which are on the lake." Then Tchatcha-em-ankh persuaded Snorfu to allow him to arrange the trip and the story tells that he brought 'twenty ebony paddles inlaid with gold and also twenty young virgins having beautiful heads of hair and lovely forms and shapely limbs and twenty nets wherein these virgins may dress themselves instead of in their own normal clothes.' The virgins were to row and sing for his Majesty. Well, believe it or not, the old king was cheered up and had a very good time, until suddenly the leader of the rowers got her hair tangled up and her favourite piece of jewellery made of 'new turquoise' fell into the river. This made her stop rowing and singing, then, because she was their leader, all the other girls stopped as well. When Snorfu found out why she was so upset he promised to recover the jewellery and called for Tchatcha-em-ankh. The magician then did a spell ('spoke certain words of power') and caused one part of the lake to fold up and over on top of the other and so found the ornament. Snorfu was well pleased and arranged a big feast to celebrate.

This story tells of the power of just one magician, although there are many other stories and they are all just as impressive and reliable as any story ever told or written anywhere. You may choose to believe them or not.

There is another story from the time of Cheops about one of his sons, called Herutataf and a powerful magician called Teta 'who is one hundred and ten years old' and knew 'how to fasten on again to its body a head that has been cut off'. At all times and in most places man has believed and feared magic, both White Magic, which is said to be for a good cause and Black Magic, which is said to be evil. This has led to all sorts of secret societies and rites and rituals, from chanting to sacrifice. Unless you have met a witch or magician yourself you either believe or you don't.

At this point, we could decide to read the Bible and get an overall picture of what was happening to the Israelites; but I will not be going into biblical details here, as I am more concerned with telling you about the ancient Egyptians. But one thing which I must mention is what happened after the Israelites got away. Whilst they were out in the desert, Moses went up a mountain to pray. When he got to the top of the mountain he saw *Yahweh* in the form of a burning bush and God spoke to his servant and told him to write down a set of ten laws, The Ten Commandments. Moses was to give them to the people so they would know how to live their lives and be able to get to heaven. Moses carved these out on stone tablets and took them back down the mountainside. Unfortunately when he got there he was horrified and very angry, because all his people had missed his leadership and reverted to worshipping idols, probably in a panic. He found them worshipping a golden calf and in his anger Moses smashed the tablets, so had to go back up and write them again. We can only hope he got them all right the second time and didn't miss any.

Moses' set of commandments have been passed down through the ages and millions and millions of people have based their lives on them, or tried to. All in all, they're not a bad set of rules to help us lead good and consistent lives without harming society around us.

As I said before, Moses was an expert with the writing materials and probably got hold of a whole load of papyrus. He put down on paper all the old stories that were passed down through the ages, about his ancestors and maybe even yours. Right from the very beginning, of how his God, *Yahweh* or *Jehovah* as we mostly call Him today, created the world out of the waters (sounds a bit like some of the Egyptian stories of the creation doesn't it?), made all the earth, sky, oceans, trees, grass, animals and birds and fishes, the lot! Then *Yahweh* made man and because man was lonely *Yahweh* made woman. He put man and woman, who he called Adam and Eve, in an absolutely beautiful garden called Eden, with all the creatures and plants. He told Adam he could eat anything he wanted, "the seed bearing herbs and the fruit bearing tree, except the fruit from the Tree of Knowledge". Up until now Adam and Eve had everything going for them and could do whatever they wanted, just wandering round naked in this beautiful Garden of Eden, in a state of innocence, with nobody bothering them. Unfortunately, like all good things, it came to an end, because a rebel angel from *Yahweh*'s heaven, who was called *Satan*, came down to earth and started crawling round the garden trying to get up to no good. Well, to cut a long story short, said Moses in his book 'Genesis', *Satan* managed to persuade Eve to try some of the fruit from the Tree of Knowledge, because, as he said "It must be good if God doesn't want you to eat it". Eve then got Adam to eat some and all the troubles of the world started. Adam and Eve suddenly became ashamed of their nakedness. God became very angry and kicked them out of the garden, saying "Go forth and multiply", which is exactly what they did and their descendants have been doing ever since.

Moses then went on to tell us that Adam and Eve had three boys, Cain, Abel and *Seth*, who became farmers and shepherds. Mankind's trouble was far from over and Cain ended up getting very jealous of Abel and killed him. Once again there is a similarity with the old Egyptian mythology, in which *Seth* killed *Osiris*. Do you think it could be the same *Seth* and maybe that *Osiris* and Abel were the same person? Who knows? It could be that Cain said *Seth* did it and *Seth* said Cain did it. Anyway, in Moses's story Cain went off and founded his own line and the descendants of *Seth*, who are listed in the Old and New Testaments, became the Israelites. A lot happened between the time of *Seth* and that of Moses but Genesis tells us not only who had (begot) whom as a son, but also how long they lived for. If you trace this back it looks like Adam and Eve were around about 4004BC

Moses went on to write the story of the Israelites leaving Egypt in his book called Exodus and then wrote books of laws and a sort of census. These books, called Leviticus, Numbers and Deuteronomy, together with Genesis and Exodus, make up the first five books of the Old Testament and, whatever your religious beliefs are, they make good reading!

Most of the writing in Ancient Egypt was, as I have said, in hieroglyphs and used by specially educated scribes. Royalty was also taught and sometimes even princesses; we know that two of Akhenaten's daughters possessed writing equipment. The scribe's writing tools consisted of a palette holding two cakes of ink, one black and the other red, a pot of water, various size brushes and a holder for the brush. The brushes were made, often by the scribe himself, by cutting short lengths of rushes and sucking one end until it became soft. Young scribes were taught a simplified version of hieroglyphics referred to as hieratic script. The difference between these two writing styles is like the difference between our modern day capital letters and handwriting. There are many pictures of scribes on the walls of tombs and statues in Cairo Museum and elsewhere. The scribes were such a valued profession that they were always respected, paid well and could afford good tombs of their own. They often acted as advisors and became knowledgeable in sciences such as astronomy, astrology, medicine, architecture and official letter writing. Parents in Egypt would have been very keen on their son becoming a scribe.

Generally the boys of the family would take up the craft of their fathers; baker's sons would become bakers, sandal-makers' sons would be sandal-makers. The teaching was done by dad. But to enter the higher ranks of society a boy would have to learn to read and write. The boy would start his lessons in these arts at a young age and probably at considerable expense to his family It was usually the nobility rather than the wealthy, who were educated best. The schooling, often at the palace, lasted ten or twelve years and would consist of hard work memorising all the characters and lots of practice writing them. There were over seven hundred different characters of hieroglyphics and one would have to remember them all.

Here is a report of a conversation of a father to his son, taken from an ancient papyrus, exhorting him to work hard:

"It is greater than any other profession. There is nothing like it on earth. I have seen a coppersmith at work at his furnace. His fingers were like the claws of the crocodile and he stank more than a fish. The jeweller...when he has completed the inlay work of amulets, his strength vanishes and he is tired out. The barber shaves until the end of evening. But he must be up early...He takes himself from street to street to seek someone to shave. He wears out his arms to fill his stomach.The potter is covered with dirt. His clothes are stiff with mud, his headwear like rag.The weaver inside the weaving house is terrible. He cannot breathe the air. If he passes just one day without weaving he is beaten with 50 lashes of the whip. He has to give food to the doorkeeper to let him come into daylight. The arrow maker is completely wretched.The furnace maker, his fingers are burnt, his eyes are inflamed because of the heaviness of the smoke. The washerman launders at the river bank near the crocodiles!" Then the father tells his son "See, I have placed you on the path of God".

So, as you can gather, there were lots of professions open to a young boy, but to be a scribe was the best.

The 700 odd hieroglyphs were little pictures of animals, birds, wavy lines and strange shapes, but each picture was meant to represent the actual object. They were carved on stele, statues, walls and doors of tombs, temples as well as on everyday possessions. Later they were written onto papyrus. It was believed that hieroglyphics were the 'words of the gods' and therefore possessed magical powers. Not only did they represent objects, but in the afterlife they would actually become the objects. In the tomb of a king's son called Rahotep, who was also a high official in the sixth dynasty, there is a list of objects and food he would need with him in the afterlife and , of course, his name and position. If the dead person was a Pharaoh then his name would be put into the oval shaped outline called the Cartouche. This is mostly how we identify relics today, although it was often the case that a later Pharaoh would wipe out the cartouche of an earlier Pharaoh. For instance nearly every cartouche of Hatshepsut was wiped clean by her step-son Tuthmosis IV who hated her for preventing him from becoming Pharaoh when he was a boy. Fortunately, several avoided the destructive chisel and so we do know a little about Hatshepsut.

In Egypt, magic spells were written on the tomb walls inside pyramids and these we have called the 'Pyramid Texts'. This practice was often reserved for royalty. Noblemen sometimes had pyramid text spells written on the inside of their coffin. These spells were meant to protect the dead person on the journey through the underworld, so that he would suffer neither hunger, nor thirst and be safe from dangers.

Later on, in the New Kingdom and about the XVIIIth dynasty, priests sold spells in 'Books of the Dead', although they were not really books, but scrolls which contained spells to be chanted at funeral ceremonies and placed in the tomb or coffin, often with a statuette of the god *Ptah-Sokaris-Osiris*.

The word 'hieroglyph' comes from the Greek name for these characters; 'hiero' is the Greek word for 'holy' and 'glyph' is the Greek word for 'carving'. Hieroglyphics were used as the language of official documentation in the time of Alexander the Great and used in Egypt up to 300 AD. Then, however, the ability to understand hieroglyphs was lost for 1500 years.

In 1799AD some troops of Napoleon found a basalt stone tablet bearing three types of script, at a place called Rosetta. This stone, which we now call the 'Rosetta Stone' contained hieroglyphics, a demotic script and Greek. It was lucky for us, because that was the key to deciphering the hieroglyphics, since people still used the same Greek letters. A man called Jean François Champollion decided to devote his time to the task of deciphering, which, even with knowledge of Greek, was not easy. It took him over twenty years and he learned eleven languages including Greek and Hebrew. Eventually, he realised it was dated as March 27th 196BC and was a decree passed by an assembly of priests conferring Honours on Pharaoh Ptolemy V. Since then, right up until now, thousands of people have been engaged in translating the many tombs, coffins, temples, pyramids, papyri and personal possessions in and on which hieroglyphics can be seen.

10

THE EIGHTEENTH DYNASTY

We are now entering the late bronze age. This was a time when Egypt was very rich. As well as building pyramids many Pharaohs built temples in all shapes and sizes all over Egypt, in particular at Karnak. Some of the temples are still partially standing and one can see very many hieroglyphics and relief's of the various Pharaohs with representations of their gods. In fact some of these temples are very impressive in themselves, in particular the temples of Luxor and Karnak (a few miles outside Luxor). Karnak temple is the biggest temple in the world in terms of ground space. It contains several chapels and halls, some fascinating stone columns representing the papyrus plant and even a Sacred Lake. There are also a couple of obelisks (like the one in London by the Thames, wrongly called 'Cleopatra's Needle' and nothing to do with any of the several Cleopatras who ruled Egypt) . It was in great temples like this that the Pharaoh was led by the priests during annual religious festivals. These places were occupied by priests and not visited by common folk.

Karnak Temple was not built by one Pharaoh, but many, spanning over a thousand years of building, including Tuthmosis, Tutankhamun, Hatshepsut, Ramesses and Seti, all of whom placed their tombs in the valley across the Nile from Thebes. I will be mentioning some of these over the next few pages.

Over the few thousand years of the Egyptian empires, the country was invaded several times by its enemies and this created a disruption in all walks of life, like any war does, on every level from government and religious beliefs, all the way to common folk and their customs. However, it has also left even worse gaps in our knowledge of what was happening and, for several periods which we call 'intermediate periods', we are completely in the dark and don't even know the Pharaohs' names. In one such period it is believed that there may have been as many as seventy different Pharaohs in one year! Although a very great and powerful nation, Egypt had times of greatness and times of weakness. It was often the case that a particular warlike ruler spent too long being preoccupied with conquering Egypt's neighbours and going off with his armies, leaving behind officials. Many of these men were corrupt and often weak. These Pharaohs ruled the country poorly and spent all the money on fighting, leaving little behind for the people, with the result that the people and administrators would become disgruntled and argue amongst themselves. Eventually the country itself would become weak and demoralised and easily invaded by foreigners. Egypt may well have been more advanced than other countries in many ways, but these Pharaohs did not always win wars and there were often major conflicts with the Assyrians, Hyksos, Hittites and later the Greeks and Romans.

In between the VIth dynasty and the XVIIth things had changed quite dramatically. There had been many Pharaohs and many battles. At some times the Pharaoh and the country were strong, at others they were weak and morale low. Eventually the country had been overrun and ruled by the Hyksos, who had set up their capital at a city called Avaris. It was a great leader called Kamose, in 1555BC, who had defeated and evicted the Hyksos kings and took the throne for himself, re-introducing a native line of Pharaohs. This led to the establishment of the XVIII dynasty, probably the most famous of all, containing names of Pharaohs which we have all heard of, like Tutankhamun, Ramesses the Great and Merne*ptah*.

Egypt was reunited by Amenophis I (Amenhotep I), 1514–1493BC. The Pharaohs of this new dynasty, the eighteenth, tried to keep the throne in the family and often a pharaoh or a pharaoh's son married his sister or even his mother. This was because the throne was passed to the husband of the eldest daughter. The parents of Ahmose (Amosis I), the first King of the dynasty, who were Seqenenre Tao II and Queen Ahhotpe, were brother and sister. Queen Ahhotpe was well respected in her day and there is a stele which was found at Karnak, which commemorates the fact that she was able to rally the armies together and put down a rebellion. Jewellery was found on the mummy of Ahhotpe, when the tomb was discovered in 1858 AD (it can be seen now in Cairo Museum). Ahmose I married his niece, Ahmose-Nefertari, who became a very powerful queen. Amenophis I (Amenhotep I), the son of Ahmose-Nefertari, made Thebes his capital .

The priests of *Amun* (also written as *Amen*) were very happy to see Thebes become the capital city and attributed the victory over the Hyksos to the support of *Amun*. Most of the eighteenth dynasty Pharaohs dedicated much effort to conquering foreign lands. Surprisingly (maybe) this was not simply to accumulate wealth and power. It was to spread the worship of their gods, in particular *Amun*. The creation myth of *Amun* told how order was spread throughout chaos and chaos was how the Pharaohs saw the foreign lands. The Pharaohs would also demonstrate their love for *Amun* by financing the building of extensions to the Temple of Karnak near Thebes. This continued for over a thousand years and so much money was given to the priests that the Temple became one of the largest financial forces in Egypt. By the middle of the New Kingdom the Temple would own one third of all the cultivated land and employ 20% of the population.

The cult and worship of *Amun* are of a delicate nature, in the twentieth century, and in even more so throughout the Christian, Moslem and Victorian eras. Actually the rituals performed in Karnak Temple were kept secret from the general populace even in Pharonic times. The rituals we can only guess at but they were thought to consist of some sort of re-enactment of the creation of the world by *Amun*. This god was believed to have created though the act of masturbation. Only the Pharaoh and his Divine Wife, also known as the Divine Hand, would enter the innermost sanctum of the Temple of *Amun*, to perform the sacred rituals. The rituals were almost certainly sexual. Many of the images of *Amun* were of an ithyphallic form, that is the god showed an erection. The erect phallus on many paintings has been carefully erased by bashful monks or discretely covered with labels by Victorian Museum Curators. They preferred not to mention the act of creation at all. In Egypt today you will see many paintings with the offending member literally chiselled out.

They now began to associate *Amun* with the powerful sun god, *Re,* who had been the predominant god of the Old Kingdom. They called him by the name *Amun-Re.* The priests even claimed that Thebes was the original first created land. Throughout the dynasty the various Pharaohs added on to the Temple of *Amun-Re* at Karnak. They also adopted a valley on the West bank of the Nile as the site for their tombs and built several temples and monuments there.

A few years later Egypt saw the first of the four Pharaohs called Tuthmosis. Tuthmosis I had been a general under Amenophis I. He had a daughter called Hatshepsut who was to become a very unique person in Egyptian history. She married her half-brother who was to become Tuthmosis II and, when he died, she herself became co-regent with Tuthmosis III, her stepson-nephew and a very cruel tyrant and a son of Tuthmosis I by a different wife.

There is a fascinating tale from these times, the sixteenth century before Christ, about a naval officer from the city of Nekheb. He served under several Pharaohs for a total of about 50 years and his story was taken from the wall of a tomb chapel at el-Kab.

"The commander Ahmose, son of Abana his mother, said "I speak to let you know what favours were granted to me. I received the Gold of Valour (gold flies) many times. I received male and female slaves and many fields. My name was put forward as a brave man which will always be known in the land of Egypt. I grew up in the town of Nekheb. My father was Baba, son of Reonet and was a soldier of the King of Upper and Lower Egypt, Seqenenre, Tao II of the Seventeenth Dynasty. I became a soldier in his place on the ship The Wild Bull, in the time of the Lord of Two Lands, Nebpehtire, the founder of the Eighteenth Dynasty. I was still a youth, before I had taken a wife. When I had established a household I was transferred to the ship Northern because I had a good record. I used to accompany the King on foot when he was in his chariot. When the town of Avaris, the Hyksos capital, was besieged, I showed bravery in front of his majesty. I was therefore appointed to the ship Rising in

Memphis. Then there was fighting in the canal 'Pedku' of Avaris. I killed a man and cut off his hand. When this was reported to the Royal Herald he gave me my first Gold of Valour. Then there was further fighting and again I took a hand. I was given the Gold of Valour a second time. Then there was fighting south of the town and I took a man as a living prisoner. This I did by going down into the water and capturing him on the city side and then crossing the water carrying him. Again a report was made to the Royal Herald and I was awarded the Gold of Valour a third time. Avaris was sacked and I took as booty one man and three women and His Majesty gave them to me as slaves. I was at the siege of Sharuhen for three years. In the sack I made captive two women and a hand and received the Gold of Valour for the fourth time. My captives were given to me as slaves. After His Majesty had destroyed the Asiatics, he went southwards to attack the Nubian nomads. He went to Khent-en-Nefer in the region of the Second Cataract. His majesty made a great slaughter amongst the Nubian Bowmen and I brought off from there as spoil, two living captives and three hands. I was awarded with the Gold of Valour for the fifth time. Then one named Aata came to the South and he brought on his own doom. His Majesty found him at Tent-taa, a place in Kush. His Majesty carried him off and kept his people as living booty. I captured two young warriors from the ship of Aata. Then I was given five persons and a portion of land in my own town. The same was done for the rest of the crew. Then came an enemy called Tetian, an Egyptian, who had rebelled against His Majesty. He was destroyed and his followers likewise. I got three slaves as my share and some more land. Next I travelled South with King Djeserkare Amenhotep I (Amenophis I), when he sailed to Kush to enlarge borders of Egypt. His Majesty smote the Nubian Bowmen, they were destroyed and placed in fetters. I was in the van of the army and I was fighting very well. His Majesty saw my work : I carried off a living captive and gave him to the King. I brought back two other female captives as well as those I had presented to His Majesty. Then I was promoted and made a Warrior of the Ruler. After the death of the King, I accompanied his successor, Pharaoh Akheperkare

Tuthmosis I, South to Khent-en-Nefer to crush rebellion throughout the Lands of the South. I helped him repel the incursions from the desert areas. I was brave in towing the ship throughout the Cataract and so I was made a commander. Then His Majesty was informed that the Nubians were attacking us again and he became enraged. He became like a cheetah of the South; he shot his arrows at the foe and they pierced the chests of his attackers. Then the foe turned to flee as they could not stand against the wearer of the Uraeus. A great slaughter was made among the Nubian Bowmen and their dependants were carried off captive to Egypt. His Majesty journeyed northwards into Egypt and landed at Iput-isut, Karnak, to the North of Thebes, having subdued the Nine Bows, the enemies of Egypt. After this Tuthmosis I and I went forth to Retinu, to assuage his heart in the foreign countries. His Majesty reached Naharain and found the enemy while they were not yet ready for battle. As a result His Majesty made of them a great slaughter. He took countless living captives. I was in the van of the army and His Majesty saw my bravery. I captured a chariot, its horse and

A NEW KINGDOM CHARIOT WITH ARCHER

he who was in it, as a living captive. When these were presented to His Majesty, I was once again given the Gold of Valour, the sixth time. Now I have reached old age. Favoured as before, I shall go to rest in the tomb that I have made."

As you can see from this story, a life of fighting and bloodshed was considered very brave in those days and very rewarding. The was also a lot of marching involved. The story also shows how it was considered important to have a tomb to go to, 'to rest' and how it was built whilst the person was still alive. Slavery was quite common throughout Egyptian history, although no doubt the treatment of slaves varied at different times.

The mummy of the Pharaoh Seqenenre was recently (1994) on display in the Cairo National Museum of Antiquities and has a nasty gash in the head, showing how violently he was killed. A lot can be seen by scientists examining mummies, not only of Pharaohs but of people in all walks of life. Many mummies reveal that a lot of people suffered from ailments such as arthritis, sometimes dying of it: a recent examination of the mummy of a royal princess revealed that she died of toothache.

Hatshepsut, (also called Hashepsowe, Hatasu, Hashepsore, Hatshopsitu), despite being a woman, was a Pharaoh. A remarkable woman, she was daughter of Tuthmosis I, married her half-brother Tuthmosis II and acted as guardian for the young Tuthmosis III. She ruled on her own from 1473 to 1458BC and became the first and only female Pharaoh, a king rather than a queen. She claimed divine birth, that her real mother was the goddess *Hathor*, which gave her divine right to the throne of Egypt. She even wore a false ceremonial beard and dressed like a man. Eventually she was overthrown by her nephew – stepson Tuthmosis III. Hatshepsut contributed to the temples of Egypt, building a large temple at Dier el-Bahari on the west bank of the Nile at Luxor, a Rock Temple at Beni Hassan, a Red Temple at Karnak and a huge obelisk.

Throughout most of the Egyptian periods women seem to have been of little importance outside of the kitchen and bedroom. Queens and other members of sometimes extensive harems probably did very little cooking, their main purpose was childbearing. However, in the New Kingdom women seemed to be awarded titles such as King's Mother, King's Wife and King's Sister, as well as God's Hand which I have already mentioned. The Pharaoh Ahmose had honoured his grandmother Queen Tetisheri (wife of Seqenre Tao I) by ordering the building of a pyramid in her memory. Many eighteenth dynasty queens had their own land and power. Sometimes a queen would act as regent for a fatherless son. This maybe was a traditional echo passed down from the Archaic Period and the Early Period. The VIth dynasty queen Ankhes-Merire had ruled on behalf of her six year old son, Pepi II. We know very little about the powerful queens of the early dynasties except their names: Neith-Hotep, Her-Neith, Meryt-Neith and Nemaathep. We know a little more about Hatshepsut.

Here is the tale of the divine birth of Hatshepsut, translated from the hieroglyphics on the northern side of the second terrace of her temple at Dier el-Bahari, known to the Ancient Egyptians as Djer-Djeseru. The temple took six years to build and decayed over the 3400 years since, but recently it has been rebuilt. The hieroglyphic texts, though, were partly destroyed by Tuthmosis II and later by Akhenaten when he decided to erase the name of the god *Amun* everywhere.

'*Amun-Re* looked at the gods and foretold the birth of Hatshepsut. He said, "I will create a queen to rule over Tamery (the Black Land of Egypt), I will unite the Two Lands in peace in her name, I will give her all lands and all countries". While he was speaking, *Thoth*, the vizier and messenger of the gods, entered. He reminded *Amun-Re* that in the palace of Pharaoh Tuthmosis I was the Queen Ahmose, who alone could be the mother of the Great Queen. So *Thoth* and *Amun-Re* proceeded to the palace, *Amun-Re* in the guise of Ahmose's husband, Tuthmosis I. It was night and Queen Ahmose was asleep on her lion-headed couch. The Queen awoke at the entry of the two gods, roused by the sweet perfumes that *Amun-Re* brought with him. Thinking she was with her husband, she sat with *Amun-Re* on a couch which was lifted from the earth and supported by two goddesses, so that their meeting would be neither on earth or in the sky. *Amun-Re* named his daughter-to-be, saying, "She shall be called Khemenet-*Amun*-Hatshepsut. She will exercise kingship over the whole land". *Amun-Re* then instructed the Creator God, *Khnum*, to form Hatshepsut on his potter's wheel, saying "For I will give her all life and satisfaction, all stability and all joy of heart forever." *Khnum* agreed to do this and said, "I will form your daughter, Makare Hatshepsut in Life, Prosperity and Health . . . . . her form will be more exalted than the gods, in her great dignity of the King of Upper and Lower Egypt." *Khnum* then took his potter's wheel and fashioned on it two children, Hatshepsut and her ka. The frog-headed goddess Heket, Goddess of Birth, kneels to the right and extends the ankh, the sign of life, to the children, so that they might live. *Khnum* then repeats his instructions and says he has carried them out and that Hatshepsut will appear as King upon the throne of *Horus*, like *Re* living forever. Six deities assist at the birth, *Khnum*, *Heket of Heru*, *Nephthys* and *Meskhenet,* the Goddess presiding at Childbirth. Also in attendance were *Taweret*, the Goddess of Childbirth appearing as a hippopotamus, or a hippo-headed woman and *Bes,* (a dwarf god), the Protector of Children.'

In due course Hatshepsut was crowned at Heliopolis by her dad, Tuthmosis I. Hatshepsut was actually a very powerful Pharaoh and controlled Egypt from the far North to the distant South and Nubia. Her capital city was Thebes. She sent her armies deep into the South, organising expeditions to the 'Land of Punt' which brought back lots of gold and metals, spices and minerals such as turquoise. This expedition is recorded on Hatshepsut's funerary temple at Dier-el-Bahari, as is her supposed divine birth. There is a scene showing her being suckled by the Goddess *Hathor* in the form of a cow.

The next Pharaoh, Amenophis II was trained as an athlete and horseman. He apparently portrayed the classic heroic figure and went to Syria to display his fighting prowess. However, later in his reign he seems to have settled into a peaceful life.

The XVIIIth dynasty continued with Tuthmosis IV,

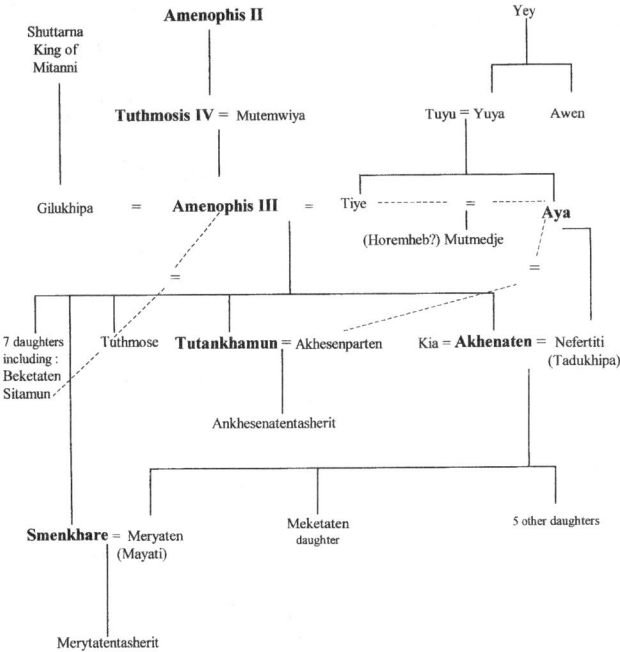

1392–1382 BC. There is an interesting story about him. One day he was out hunting in the area around the pyramids and Sphinx and decided to take a rest. In those days, at least eleven hundred years after the three large pyramids had been built at Giza, the Sphinx was largely covered with sand, with only the top of the head sticking out – a whole lot of sand considering the Sphinx is much taller than most modern houses. Well, Tuthmosis IV fell asleep next to the Sphinx and had a dream in which the Sphinx spoke to him and told him that if he ordered his men to clear all the sand away, he would become a truly great and powerful warrior. So this was exactly what Tuthmosis IV did and, after finding all the men and buckets and shovels, the sand was finally cleared. Even today in Egypt, sand is a big problem at Giza and everyday parties of workmen have to go out and sweep up the sand from around the Sphinx, but now it's for the tourists. I've never heard of anyone else having a dream like that, but it was so important to Tuthmosis that he left a stone tablet, or Stele, commemorating the episode. He certainly became a very great and powerful Pharaoh.

The Pharaoh Amenophis III, also known as Amenhotep III, 1382–1344BC, was very different to his ancestors because he married a lady of more humble origins, that is, she was not of Egyptian royal blood. Her name was Tiy, or Tiye and she was unique at this time because she appeared so often besides the Pharaoh in paintings in the tombs of nobles of the time. At Thebes, in the tomb of Heruef, she is depicted as a female sphinx trampling on an enemy woman. The inscription reads "The Principal Royal Wife, his beloved (Tiy) may she live, may she endure, may she flourish every day, who crushes every foreign land". On a stele set up by a man called Kay he requests that praise be given to *Osiris* and *Isis*, Amenhotep III and Tiy. The cult of worshipping the *Apis* bull developed again during this reign.

After the death of the Pharaoh, Queen Tiy seems to have been co-ruler with the eldest surviving son, Amenophis IV, who was soon to try to bring about major changes in Egypt; but, for a while Queen Tiy was considered sole ruler. Later she retired to the Fayyum Oasis. Queen Tiy was also exceptional in this age because she was worshipped within her lifetime and was proclaimed Divine Heiress. King Tushratta of Mitanni wrote to her after the death of Amenophis III, asking that the good relations between the two countries be allowed to continue under the rule of her son. Tiy's name even survives today in a slightly different form, Tahta, a town in Egypt. Amenophis III had two other wives, Queen Henut and Queen Nebet-Nuhe.

By the time Amenophis II came to the throne of Egypt the Pharaoh, therefore thecountry, had become extremely rich through both conquest and trade. There seemed no need to expand further and much effort was devoted to monument and temple construction.

Amenophis III built a large funerary temple on the West Bank, but unfortunately little remains to be seen today except two very impressive and colossal statues of the king, now known as the Greek named 'Colossi of Memnon'. They were so called by the Greeks because it was believed the statues represented the son of Tithonus and Aurora, about whom nothing is known but their names. These two huge and cracked statues which were once on either side of the temple, are the famous singing statues – a noise can (apparently) be heard resembling singing, at dawn, Whether it is supernatural, or if the scientific explanation of the sound being caused by internal vibrations created by the temperature and humidity changes at dawn, is closer to the truth, is open to question. The statues were repaired in the time of Septimus Severus, a Roman Emperor.

The mummy of Amenophis III was found in the tomb of Amenophis II, where it had been moved after tomb robbers had partly destroyed it in their frantic search for treasures. Upon examination of the mummy it was seen that he had been about 5 foot 2 inches tall, almost bald when he died and suffering terribly from toothache.

The last of the four Amenophis's was a very unusual man about whom little is known for sure but much is speculated. In fact he was one of the most interesting of all the Pharaohs, being far ahead of his time and something of a poet and philosopher, rather than a warrior. His name was Amenophis IV and he later changed his name to Akhenaten and ruled from 1352 to 1344BC. Throughout the rest of the Pharonic times Akhenaten was regarded very much as an evil heretic who worshipped a false god. However, evidence shows that he appreciated many of the finer experiences of life. In the Cairo museum there are several statues of Akhenaten showing him as a deformed character (with a face very different from those of all the other Pharaohs). Either he was a truly ugly king, or he didn't consider himself very handsome; whichever the case, he certainly changed art in Egypt, if only for a short while. Akhenaten, as Amenophis IV, was a pale and sickly youth with a large head and big eyes; his physical vulnerability may have led to his preoccupation with religion, sending him often into solitary retreat for contemplation. Freud considered him as the possible mentor of Moses, although evidence now suggests that Moses had died long before the birth of Akhenaten. Maybe Akhenaten had read about Moses.

It remains arguable at what age Amenophis IV ascended

the throne, probably as co-regent initially with his mother, Queen Tiy. He took as his main wife a lady called Nefertiti and, like his father, was often portrayed with his wife and sometimes with their children. Amenophis IV – Akhenaten and Nefertiti had six daughters and the number of daughters appearing in a picture is used as a clue to the chronology of events during the reign. Amenophis IV changed his name to Akhenaten in the 5th or 6th year of his reign and began proclaiming that *Aten*, represented as the sun disk, was the one and only God. He started to close the temples to all the other gods Egyptians had worshipped for so long, removing the priests and building temples to *Aten*. His belief in one supreme God led him to become a pacifist and a writer of psalm-like poems of praise.

However, the end result was that his attitude weakened Egypt as a military power. He had inherited problems from his father, mostly in Syria and Nubia. Egypt's ally, the king of Mitanni, was under attack from the Hittites and begged Akhenaten for military help, but, instead of helping, Akhenaten immersed himself in his philosophy. These attitudes made him unpopular with both priests and army.

The eldest of the six daughters of Akhenaten and Nefertiti was called Meritaten and married Smenkhkare, who would soon become Pharaoh himself. The second daughter, Meketaten, died before Akhenaten himself. The third daughter was called Akhsenpaaten and married the young Tutankhaten who was to become Tutankhamun. Nothing is known of the other three. It is thought that they had no sons, although a letter amongst the 'Tel el-Amarna letters' found in the records office at his city, suggest that they did. He had one other wife, Queen Kia, who is depicted on a pot now in the British Museum , but nothing more is known about her.

It is apparent that Akhenaten was entirely devoted to his first wife. As he began to build his new city, Akhetaten, which meant 'the Horizon of *Aten*', he inscribed to Nefertiti on a boundary stele, the words "Fair of Face, Joyous with the Double Plume, Mistress of Happiness, Endowed with Favour, at hearing whose voice one rejoices, Lady of Grace, Great of Love, whose disposition cheers the Lord of the Two Lands".

In 1887AD an old Egyptian lady discovered the Royal Records office and hundreds of cuneiform tablets, at Tell el-Amarna. By the time the authenticity of these was accepted, though, only 350 were left. They turned out to be letters between Akhenaten and the rulers of other lands, such as Anatolia, Assyria, Babylon, Cyprus and Mitaani. These became collectively known as the Amarna Letters. The area was excavated by Petrie in 1891 and 1892 with the help of a young Howard Carter. The major part of this large and ancient city was uncovered by the German excavation teams of 1907-14 and 1921-36. The tomb of Akhenaten, which he had built for himself, was in the cliffs behind Tell el-Amarna.

Shortly after the mysterious death of Akhenaten, whose mummy has never been identified, a young boy called Tutankhaten ascended to the throne. This boy is better know as Tutankhamunn who's whose tomb became so famous, after it was discovered in the Valley of the Kings, by Howard Carter in 1922. The tomb had escaped robbery and was filled with incredible wealth, impressive even by today's standards. Remember this was a comparatively unimportant Pharaoh who died at the age of nineteen. Think how much more wealth the other Pharaohs may have had and consider that the average person could often hardly afford to eat. This one-sided distribution of wealth is common throughout almost all of human history, even today.

Howard Carter recorded his exciting experience in his journals. He wrote :

"3000, 4000 years maybe, have passed and gone since human feet last trod the floor on which you stand...yet you feel it might have been yesterday".

"As details of the room emerged", he said, "slowly from the mists, strange animals, statues and gold – everywhere, the glint of gold".

At first, they had drilled a hole through and enlarged it and shone in their lanterns. Then, they made an entry and inside a small room they found life-size figures, vases, bouquets, bedsteads, a throne and a pile of chariots, but no sarcophagus. Then they found another little room and inside this was an eight foot high golden chest and a statue of the god Anubis, with jackal's head. Also there was a life-size bull's head made of gold, two chariots, thirty caskets, jewellery, statuettes and gilt couches and jewelled beds. There was also a huge coffin with a granite slab weighing 1.25 tons, over the top. They removed the top and underneath found a series of linen shrouds. Carter wrote "As the last was removed a gasp escaped our lips, so gorgeous was the sight that met our eyes; a golden effigy of the young boy king". But this was not all! Under the effigy were three coffins, one inside another. The third coffin had a lid made of 2440 pounds of gold and under this was the incredible death mask, which is so famous today.

"The face is a portrait,", wrote Carter, "his garments are encrusted with semi-precious stones, such as carnelian, turquoise and lapis lazuli".

It must have been an incredibly exciting time for Howard Carter and his helpers after years of searching for the missing tomb; it had been found more or less accidentally by a workman who was clearing away rubble and spotted a step. Today much of this wealth has been taken to exhibitions around the world, to help raise funds to preserve the ancient tombs and monuments which are decaying badly. The remainder, including the gold coffins and death mask, is on display in several rooms of Cairo Museum. The mummy of Tutankhamun is one of a few which still rests in peace in the original tomb in the Valley of the Kings. It will be a memorable experience for you if you can visit an exhibition of some of Howard Carter's fascinating finds, and see for yourself some of the splendours of the eighteenth dynasty, a time when the population of Egypt was between two and three million.

After the boy Tutankhamun died his throne and his wife were inherited by one of his old generals, Ay , Aye or Aya. No mummy of Ay has been found and, once again , we have to rely on sparse evidence such as tomb paintings for what little we can guess of him . It is thought that his father was called Yuya whose tomb is also in the Valley. However Ay did not survive for very long and was replaced by a general called Horemheb. This Pharaoh is famous for having started the building of the Hypostyle Hall at Karnak Temple, a task which was later completed by Ramesses the Great.

The eighteenth dynasty Pharaohs had gone to great lengths to have their tombs dug out of the valley side. Tomb entrances were sealed up, plans and locations known to only a few priests. Many labourers, having performed such an honourable task for the Pharaoh, were executed under the belief that the Pharaoh would secure their places in the underworld. But however well the authorities tried to keep the locations secret, knowledge leaked out and the tombs were robbed. When the tombs were entered in recent years almost all were empty, even the mummies missing. It caused tremendous excitement when caches of many royal mummies which must have been moved by priests for safekeeping, were rediscovered at the end of the nineteenth century of our era. The discovery by Howard Carter was much more exciting as the mummy was still in the tomb, within the several beautiful golden coffins and, although the tomb had been disarrayed, in what is now believed to have been a disturbed robbery attempt, it must have appeared much like it did before the tomb was sealed. Pure chance had hidden the tomb entrance under piles of rubble from a later tomb dug higher in the valley side.

11

RAMESSES THE GREAT, THE 19TH DYNASTY

During the reign of Akhenaten there had been great changes to all the temples throughout Egypt, many of which were closed down. But after Tutankhamun had ruled and then died, the throne was inherited by Ay (who was probably the father of Nefertiti, the consort of both Akhenaten and Tutankhamun) the religion reverted to *Amum*. The temples of *Amun* at Thebes were reopened, the priests re-instated and Akhenaten became regarded as a heretic.

The Pharaoh Haremheb took over the throne from 1323 to 1295BC and he was most definitely a worshipper of Amum and despised Akhenaten and his god *Aten*. Haremheb dismantled a temple Akhenaten had had built at Karnak and ensured that his own tomb would be in the Valley of the Kings. It is one of the tombs you can see if you ever go there and, like many of the others, has impressive paintings on the walls, although no mummy has ever been found. Haremheb improved the administration and began to restore order and prosperity to Egypt. He removed the names of Akhenaten, Tutankhamun and Ay from the lists of Pharaohs and began dismantling Akhetaten (the city) and using the stone for building elsewhere. He made supreme efforts to wipe out all trace of Akhenaten who was now considered evil and heretic.

Haremheb had a very strong general of his armies, a man called Menpehtire, who became Pharaoh and called himself Ramesses I. Ramesses I built the new city of Pi-Ramesse as his capital, but although establishing the XIXth dynasty, one of the most famous in Egyptian history, he only ruled for one year.

Ramesses I had a son who inherited the throne from him, Seti 1 Menma'atre, later called Sethos I by the Greeks when they wrote their history. Now pause for a moment and look at these names. Are there any hints of names of the old

Egyptian gods? Well, within the name Ramesses there is of course the name of the powerfully worshipped sun god *Ra* or *Re*. In fact if you look at the cartouche names of the Pharaohs you will see the 're' bit occurring quite frequently, which shows just how widespread and accepted this particular belief was and for so long, actually far longer than Christianity. In fact the Pharaohs were considered to be the House of *Ra*. With Seti we see the name of the god *Seth*, the one who was said to have killed *Osiris*. *Seth* was generally regarded, by the Egyptians, as an evil god who manifested in mostly unpleasant forms, like pig (they seldom ate pig), boar, snake and an unknown animal. Even so, the people accepted *Seth* as a powerful god who deserved respect and worship. He was not regarded at all like our concept of the devil, Satan and accumulated so much respect that Ramesses' son, Seti, took the name.

Seti 1 was a very active Pharaoh and tried to expand his kingdom by sending military expeditions as far as Palestine and Syria. He fought a bloodthirsty but indecisive battle with the Hittites at a place called Qadesh, sometimes spelt Kadesh. In addition to battling, Seti had time to organise several major building projects, including the 'hypostyle hall' within Karnak Temple and two new temples of his own, one on the West Bank at Thebes and the other at Abydos.

In addition to all this Seti had plenty of time to spend with his wives and consorts and had no less than 198 (yes, one hundred and ninety-eight!) children. One of his sons became Ramesses II, whom we now call Ramesses the Great.

Seti I and the Princess Tuaa, who was described on monuments as 'Royal wife, Royal mother and heiress and sharer of the throne' and may have been a descendent from the eighteenth dynasty, had a son. This was Ramesses II, whose cartouche name was User'ma'tre'setepenre and he reigned strong for sixty-six years, 1279 to 1213BC. Ramesses II seems to have been born a king. Some inscriptions show him being paid homage even before he was born. A temple at Abydos depicts Seti I showing the baby Ramesses to the people as their king, with an inscription 'he was commander of the bodyguard and the brigade of charioteers'. By the age of twelve he certainly ruled alongside his father. One stele records 'You were a boy wearing the side-lock and no monument was erected and no order was given without you. You were a youth aged ten years and all the public works were in your hands, laying their foundations'.

He probably took the throne himself at the age of about thirty, when his father died, although we are not certain of this because his reign is dated only as year 1 from the time he sat on the throne alone. He must have thought very highly of himself, because although all the Pharaohs were generally considered divine, Ramesses II actually proclaimed himself as a god and demanded worship. There is a inscription which shows Ramesses the Pharaoh burning incense before Ramesses the god! He busily employed the Israelites as slaves and became one of the most prolific builders since Cheops. The Bible records that a Pharaoh came to the throne, who became alarmed at the increase in numbers of the Israelites and ordered the death of all male infants. This could well have been Ramesses II, although all in all, things considered, he was probably no better or worse than the average Pharaoh. Remember that it is not certain who the Pharaoh of the biblical story of Moses really was; it may not have been Ramesses II at all.

One huge and famous temple was built at Abu Simbel and contained two massive 22 metre stone statues of himself and his beloved wife *Nefertari*. It is interesting to see how small Nefertari's statue is, standing next to Ramesses the Great. Nefertari's tomb is on the West Bank at Luxor and is filled with beautiful wall paintings. It is a shame but a fact, though, that after being sealed up for so many years, the paintings have suffered since the tomb was opened to the public and so many have visited. This is not due to vandalism, or any deliberate act, but due to the moisture on the tourists' breath causing salt crystals to form on the rock beneath the paint, causing the paint to flake off. This type of damage is causing devastation to monuments all over Egypt and even the Sphinx and pyramids are now beginning to crumble away. If you go to Egypt and visit these tombs and monuments, you will probably have to pay entrance fees; not a lot in terms of our money, but this is how the Department of Antiquities in Egypt raises money to help the monuments survive.

We have some ideas of what Ramesses II did and when he did it during his 66 year sovereignty. He was certainly a very great conqueror. In his second, fourth and fifth years he campaigned in Syria. In the year in between, his third alone on the throne, he marched victoriously into Ethiopia; one stele records 'the bull powerful against Ethiopia, the griffin furious against the Negroes'. In his fifth year he had his famous 'single handed fight' in sight of both armies, when he slayed many and obtained his reputation as invincible. In his eleventh year he took the coastal city of Ascalon and Jerusalem.

In his twenty-first year Ramesses II made a historical treaty, the first recorded example of an extradition treaty, with Khetasira, Prince of the Kheta tribe of the Hittites. Inscriptions carved on a wall adjoining the Great Hall at Karnak, recording the peace treaty, read 'Ramesses, Chief of Rulers, who fixes his frontiers where he pleases...'. It is a fact that political fugitives were exchanged with guarantees of safe conduct; 'Whosoever shall be so delivered up, himself, his wives, his children, let him not be smitten to death; moreover, let him not suffer in his eyes, in his mouth, in his feet; moreover, let not any crime be set against him'. The treaty was placed under the protection of the gods of both countries, 'Sutekh of Kheta, *Amun* of Egypt and all the thousand gods, the gods male and female, of rivers, of the great sea, of the winds and the clouds, of the land of Kheta and the land of Egypt'. After this Ramesses II married a Khetan Princess and there were no more wars between Ramesses II and the Hittites, producing forty- six years of peace.

This was when Ramesses II developed his passion for building great monuments, some of which I have already mentioned, as well as new cities, statues, temples, dykes, canals and wells through the stone of the desert. His additions to existing monuments were often so extensive that his works dwarfed the originals. No enterprise seemed too difficult for Ramesses II and he used, very cruelly, slaves from Ethiopia and elsewhere, who often were worked to death and had to make their own bricks out of straw and mud. Well, at least they had straw, which, according to Moses' Book of Exodus, not all slaves had! The Bible records two treasure cities being built, those of Pi-Ramesse and Pa-Tum. Pi-Ramesse is where Ramesses II set out to fight the Asiatics at the Battle of Qadesh, from which he obtained a great reputation.

Ramesses II also built a very impressive mortuary temple on the West Bank at Thebes, added to the temple at Luxor, built the Great Hall in the temple at Karnak and lots of statues of himself. His battle with the Hittites at the Battle of Qadesh is referred to in wall carvings at some of his constructions. He is often depicted with a bow and arrow.

There are tombs belonging to Kauiser and Keniamon, two scribes from this time who must have seen Ramesses the Great and maybe even Moses face to face. Papyrus scripts, now in museums, reveal that accurate records were kept of workers and captives, date tax, the transport and taxation of corn, payment of wages as well as the sale of land for burials.

The first historian in Egyptian times was alive during the time of Ramesses II. He was Khaemwese, a High Priest of *Amun* and a Magician of the Pharaoh. It is known that he 'loved restoring the Ancient Monuments' – remember that by now the pyramids were nearly two thousand years old, older to Khaemwese than the Colosseum in Rome is to us. He also visited the Step Pyramid at Saqqara and discovered that the name of the pharaoh who had built it, which was believed to have been Unas (also written as Wenis), was nowhere to be seen. So he carved it on the side! This could be an example of misleading information or of the truth preserved.

Ramesses II was probably over one hundred years old when he died and had many sons. At least two of these were to become Pharaohs, Seti II and Merneptah, the one mentioned as the possible Pharaoh at the time of the Exodus and Moses. Merne*ptah*, who ruled 1213 to 1203BC had the Cartouche name *Baenre'hotephirma'at*. He fought the Hittites again, in Syria. One indication that he was the biblical Pharaoh consists of a Stele, or stone tablet, in Cairo Museum, taken from Thebes, which mentions his struggles with the Israelites, in which Merneptah was triumphant. As it is well known, history is nearly always written either a long time after the events and relies on stories, or is written by historians specifically employed by those in power, normally the victors of war. Hence, if for instance, if Merneptah had lost against Israel but retained his personal position of power, it would be unlikely that he would record defeat. On the other hand Israel would record the victory. The reverse would be true too, if Merneptah won he would glorify his victory, whereas Israel may not mention it. On top of that, it is always possible for the loser to claim victory, simply telling untruths. Much the same happened, for instance, since the 1991 Gulf War. Although we in the western world, with all our modern technology and communications, consider ourselves well and honestly informed by the media, Saddam Hussein told *his* people that Iraq had won the war. If Iraq was to fight and win a major war, it could happen that the defeat of Iraq would never be mentioned in Iraqi history books; everybody who witnessed the 1991 war would be dead and people of the age will be reading a very false history.

The same can be said for books of religion, in particular the Bible. The Bible is actually a collection of lots of different books, gospels and letters (epistles) written at different times, in different places, by different people. You have heard about the five books written by Moses already. When King James of England arranged for the Bible to be published, it was his ministers who decided which books to include and which to ignore and that depended on what they personally believed; some people would disagree with my use of the word 'believed' and say those men were actually 'divinely inspired or led'. Nevertheless the Bible was a 'selection' of previously written materials. I'm not talking about the truth contained in the Bible, or how much is true, or the quality, but emphasising that it is a collection of selected materials. Other books were also available and not chosen for inclusion. Some of these can be read elsewhere, such as in the Apocrypha, which is in itself a collection of books, that are now omitted from the Old Testament. The word 'apocrypha' is derived from Greek and means 'hidden things'. In these cases the books have been translated from old languages, hundreds of years later. So, in short, what I am saying is that, regrettably, the history we read may not all be true and it is up to us as individuals to believe what we choose. On the other hand the gist of history is true, probably.

So, after this brief philosophical interlude, let us get into the best time-travelling machine we have available – our imaginations – and quickly fly back to 1196BC.

After the rule of the Pharaoh Merneptah, Egypt was ruled for short times by several Pharaohs, Seti II (1214–1204), Amenesse (for a year), Siptah (1204–1198), Queen Twosre (1198–1196) and Sethnakhte (1196–1194). There was a lot of civil unrest leading to a civil war and the downfall of the dynasty.

The XXth (20th) dynasty was founded and Egypt was ruled by Sethnakhte (the name of *Seth* again), who took power with the consent of the country's civil authorities. He may have been a distant relative of the reigning house. He managed, in his two years, to restore some sort of order back to Egypt after the civil war.

12

MORE RAMESSES

Sethnakhte had a son who became Ramesses III. His full name was Usermare Meryamun Ramesses Hahaon and his *Horus* name was – wait for it and take a deep breath – Ka-Nekht-Mah-Pehti-**Nekht-A-Neb**-Khepesh-Sati. Can you spot any gods' names in Ramesses III's ? There is *Ma'at, Re* and *Amun*, which confirms that some Pharaohs worshipped many gods and, if you look back at some of the other cartouche names I have told you, the same can be seen.

For anyone following literally the dates I have supplied so far, you are in for a disappointment. They may all be wrong by hundreds of years! Don't say I never warned you!

Ramesses III has been placed, along with the rest of the XXth dynasty, by Egyptologists, in the twelfth centuryBC. This was largely based on work by previous historians, written long before hieroglyphs were deciphered. Now that we understand some of the inscriptions, however, we can test the reliability of the generally accepted chronology. Everything is not well.

In his book 'Peoples of the Sea' Immanuel Velikovsky presents us with a different chronology and compares inscriptions found at Medinet Habu (which I will mention again shortly) with writings of Greek authors such as Herodotus and Diodorus. Herodotus himself, although providing beautiful insights into the history of Egypt, relied on stories told to him mostly by priests in Egypt, sometimes possibly embellishing the story himself. Velikovsky claims that Ramesses III actually reigned some 800 years later, just after the end of the Persian conquest of Egypt, in the fourth centuryBC. Furthermore Velikovsky claims that Ramesses III was the same Pharaoh as the ruler known as Nectanebo I. If we look at the *Horus* name of Ramesses II again – *Ka-Nekht-Mah-Pehti-**Nekht-A-Neb**-Khepesh-Sati* – we see that there, in the middle of it, are the syllables **Nekht-A-Neb**, very close to the name Nectanebo! If this is true then a great deal of history will need rewriting. I will echo Velikovsky's parallels between Ramesses II and Nectanebo I shortly; first let us see something about Ramesses II himself.

Ramesses III was another truly great Pharaoh and one of the richest. It was said he had more silver than anyone else who had ever lived. He is a hero as portrayed by Herodotus who interpreted inscriptions at Medinet Habu on the West Bank at Thebes. This claimed that Ramesses III descended into the underworld whilst he was still alive and played a game of draughts with a goddess, from whom he won a gold napkin. Plutarch named the goddess as *Isis* in his version of the story.

At Medinet Habu there are many bas-reliefs of religious, military and domestic life during the time of Ramesses III. He is shown smiting prisoners, playing draughts with a maiden in his harem and declaring his victory over the enemies – Sicilians, Sardinians, Etruscans, Libyans. It appears that these peple were regarded as low-life, whereas the European enemies were described as 'Great' even after their defeat. Ramesses III says "Behold I have taken their frontiers as my frontiers! I have devastated their towns, burned their crops, trampled their people underfoot. Rejoice, O Egypt! Exalt thy voice to the heavens for behold I reign over all the lands of the barbarians. I, King of Upper and Lower Egypt, Ramesses III"

Ramesses III sent his huge army off to do battle with a whole range of tribes from around the Mediterranean. These included folk from Crete, Philistia, Cyprus, the northern Mediterranean and Libya and were referred to en masse as the 'Sea Peoples'. This list of formidable opponents caused Ramesses to reorganise his administration and armies and the Sea Peoples were driven off. Ramesses III also reopened some of the old quarries in Egypt to get a lot more building done. He ruled thirty-one years, 1184–1153BC. During the later part of his reign there seems to have been persistent economic difficulties, which so often occur after expensive battles. Also the High Priest of *Amun* began to exercise direct power on parts of Egypt.

About these events Immanuel Velikovsky has a lot to suggest. He sees it as strange that although such great battles are displayed at Medinet Habu depicting Ramesses as a great warrior, accounts from records of events as belonging to the defeated peoples do not seem to mention the battles at all. However, in the fourth century, there are reports of battles in the Nile Delta between what appears to be the same Sea Peoples and a King of Egypt called Nectanebo I. At Medinet Habu the enemy are described as Pereset people, Velikovsky equates these with Persians. Nectanebo I does not mention this battle on his few monuments. These puzzling and serious omissions from differing people's histories can be solved if Ramesses III and Nectanebo I were the same Pharaoh, using different parts of his name on different monuments and referred to as only one name by foreigners of the time. When we read the descriptions of the battles of Ramesses III and the battles between Persians and Nectanebo I are startlingly similar, in the descriptions of the various warriors, the scenes and events of the battles and the events after the Pharaoh's victory. Velikovsky's argument is very convincing; all we have to do is move Ramesses III and the XXth dynasty forwards in time by about 800 years! A momentous task. This would involve finding out which of Ramesses III's successors matched which of Nectanebo I's. In his remarkable work Velikovsky achieves some considerable successes here too.

Ramesses III, like nearly all the Pharaohs of the XVIII, XIX and XXth dynasties, was buried in the Valley of the Kings. His tomb was discovered in 1768 by James Bruce, but Bruce didn't know it had been Ramesses III's, because he was unable to read the hieroglyphs in the Cartouche. It was a few years before this was understood. An interesting point about Ramesses III is that his mummy was buried three times. This was because in those days tomb robbing had become a popular pastime (and so, presumably, had the execution of those criminals who were captured) and Ramesses III was not safe anywhere after he was dead, which shows how law and order must have been breaking down in those days.

The next Pharaoh, Ramesses IV, Velikovsky equates with the Pharaoh whom the Greeks referred to as Teos or Tachos. Ramesses IV is recorded as praying to the god *Osiris* 'It is

Thou who wilt rejoice me with such length of reign as Ramesses II, the great god, in his sixty-seven years. It is Thou who wilt give me the long duration of this great reign'.

Ramesses V is a Pharaoh about whom very little is know. He is said to have died of smallpox.

Ramesses VII is another Pharaoh whom has been placed in the fourth century by Velikovsky. His *Horus* name was Nebmare-Meryamun-Ramesses-Itamun-Nutehekaon. He seems to have erased the name of Ramesses IV from monuments and inscribed his own. Velikovsky considers Ramesses VI to be the same person as Nectanebo II.

There followed a series of Ramesses, each one with a different Cartouche name. By the time of Ramesses IX the High Priest of Egypt had apparently become as important as the Pharaoh himself, and the two men are portrayed as the same height on monuments. But we will jump through time, to Ramesses X and XI, 1131 to 1070BC.

During the time of Ramesses X, at 1103BC, Chinese historians were writing about the arrival in China, from Japan, of boats made by the peoples of 'Nili', which is almost certainly the Nile. So by this time people were sailing all round the known world, as well as travelling overland. It is not known whether Egyptians were on the boats or not. Yet the journey from Egypt to China via Japan would seem to have been very difficult, even with good boats, as there was no Suez Canal. Nevertheless it may be even harder to doubt the abilities of the descendants of pyramid builders. Discoveries of tobacco and cocaine in the hair of mummies, announced in 1996, are believed by some to be equally indicative of world-wide sea voyages by the ancient Egyptians. Although it is possibly that plants similar to tobacco and coca were grown at those times but are now extinct, there are no traces and they were never mentioned. Both these plants come from South America; could it be that the Egyptians visited that continent too, returning to Egypt with intoxicants?

By this time tomb robbing at Thebes had reached scandalous proportions and something unusual had to be done, not so much to protect the riches but more to protect the mummies. The robbers seemed to have had no respect for mummies and often dug into the cadaver searching for expensive amulets, bangles, scarabs, etc, that had been wrapped with the mummy. At this time it was decided to move many of the mummies of Pharaohs from their individual tombs into new hiding places, which is why Ramesses III had to be buried three times. Such huge amounts spent on the dead did not please the populace. They were becoming increasingly unhappy and soon the civil war started again.

From 1080 to 1072BC the North of Egypt was ruled quite efficiently by Herihor, who had been a powerful general in the army of Ramesses XI and had overthrown the Viceroy of Nubia. Herihor ruled as High Priest for a while and then as Pharaoh. However, to the South at Thebes, the Priests of *Amun* had taken control under the rule of Pinedjem I. Throughout Egyptian history it happened that sometimes rule would not pass direct to a blood relative, but to a general or vizier. It was traditional that when the Pharaoh died the throne would be claimed, normally by the eldest son but, as I say, not always. In fact claims could be laid by anyone in the court who was physically present; it was often the case that a vizier or ruler or a close friend of the living Pharaoh, would persuade him to send his sons off on some adventure or task, the longer the better, supposedly to gain fame and fortune for the Pharaoh. Communications in those days were, of course, very slow, especially if delaying tactics were used and so it was often the case that the true successor to the throne would not get news that his Pharaoh was dead or put in his claim, until long after the sly and ambitious vizier or general had been made Pharaoh by the priests. This was convenient for the power seeking priests of *Amun*, because they would then have a very co-operative ruler on the throne, a man we would call a puppet. From 1070BC, with the overthrow and death of Herihor, we enter the XXIst dynasty and the Third Intermediate Period. During these years Egypt was divided again and different rulers ruled the North from Tanis and the South from Thebes. Pinedjem I, who was actually a High Priest, ruled from 1070 until 1026, from Thebes while Smendes ruled from Tanis, 1069 to 1063. His dynasty was largely recognised at Thebes, but further South remained more or less independent. A number of tombs were built at Tanis and many have been found recently, including one belonging to Psusennes I (1040–992) with a mummy with twenty-seven bangles and twenty-seven rings, now in museums.

The Third Intermediate Period is another time when several weak Pharaohs ruled in the North and priests ruled in the South. There are only a few I will mention here but a great many more existed.

From 978 to 959BC Egypt in the North was ruled by Siamun, another Pharaoh whose tomb was at Tanis. A while after him came Psusennes II and Sheshonq I (945–924). Sheshonq I founded the XXIInd dynasty and built extensions to the now famous Temple at Karnak and proclaimed himself 'Great Chief of the Me'; the 'Me' were Meshwesh Libyans. Thebes was now firmly back under control of the Pharaoh although local magnates still tried to resist the ruling house, especially in the reign of Sheshonq III (825–773).

It was during the reign of these foreign Pharaohs that a very famous king was ruling in Israel and Judah, King Solomon, a man with a reputation for wisdom. Since leaving Egypt (Exodus) the Israelites had continued to have contact with the Egyptians, whether through fighting or trading. Another Pharaoh, Sheshonq III, of the XXIInd dynasty, is the only Pharaoh actually named in the Old Testament (I Kings 14:25), under the name Shishak. Sheshonq III tried to split Egypt into four regions, each with their own rulers and all answerable to him. It was not long after the death of Solomon the Wise that Sheshonq III decided to attack Judah and sent in his armies who successfully sacked Jerusalem and plundered the Holy Temple of the Jews there.

By the end of the XXIInd dynasty, Egypt had become fragmented yet again while Nubia, which had been growing in strength for three hundred years, began to exercise its influence over the northern Nile Valley. Egypt went through a long period of anarchy whilst being ineffectively ruled by the Libyan Kings of the XXIIIrd and XXIVth dynasties, 818–712BC.

Despite being victorious in her foreign wars Egypt remained a divided land until it was united by a Nubian called Shabaka in 716, founding the XXVth dynasty and starting an era we now call the Late Period. He managed to unite Egypt by allowing Thebes a certain amount of independence, under the ruling hand of a royal representative called the 'Divine Votaress of *Amun*'.

Obviously not all the Pharaohs were popular men; some weren't liked by the people and others fell out of favour with the court. Sometimes the ambitions of the Pharaoh's overseers led them to spread false stories about the Pharaoh and to try to seize power for themselves. Sometimes they succeeded and at others, as in the following story, they failed. There is story (taken from the DevÈria 'Le Papyrus Judiciaire de Turin' in Journal Asiatique 1865, & Chabras 'Le Papyrus Magique Harris') about events during the reign of Ramesses III, when his high officials and scribes, including the Overseer of the Treasury, conspired to spread dissatisfaction throughout the kingdom and took in their trust a number of women in the royal harem and court. One was told to 'Carry abroad these words to the mothers and sisters, who will stir up the men and incite malefactors to do wrong to their Lord'. Another was appointed as a ringleader, another to listen to and report conversations. One particular high official, named Hui, the Overseer of Royal Cattle, decided to do more and used magic. He obtained formulae from books in the royal library and learned 'divine power' in order to put spells on people. He found a secret place to work in and made wax figures of men and inscribed amulets with magic symbols. He arranged for them to be taken into the palace, so that whoever carried or received them would become entranced. By means of an official called Athirma he tried to get them to Ramesses. Hui had studied his magic and was able to do 'horrible things and all the wickedness his heart could imagine', making men terrified and crazy. In the end, even the gods and goddesses were appalled and decreed that the only punishment could be death. Hui had made figures of gods and men from the same wax, which caused the men to become paralysed. Fortunately for Ramesses III the conspiracy was discovered and he set up two small courts from amongst his personal friends and companions, to investigate, saying "those guilty shall die by their own hands and tell me nothing whatever about it". So many of the conspirators, including Hui, were forced to commit suicide, a dreaded sin.

13

THE LATE PERIOD AND THE GREEKS

Just before 712BC, some 2700 years ago, Egypt was being ruled by an unpopular Pharaoh called Bocchoris and he was overthrown by a man who must have been quite ruthless. According to the historian Manetho, Bocchoris was burned alive by his successor, Shabaka, who came from Nubia in the far South of Egypt. Shabaka, however, turned out to be powerful enough to reunite Upper and Lower Egypt once again.

Shabaka managed to move the capital to Napata near the Fourth Cateract in the Sudan. However, despite the end of civil war, the XXVth dynasty saw a lot of conflict both between different parts of Egypt and with her neighbours. From 690 to 664BC a Pharaoh called Taharqa ruled. He was a religious man and built extensions to the now long-standing Temple of Karnak.

During the reign of Taharqa, Egypt began to lose control of Asia again, which resulted in two attempts at invasion by the Syrian King Esarhaddon. He was unsuccessful in 674BC, but three years later he tried again, devastated Thebes and drove the XXVth dynasty back to Nubia, Taharqa fleeing South.

The Pharaoh Tantamani, 664–657BC, was also forced to run away to the South to save his life, but this time trouble came from outside Egypt in the form of Assurbanipal of Syria. Assurbanipal, to say his name again just to give you the practice, marched his armies all the way down to Thebes which he sacked and took control of. But it was not long before he was defeated by Psammetichus I, also known as Psamtik, who founded the XXVIth dynasty. Psamtik tried to solve the problem of these troublesome local rulers up and down Egypt by getting rid of them for good! He eliminated them all and employed mercenaries from Greece, to help him keep control and to persuade the principalities to acknowledge the sovereignty of the ruling house in Sais, yet another new capital city. This was in 664BC and by the end of his reign in 610BC Egypt had recovered enough of her strength to send her armies off to attack someone else again and so the cycle continued.

It was Necho II, 610–595BC who attacked King Nebuchadnezzar II, another name which is mentioned in the Old Testament and a very powerful ruler. Necho II won that battle with the help of Greek mercenaries, destroying the cities of Joshua and Judaea and conquering Syria. This was a case of one powerful empire, Egypt, snatching lands from the grasp of another powerful empire, Babylon, which had itself invaded and snatched the land from the people who lived there. After his success at fighting, Necho II set the hands of his slaves to building the Red Sea Canal. It was not completed in his lifetime though. He ruled for fifteen years.

The last two Pharaohs of this dynasty were Amasis, who is recorded as being a drunkard yet reigned for forty-four years and finally Psammeticus III, who only lasted a year despite being sober.

During this dynasty, the XXVIth, Greeks were beginning to settle in northern Egypt and were granted the site of Naucratis, in the western Delta, as a homeland. Many of them became soldiers in the Pharaohs' armies.

Egypt was now trading and negotiating more with other Mediterranean countries. Throughout the dynasty, the Pharaoh was forced to keep a close eye on Egypt's borders, especially the border with Nubia. Psamtik II (595–589BC) had to deal with rebellions in the South and managed to secure the country against successive invasions from Assyria and Babylon.

In 525BC yet another powerful empire came into serious play and attacked and took Egypt, under the leadership of Cambyses of Persia. Egypt became a province of Persia, known as the Achaemenid Empire. This was the end of the Saite dynasty and athough the Egyptians didn't like being ordered about by Persians, they were unable to do anything about it. Cambyses founded the XXVIIth dynasty and the early kings of this dynasty adopted the traditional style of the Pharaohs towards their subjects. Herodotus wrote that Cambyses was "raving mad, destroyed religious relics and children".

A revealing letter known as the Papyrus of Ourmai tells a disturbing story of what life was like during the struggles and wars of those days. Although the papyrus is thought to have originated in the XXIst dynasty it is possible that it actually came from the XXVIIth dynasty. In the letter Ourmai tells us that Egypt had just been conquered. Listen to his lament:

"I was carried away unjustly, I am bereft of all, I am speechless, I am robbed, though I did no wrong; I am thrown out of my city, the property is seized, nothing is left. I am before the mighty wrongdoers... They are torn away from me; their wives are killed; their children are dispersed, some thrown into prison, others seized as prey. I am thrown out of my domicile, compelled to roam in harsh wanderings. The land is engulfed by enemy's fire. South, North, West and East belong to him. Bodies and bones thrown out upon the ground, and who will cover them? Their altars disappeared and offerings of salt, natron, vegetables. Thy power, O lord creator, should manifest itself. Come, save me from them."

In 521BC Darius I from Persia took the throne and sent his men off to complete the Red Sea canal that Necho II had started. Darius I also seems to have another claim to fame, evidence of which can still be seen in Egypt; he introduced the camel. The Persians had used the camel for transport for many years, but few Egyptians had ever seen such a beast. The main beast of burden previously used in Egypt was the donkey. Cambyses and Darius were the only Persian Kings who seem to have visited Egypt personally.

Darius I reigned for thirty-four years and he was succeeded by Xerxes I (486–466BC) During this reign there lived a man who was to become a great and famous Greek historian, Herodotus (484–436BC). Herodotus went to Egypt and listened to the people, writing down stories that had been passed down through the generations. He made some valuable comments about life at this time. He wrote 'Some kinds of fish they eat raw, either dried in the sun or salted; they also eat quails raw, as well as ducks and various small birds, after pickling them in brine; other kinds of birds and fish (except those which are considered sacred), they either roast or boil. When the wealthy give a party and the banquet is finished, a man carries round amongst the guests a wooden image of a corpse in a coffin, carved and painted to resemble the real thing as closely as possible...he shows it to each guest in turn and says "Look on this body, as you drink and make merry, since you will be just like it when you are dead!" Herodotus also wrote about the sacred animals in Egypt and left a wealth of information about the Egypt of his day and the Egypt that was already passed. His writings have been revered by many other historians and have helped fill many gaps in our understanding of everyday life in that period.

Egypt remained under Persian rule throughout the XXVIIth and XXVIIIth dynasties. Under the reign of Artaxercius (465–424BC) there was an anti- Persian revolt led by two men, Inaros of Libya and Amyrtaeus from Sais, supported by Athens. The city of Memphis was under siege for eighteen months before the rebels were finally defeated. The throne was usurped by Nepherites I, from Mendes, in 399BC, establishing the XXIXth dynasty, which only lasted nineteen years. In those days it must have been difficult to remember who the Pharaoh was when you got up in the morning!

The XXXth dynasty seems to have started with the Pharaoh called Nectanebo I. You will remember this name from our discussion of the work of Velikovsky on Ramesses III. Velikovsky claims that these two names belong to the same Pharaoh, thus bringing Ramesses III forwards in time by 800 or so years. Nectanebo I's great victories were those recorded by Greek historians.

In 380BC when a general from Sebennytos in the Delta, took the throne and reigned for ten years. His cousin, Teos was installed as virtual governor of Egypt and ruled from 365 to 360BC and gave the people a short, sharp and unpleasant taste of the hardships which were to come. Teos used his Greek mercenaries to go against Palestine and, in order to pay the wages, raised taxes uncomfortably high.

In 360BC Nectanebo II (360–343BC) seized the throne. Velikovsky equates him with Ramesses VI. He defeated an invasion by the Persian Artaxerxes II Ochus, who later attacked again and won, in 342BC, founding the second Persian period, the XXXIst dynasty.

The XXXIst dynasty was, however, very turbulent and brief and in 332BC Darius III Codoman (335–332BC) was crushed by the armies of the greatest conqueror the world had ever seen, Alexander of Macedonia, 'Alexander the Great'.

Alexander was born about 356BC and by the time he entered Egypt he had already subdued many other people, including the Persians and Scythians. In 334BC he had convinced the people that he was the destined conqueror of Asia by cutting the Gordian knot with his sword. He cut the knot of rawhide at the city of Gordium, although the knot belonged to a Phrygian called Gordius. Although a terrifying enemy, even cruel at times, he seems to have shown respect to religion. In Egypt he travelled 300 miles into the desert to pay homage at the temple of Zeus Ammon, and was saluted by the priests as a son of god. He won great respect from the priests of Egypt by not slaying the sacred Apis bull.

No forces seemed capable of standing against Alexander's armies; he fought with such ferocity and cunning, adding Egypt to his territory. He ruled with a glove of iron. The Greeks brought with them their own gods and these took on some of the roles of the old Egyptian gods; there are many parallels in the mythologies of Egypt, Greece and Celtic Europe. Alexander was not popular with the priesthood of Egypt and when he died, in 323BC, the priests from Memphis refused to inter his body.

Before dying though, Alexander had founded a completely new capital city, on the Mediterranean coast and within easy sailing of Greece and had named it after himself, Alexandria, which has thrived ever since. The city was on a ridge that separates the Mediterranean from Lake Mareotis. A breakwater, made of stones and nearly one mile (1.6 km) in length, was built to the Island of Pharos; this was called the Heptastadium ('seven furlongs') and enclosed a spacious harbour. The city itself was built on a regular pattern, with roads and streets intersecting and crossing at right angles. To the West there was Serapeion, the temple of Serapis. Upon the Island of Pharos was constructed one of the Seven

Wonders of the Ancient World – the Pharos Lighthouse. The city rapidly expanded and soon housed over 300,000 free citizens (that is, not counting slaves). Under the Ptolemies Alexandria would become the literary and scientific center of the world.

As this present book is being completed there have been major discoveries in the sea off Alexandria. It appears that the sea has hidden from our view, many building, palaces, statues and even the ruins of the great Pharos Lighthouse itself. We can only wait in anticipation of the information and clues which will be gathered over the years to come.

Alexandria thrives today. After the death of Cleopatra, however, the city lost some of its prosperity, suffering also from much destruction during the Jewish Revolt of 116 AD. In 215 AD the Roman Emperor Caracella ordered the killing of all the male inhabitants of Alexandria, but we know not why. Invading Muslims destroyed much of the city in 638 and 646 AD , under Amr ibn-al-As.

Alexander also built a Temple of *Thoth* at el-Ashmunein. There are many good books devoted to stories of Alexander as a boy and as a man.

After Alexander died the country started to fall apart again and when the nominal rule of his successors came to an end in 305BC, control passed to Ptolemy I Soter, son of Lagos. He had been, in effect, running the country since 323BC and continued to do so until 282BC, altogether forty-one years. This was the foundation of the last of the great dynasties of Egypt, the Ptolemaic Dynasty, which continued until it was itself defeated by the Romans, three hundred years later. Over these years the Greeks established themselves as the ruling and upper class and exploited the country economically.

14

THE PTOLEMIES

No less than fifteen kings called Ptolemy and a few Cleopatras, before we come to the very famous Cleo. Fortunately for us they all have other names by which they were known. Their names and dates are:

Ptolemy I Soter ('The Saviour')	304–284
Ptolemy II Philadelphus ('Lover of his Sister')	285–246
Ptolemy III Euergetes I ('The Benefactor')	247–222
Ptolemy IV Philopator ('Lover of his Father')	222–205
Ptolemy V Epiphanes ('God Manifest')	205–180
Ptolemy VI Philometer ('Lover of his Mother')	180–164 & 145–116
Antichus IV	168
Ptolemy VII Neos Philopator Physko	145
Ptolemy VIII Euergetes II ('The Benefactor')	170–163 & 145–116
Ptolemy IX Soter II Lathyro	116–110, 109–107 & 88–80
Cleopatra III	116–88
Ptolemy X Alexander I 'The Vetch'	110-109 and 107–88
Ptolemy XI Alexander II	80
Ptolemy XII Neos Dionysus('The Piper')Auletes	80–67 and 55–51
Berenice IV (Queen)	58–55
Ptolemy XIII	51–47
Cleopatra VII	51–30
Ptolemy XIV	47–42
Ptolemy XV Caesarion	36–30

The Ptolemies were frequently at war with their neighbours and amongst their own families, often assassinating their relatives for the sake of gaining power. Although there was some interest in building, it seems that many of this dynasty were content to wallow in drunkenness.

Ptolemy I Soter started a temple at Edfu, South of Thebes on the Nile. Work continued on this for several hundred years. The temple is still visited by tourists by the boatload.

Ptolemy II was Pharaoh from 285 to 246BC although there were times when more than one ruled as co-regents. He was called Philadelphus meaning 'Lover of his Sister' and he was the builder of one of the Seven Wonders of the Ancient World, of which little now remains. He employed an architect called Sostratus to build a lighthouse at Alexandria, no less than 400 feet high, an impressive achievement in those days. This became known as the Pharos Lighthouse. Some pieces of this lighthouse, which, when intact, was said to have been visible for a thousand miles, were discovered in the sea near Alexandra in 1995.

Egypt was the predominant naval power in the East Mediterranean and during times of less fighting the Greeks were able to build a court in Alexandria and patronise the arts. Ptolemy II built two major temples in Egypt, both at Qift, one devoted to *Min* and *Isis*. He surveyed the land for crop suitability, importing foreign strains of wheat into Egypt and introducing the practice of crop rotation.

Ptolemy III Philadelphus Euergetes, who ruled from 246 to 221BC, was called 'The Benefactor'; he raided as far as Babylon and sent out an unsuccessful expedition to try to discover the source of the Nile. It was during this time that Manetho, another Greek historian, went down to Egypt and examined some of the relief's on temple and tomb walls. From his work he produced the first 'King's List', a list of many of the Pharaohs throughout the dynasties, which is where a lot of later historians have obtained their information. He wrote, of course, in Greek. It was said that Ptolemy III was murdered by his son Ptolemy IV, who also, at one time or another, seemed to have planned the murder of his brother Magas, his uncle Lysimachus, his mother Berenice and his wife Arsinoe. Murdering one's own family was not uncommon amongst the Ptolemies.

Ptolemy IV Philopator (222/1–205BC), meaning 'Lover of his Father', continued his predecessor's wars with Egypt's enemies and won a crucial victory at Raphia in 217BC. This caused a great upsurge in nationalistic feelings within Egypt, resulting in a twenty year rebellion which led to the decline of the dynasty. After this there were many family quarrels (featuring many of the murder attempts mentioned above) and the dynasty fell more and more under the influence of another very powerful and fast growing empire, Rome.

Ptolemy V Epiphanes (205–180BC), meaning 'God Manifest', was a very cruel tyrant and during his twenty-five years the throne was usurped twice by natives, Harwennofrea and 'Ankhwennofre. Notice the familiar sound of the Egyptian names, quite distinct from the Greek and Roman, or even Assyrians and Babylonian languages. Both names contain the name of the god *Ra* (*Re*). It was also during the reign of Ptolemy V that a proclamation was written on stone in three different languages. The Rosetta Stone, so called because it was found at a place called Rosetta, contained both Greek, hieratic and hieroglyphic characters and it is thanks to this that we have been able to read the ancient inscriptions and papyri found throughout Egypt.

Ptolemy VI Philometer, meaning 'Lover of his Mother', built the Temple of *Khnum* at Esna, a temple which has been badly damaged over the years due to water levels rising.

Ptolemy VII Neos Philopator Physko ruled in 145BC for less than a year and was said to have had the Egyptian vice of drunken riotousness. Apparently, though, he did not share the family fondness for shedding blood.

Ptolemy VIII was nicknamed 'Fatty' because of his obesity. He murdered his young nephew, the heir to the throne and married the boy's mother, Cleopatra II, who shortly afterwards, gave him a baby who was called Memphites. Later, apparently, Ptolemy VIII killed the boy child and married his own niece, Cleopatra III who, in turn, bore him a son who was to become Ptolemy XI. Cleopatra III killed Cleopatra II, after her own widowhood! Ptolemy XI ended up killing his mother, Cleopatra III. These murders are examples of the struggles for power in a nation which was slowly becoming more and more dominated by external influences such as those of Rome. Few of the rulers of Egypt at these unsettled times possessed either the strength of character, or the loyalty of others, to govern effectively without help. It seems that some of the dynasty were not interested in ruling at all; these Pharaohs seem to have been content with the illusion of power.

Ptolemy IX Soter II Lathyro was co-regent with Cleopatra III. This was not the great Cleopatra (VII) to be born soon. Cleopatra III reigned 116–88BC After her unsuccessful attempt at assassinating Ptolemy IX, he killed her off.

Ptolemy X Alexander I reigned from 110–109BC and came back to the throne from 107 to 88BC.

Ptolemy XI Alexander II (80–67BC and 55–51BC) married his step-mother and then murdered her. He was himself killed by a mob in Alexandria. Certainly the Pharaohs has lost much respect and come down in status.

The throne of Egypt then passed to his cousin, Ptolemy XII Neos *Dionysus* Auletes 'The Piper', who ruled for twenty-nine years, from 80 to 51BC. Having married his step-mother, he then killed her. He was said to have been a weak drunkard, detested by the people, with a very high opinion of himself. He called himself 'Neos *Dionysus*' which means the 'new god of wine' and he built a temple at Dendera. He had 6 children: Cleopatra VI Tryphaena, Berenice IV, Cleopatra VII, Arsinoe IV, Ptolemy XIII and Ptolemy XIV. He was overthrown by Berenice IV, his daughter, whilst he was away in Rome, no doubt as a result of some sort of conspiracy. Queen Berenice IV made the people even more restless by increasing taxation and devaluing the currency. She had control for only three years, 58–55BC before her father, Ptolemy XII, returned. Although a drunkard, Ptolemy XII was an ideal puppet – ruler for Rome and was re-instated with the help of Pompey of Rome, who had visited Egypt in 63BC.

In 51BC the throne passed to Ptolemy XIII, a degenerate. Ptolemy XIII lasted only four years and in 47BC Ptolemy XIV, husband and brother of Cleopatra VII, took the throne.

The famous Cleopatra, of 'Anthony and Cleopatra' fame, ruled Egypt 51 30BC, , first as a co-regent and later alone. Cleopatra VII, although not born native to Egypt, was the only powerful Pharaoh of the dynasty, possessing great intelligence and beauty, able to win favour from foreigners and respect from Lower Egypt. She was a truly great ruler, able to regain control of the country, at least in her early years as Queen of Egypt.

After Cleopatra had died her son, Ptolemy XV Caesarion, who had ruled alongside his mother for 6 years, 36–30BC, was being killed by Octavian. The throne then passed to a series of Roman rulers.

THE GENEALOGY OF THE PTOLEMIES

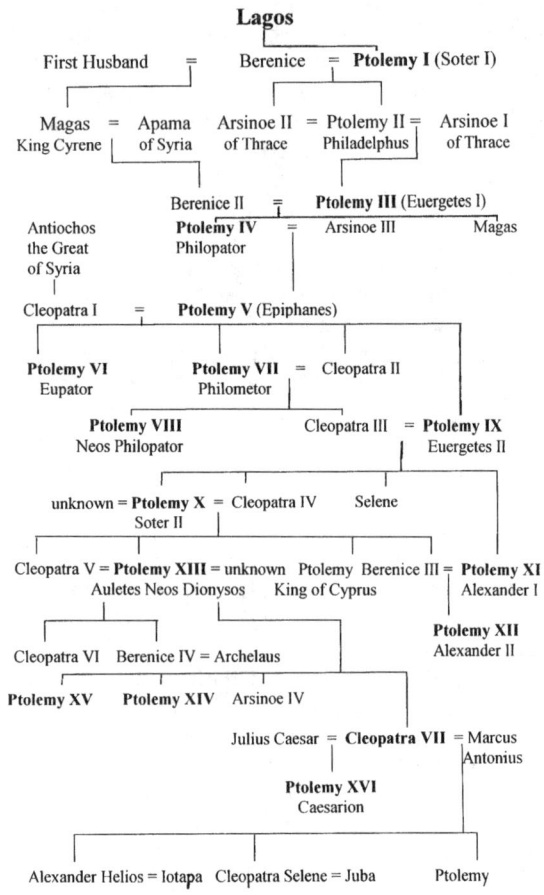

15

CLEOPATRA, JULIUS AND MARCUS

The Ptolemaic dynasty drew to a close with the life and death of Queen Cleopatra VII. Her father, Ptolemy XII Auletes, introduced her to the throne as co-regent in 51BC and then she ruled as co-regent with her brothers, Ptolemy XIII and Ptolemy XIV, both of whom she also married.

Ptolemy XIII was a drunkard; in fact he was almost fanatical about alcohol and thought that everyone around him should also get drunk. On one occasion the philosopher Demetrius had to drink himself silly, in public, to save his life.

Because Ptolemy XII had left a will putting Egypt under the care of Rome, Ptolemy XIII intended to set out for Rome to seek support for his sovereignty, taking with him huge sums of money for bribes. Although the people of Alexandria accepted him, he was driven out of Egypt as a result of increased taxes needed to pay his debts and bribes. He also visited Rhodes seeking support. Whilst Ptolemy XIII was absent from Egypt the throne was seized by Berenice IV. When he reached Rome Ptolemy XIII met Pompey and asked for the Emperor's support.

Sensing that war was imminent, the people of Alexandria sent over one hundred delegates to plead for no interference, but most of these were either killed on route or bribed. But a warning was found in the Sibylline, the most famous of the Roman Oracles "If a King of Egypt comes begging for help, he should be aided with friendship, but not with arms". Eventually Aulus Gabinius, Roman Governor of Syria, offered military help, at a charge of 10,000 talents (about £2 million). By this time Berenice had married a High Priest, Archelaus. Gabinius declared war on Berenice and Archelaus and marched his army, which contained a young Marcus Antonius, into Egypt and Alexandria. Archelaus was killed, Ptolemy restored to the throne and Berenice IV executed.

Cleopatra was now 14 and had just met Marcus Antonius for the first time. Such a fine, strong, Roman soldier won her heart immediately.

The victorious Roman soldiers, with Celtic and Germanic cavalry, occupied Alexandria and Ribirius Postumus was appointed Chancellor of the Exchequer with the task of raising the taxes necessary to cover the costs of the occupying army. In 54BC the Alexandrians drove Ribirius out of their city.

Ptolemy XIII died three years later, leaving four children from his second marriage; the oldest being Cleopatra VII, now 18. Her sister, Arsinoe, was about fifteen years old. She also had a brother of about ten or eleven, who was to become Ptolemy XIV and a younger one of about eight, later to become Ptolemy XV. Their father, Ptolemy XIII, had left a will clearly stating that he wished the throne to be occupied jointly by Cleopatra VII and Ptolemy XIV under the protection of the Roman Empire. Cleopatra and Ptolemy XIV, sister and brother, were to be married, a practice common throughout Egyptian history and perfectly acceptable in those days when they were not fully aware of the dangers of incest, although most marriages of this type were mere formalities enabling the oldest son to become uncontested heir, by marriage to the eldest daughter through whom the line was passed down. Actually the wedding was postponed as Ptolemy was still only about eleven years old, under the care of a eunuch, Potheinos and taught by a Greek called Theodotos and an unscrupulous Egyptian soldier called Achillas. Together they exercised a lot of power, greater than that of the still young Cleopatra who had weaker advisors.

Cleopatra VII developed a bad reputation, possibly originating from her enemy Octavian and her other opponents, and this reputation seems to have followed her, to some extent, through history. Plutarch was one of the few historians who saw her in a more or less favourable light, obtaining his information from Olympis, her doctor's, journals. As for her liaison with Julius Caesar, it is normally believed that she seduced him, yet she was still only twenty-one and he was a much travelled and experienced soldier of over fifty, with a reputation for destroying marriages. Cleopatra had no such reputation and was as yet unmarried. Throughout her life it seems she had only two relationships, one with Caesar with whom she lived as wife and, after his death, with Marcus Antonius.

The name Cleopatra, actually CLEOPADRA in Greek, means 'Glory of Her Race'. As for Cleopatra's appearance we have little to go on. There are a few coins in the British Museum which bear her portrait and a poor quality bust, also in the British Museum. Wall reliefs at Denderah are of little use since they were not meant as portraits. There is no mummy to examine. But we know she was a slight woman, small in height and although not an outstanding beauty she had an extremely attractive charisma. Being a Macedonian she looked more Greek than Egyptian. We do not know the colour of her eyes, hair or skin; she may well have been brunette. Plutarch wrote 'her beauty was not in itself altogether incomparable nor such as to strike those who saw her.' Dion Cassius wrote 'She was splendid to hear and see. Her charm of speech was such that she won all who listened.'. It is known that she was very intelligent and spoke many languages, including Egyptian (being the only member of her dynasty who bothered to learn it); she seldom needed a translator in international discussions. She was a patron of the Arts and Sciences and persuaded Marcus Antonius to donate over 200,000 books from the collection of the defeated Pergamum to the library in Alexandria. Her subject, Photinus, wrote a book called 'The Canon of Cleopatra', a work of arithmetic and geometry. She had a close friend in Dioscorides, an important physician, who attended her and another in Sosigenes, an astronomer.

She was certainly no more ruthless than any other of her dynasty or rank, but did kill her sister Arsinoe and some conspirators. She also executed King Artavasdes of Armenia, as a political act. She tested the efficiency of poisons on prisoners and criminals, an act which many considered merciful compared with spending their lives in the dreadful conditions of an Alexandrine prison. She accepted the powers of the gods (unlike Caesar) and her own divine affiliations, sometimes wearing the ceremonial robes of *Isis*, or maybe those of Aphrodite. She tended to demand heavy taxes and took funds from the temples, regarding it as hers by right, to pay for her battles. Bearing in mind her huge wealth and power, she was a very attractive young queen, who many a leader would have been as anxious as Caesar to liaise with.

The capital city, Alexandria, was surprisingly cut off from the rest of Egypt and the Ptolemies seldom, if ever, travelled into the country proper. It is doubtful any of them bothered to visit Giza and the Pyramids; there is certainly no record of such a visit. Alexandria would have looked more like an Italian or Greek city than Egyptian, full of palaces and villas, with galleries, gardens, the famous library, a gymnasium and a museum where science was studied. It was the most important port in the world, trading with Rome, Greece, Turkey and India. It was the biggest corn market in the world. The city was cut off from the Delta by a lake, Mareotis and set on the Mediterranean coast. On the side of the port stood the wondrous Pharos Lighthouse, the base of which had been discovered whilst this book was being prepared in 1994.

There must have been a very serious quarrel between Cleopatra VII and Ptolemy XIV in 48BC as Cleo was driven out of Egypt, although there is no direct historical record of such a row. Ptolemy XIV proclaimed himself sole King of Egypt. Cleopatra went to Syria and raised an army, preparing to march back to Alexandria and retake the throne. Her army met the opposing force of her brother- husband at Pelusium, an easterly Egyptian port and stronghold in the Delta.

At the same time there were also quarrels amongst the Romans and Julius Caesar had fought and beaten Pompey at the Battle of Pharsalia in 47BC. Julius chased Pompey to Egypt and Cleopatra, who had just been evicted by her brother sent messages to Julius asking for his help. Whilst the armies of Cleopatra and Ptolemy XIV faced each other, who should arrive by boat, but Pompey himself, seeking refuge with his friend Ptolemy XIV. Or rather he thought he was his friend because, acting on the advice of Theodotus, Ptolemy had Pompey killed, in order to gain favour with Caesar. He cut off Pompey's head and threw the body in the sea. The body was later secretly recovered and buried.

Whilst Ptolemy was still away Julius Caesar arrived in Alexandria and made himself at home in the Palace. He sent messages to the brother and sister to cease fighting, return to Alexandria and present their cases to him. He had heard about the murder of his enemy, Pompey and was severely displeased. Theodotus fled Egypt – years later he was captured and crucified by Marcus Brutus. Julius had taken about 4000 troops with him into Alexandria. The younger Ptolemy and Arsinoe were still in the palace when the troops arrived . The local population, including Egyptian troops and renegades, showed their disapproval by rioting for several days. Caesar remained unaffected and lived in luxury in the royal apartments.

Julius Caesar was demonstratively powerful, Master of Rome, the man of the moment. Ptolemy XIV returned to Alexandria immediately, but Cleopatra, fearing assassination, had to return in a small boat in secret. She entered the palace by getting Apollodorus, a faithful man, to roll her up in blankets and carry her over his shoulder, an easy task considering how small she was. Apollodorus presented the bundle to Caesar and of course when it was unrolled, out came the gorgeous Cleopatra, probably laughing. Cleopatra must have used all of her considerable charms on him. The attraction between Caesar and Cleopatra led to one of the most famous romances in history.

At this time Julius Caesar was just over fifty-four. He was full of confidence, a fearless and expert horse rider, an experienced and ferociously brave soldier. He must have been a relatively slight man of about ten stone; he was always clean shaven and immaculately dressed and groomed. He was always quiet of speech, but a great orator, direct and straightforward, a perfect aristocrat. However, he had a reputation of licentiousness as well as bravery. He held to no particular religion and was often less than scrupulous, able to turn against his friends as circumstances demanded and capable of extreme cruelty to his conquered enemies. He was probably one of the most ambitious men the world had ever seen, he desired absolute power. It was said that he cried aloud when reading about Alexander the Great, because

Alexander had conquered the world by the age of thirty, whereas Caesar, at that age, had done nothing but live the life of a debauched dandy in Rome. But, by the age of 54, Caesar had taken over eight hundred towns and subdued three hundred states; in Gaul he was responsible for the deaths of over a million men, enslaving as many again. After defeating the Usipetes and Tencteri tribes and concluding peace, he then slaughtered over 400,000 men, women and children. At Uxellodunum he maimed thousands of prisoners by cutting a hand off each.

On the other hand he was much loved and admired by his men whom he had spurred to many great victories. One story tells how he spotted a standard bearer running from the enemy and calmly stopped the chap to explain that the enemy was in fact the other way, after which the man proudly raised the standard and marched back into battle. He always shared the hardships and rations with the men, keeping nothing special for himself, which must have been quite a sacrifice considering his previous lavish lifestyle in Rome, although it appears that he was no gourmet. Another story relates how his dinner was once covered with ointment by mistake, instead of sauce; Caesar ate it, apparently without noticing!

Caesar was now in the palace with Cleopatra, whom he interviewed all night. She pleaded with him, using all her charm, explaining that a co-regency was the will of her late father. It was during this first meeting that he must have weighed up the pleasurable and political benefits of forming a liaison with the Queen of Egypt. By the end of the night he declared that Cleopatra should return to the throne, to rule alongside Ptolemy XIV. Ptolemy, however, was entirely displeased with this; all his plans had been thwarted and he had a tantrum, after which he and his minister Potheinos became largely disregarded. The population of Alexandria were also still agitated and Caesar tried to placate them by presenting Egypt with a gift – Cyprus! – in the names of the two younger royal children, Arsinoe and Prince Ptolemy. Potheinos, working against Caesar and Cleopatra, melted down the royal dishes of gold and replaced them with earthenware and wood, claiming to be raising funds to pay for

Cyprus. He also fed the army with the very lowest grade of grain, telling them that under the circumstance they were lucky to get anything. Caesar, sensing the growing hostility, responded by burning the ships of Ptolemy XIV, which stood in the harbour, destroying fifty warships, twenty-two guard ships and thirty-eight others, leaving Ptolemy with little afloat and securing his own escape route out to sea if necessary. It was said that part of the library was destroyed by the fires. He also seized the Pharos lighthouse, with which he was ensured complete control of the great harbour entrance.

While Caesar and Cleopatra were spending their time entertaining and impressing each other, no doubt falling in love, within the besieged palace in Alexandria, Cleopatra's sister Arsinoe made an escape with her male nurse, Ganymedes. They made for the headquarters of the Egyptian army and attempted to bribe the officials into putting Arsinoe on the throne. As you will see this was a time when brother and sister, sister and sister and all relationships, even mother and son, were to break down, leading to many political assassinations. Achillas, who was still loyal to Ptolemy XIV, was promptly assassinated by Ganymedes. Potheinos, the eunuch, who had been secretly conspiring with Achillas to arrange an escape route for the boy should Arsinoe gain the throne, was discovered by Caesar and beheaded. The Egyptians now attempted to poison the water supply to the palace. Caesar had to order the sinking of new wells to look for a safe supply. Fortunately plenty of fresh, good water was to be found beneath the palace grounds.

In the midst of all this, Caesar's reinforcements – the 27th Legion – arrived and he calmly sailed out to meet them, proving that he had been in no danger at all. Upon his return he easily destroyed the Egyptian vessels in the harbour and then attacked the Egyptian fleet in its home port at Heptastadium and landed on the end of Pharos Island (which today is part of the mainland) capturing the forts which overlooked the harbour. His plan was to attack across Heptastadium and drive a wedge into the city, but he was foiled on this occasion by a counter-attack in the North, which drove his forces back into the water, resulting in the loss of many lives. In fact, in making his own escape, he boarded a raft which became overcrowded. It capsized and Caesar himself was thrown into the water and had to swim for his life, under a barrage of hurled missiles, losing his beautiful cloak of office in the process. Over four hundred legionaries and more seamen were killed.

Caesar must have realised that the war was more serious than he'd imagined. Well, maybe the loss of life and his proximity to his own death in such a helpless manner brought home some reality and burst the bubble which was forming around him, convincing him of his own invulnerability. He certainly could have sailed off to Cyprus or Rome in safety, had he so desired. However, he decided to stay on at the palace with his beloved Cleo. He heard news of a strong army of reinforcements marching to his aid from Syria and became confident of victory. Rather than destroy Ptolemy XIV as a captive, he preferred to kill him as an enemy and suddenly handed him over to the Egyptian forces.

After some clever manoeuvres the Romans gained a complete victory and drove the Egyptians back beyond Memphis. Ptolemy XIV, seeing the approaching Romans, tried to escape by jumping onto a boat on the Nile, an act copied by vast numbers of his men and, as with Caesar's recent experience, the boat sank and Ptolemy was forced to swim for his life. Unlike Caesar though, the now fifteen year old Ptolemy XIV apparently failed and drowned. He was never seen again, although some years later a young man claiming to be him rose and sought support for another attempt at the throne. Caesar marched into Alexandria in triumph and Princess Arsinoe was handed over as a prisoner. Now that Ptolemy XIV was assumed dead, the young brother, Ptolemy XV, was raised to the throne alongside Cleopatra; he was now eleven.

Not only did Ptolemy XIV drown in the Nile, but Cleopatra regained the throne. She was pregnant by Caesar and persuaded him to become the Royal Consort. A marriage ceremony of sorts was held, although Caesar still had a wife under Roman law in Rome. Cleopatra spread rumours that Caesar was the Great God of Egypt and a manifestation of *Amun*. As Queen of Egypt, she was considered divine, daughter of the sun and sister of the moon and she was now married to a man said to be descended from Venus and the Olympian gods. Their child, if a boy, would become ruler of the world and fears of Egypt becoming a province of Rome would disappear. Caesar's and Cleopatra's ambitions matched perfectly and a strong political alliance developed as well as an apparently loving relationship.

Caesar was not prepared to leave Egypt until the child was born. A trip down the Nile was arranged for the Queen and her new consort, accompanied by no less than four hundred vessels, carrying his own legionaries and Cleopatra's troops. There must have been several thousand troops and it may have been his plan to sail right down to Sudan, although in the end they did not pass the first cataract, which would have required remarkable force to drag the royal house-boat over. This boat, called a Dahabiyeh was splendid, containing even several banqueting halls. They sailed past Giza, where they probably saw the Great Pyramid for the first time and visited many temples such as that at Karnak, where Cleopatra ordered the fallen obelisk to be transported to Alexandria (the same one now standing on the Thames Embankment in London and wrongly called 'Cleopatra's Needle'); an inscription commemorating the re-erection was carved at its base. Not long afterwards a child was born.

The boy was called Caesarion and became Ptolemy XVI, jointly ruling Egypt with his mum, from 36BC.

Not only was Cleopatra pretty, she was also very clever! She was the only ruler of the Ptolemaic dynasty to learn to speak native Egyptian and she was an ambitious politician , determined to keep Egypt safe from other invasions. Having Julius Caesar under her thumb, so to speak, she decided to seek extra support from other powerful Romans and probably met Marcus Antonius whom we know as Mark Antony, at about this time. Caesar then left Alexandria and headed to Rome, a trip which took about a year since he visited Antioch, rushing to the assistance of Domitius Calvinus at Zela, where he rapidly beat down the enemy, Pharnakes, son of Mithridates the Great. It is from there Caesar is said to have written to a friend, Amantis, in Rome, saying "Veni, vidi, vici", which means 'I came, I saw, I conquered'. He then sailed to Rome. Shortly afterwards he was drawn to another battle, this time against Pompeians at Tharsus in North Africa. Caesar was victor.

After returning in triumph to Rome in 46BC, Caesar finally sent for Cleopatra. Caesar was elected Dictator of the Roman world for the third time. He also sent for the prisoners Arsinoe, Ganymedes and the young brother ,who it was feared, might follow family tradition and try to claim the throne for himself in Cleopatra's absence. Caesar and his Egyptian Queen arrived amid great pomp and glory and made sure the world could see their heir, the baby Caesarion. At the celebrations Princess Arsinoe was led through the streets in gold chains and Ganymedes was executed. Soon afterwards Caesar consecrated a temple to his ancestor, Venus Genetrix and within the sanctuary placed a statue of Cleopatra, clothed as the goddess *Isis-Aphrodite,* thus proclaiming her divinity. As part of the ongoing celebrations over twenty-two thousand people were feasted and entertained with gladiator shows and a small sea battle on the artificial lake. Most of the populace readily accepted Cleopatra as an incarnation of Venus; in fact the worship of *Isis* had already been popular amongst the lower classes in Rome for some time.

It was about this time that Caesar instigated changes to the calendar. With the help of Egyptian astronomers brought over by Cleopatra, including her friend Sosigenes, the decision was made to extend the present year, 46BC, by three months (to fifteen months), thereby bringing the date in line with the actual seasons. The Julian Calendar was introduced, more or less the same calendar which we use today.

Caesar was then made 'Consul for Ten Years' and became a ruler of almost irrevocable power, regarding foreign capitals as seats of local government within his own kingdom. But, by this time, the burden of responsibility which he refused to share was taking its toll on his health. He had suffered epileptic fits all his life, but now the frequency of his suffering quickened: he was becoming more irritable and physically weaker. Doubtless Cleopatra was the only person capable of influencing him now. Together they planned to become King and Queen of Rome and the whole world.

At about this time Cleopatra's younger brother, Ptolemy XV mysteriously passed from history; we know nothing more of him. Ptolemy XVI, Caesarion, became an uncrowned King of Egypt, although still very young. It may be that Cleopatra disposed of her young brother for political reasons, but there is no solid evidence.

Caesar erected a royal statue of himself alongside the statues of the seven Royal Kings of Rome. He had sat on a golden throne in the Senate and had his head placed on coins in the classical royal pose. He made no attempt to hide his desire for the throne of Rome and , in short, was proclaiming himself divine, as a manifestation of Jupiter.

Some time before February 44BC Caesar was made 'Dictator for Life'. But the more powerful he became, the more his isolation grew and the more self-opinionated he became. He lost his temper when his orders were questioned; he expected all to rise upon his entrance but he remained seated for everyone else. He was reported to have said 'Men ought to look upon what I say as Law'. Opposition was growing, mostly in secret. In the Senate, there was a faction against him, partly because of his use of Egyptians in his court and other fears that he might move his capital to Alexandria. He certainly seemed to favour Egypt; as well as introducing the Egyptian calendar he had started using the Egyptian mint to make coins and even hiring Egyptians for public entertainment. His plans included control over everywhere and he personally supervised everything, from the building of the Corinth canal, to the placing of public libraries in Rome, as well as preparing to battle against the Parthians. He planned to return victorious after conquering Asia, then to become King of the World. This was entirely in keeping with Cleopatra's own plans for her country and her son.

However, before Caesar could leave he was invited to the senate, by a good friend (or so he thought), with the suggestion that he was about to be offered the throne. Despite warnings of 'Beware the Ides of March', he went along. Between February and March 44BC sixty to eighty senators, including many supposed friends, had plotted together to assassinate him that day. He died as a result of very many stabs from them all, including Brutus, his son (although apparently Brutus never knew it) and died on the floor. This was when he uttered his famous 'You too Brutus?' or 'Et tu Brutus'.

Caesar and Cleopatra had not been legally married under Roman law; he had probably planned to marry on his return from India. So the rulership was destined to pass to his nearest male heir, his nephew, Octavian. Cleopatra's hopes for her son were dashed.

During her months in Rome, Marcus Antonius was a frequent visitor to Caesar's palace, being a right – hand man and trusted companion; doubtless Caesar had mentioned Marcus' strengths and weaknesses to the Queen of Egypt. Marcus Antonius declared Caesarion as Caesar's son in the Senate, in an attempt to put him in Caesar's place and both the Senate and the city became divided. Civil war was about to start when Cleopatra, wisely, decided to return to Alexandria. Octavian, now nineteen years old, returned to Rome and was advised by a confident Marcus to wait before making his claims to the throne.

Marcus Antonius, whom I shall refer to as Marcus, was a man well thought of by his allies and soldiers, but much feared by his enemies. He was the opposite of Caesar, being a rougher and more down-to-earth man, of heavy build with curly hair, very much like paintings of Hercules, from whom he claimed descent. As can be seen from his bust, he had a good humoured face. With an almost lovable nature he was adored by his soldiers and irresistible to women. In battle he reigned supreme, yet he often showed mercy and honour to defeated leaders.

When Cleopatra was brought to Marcus, he was at the height of his power, master of the East, a possible future ruler of Rome and even King of the World. Having already met Marcus and heard about his virtues and faults from Caesar, Cleopatra was well prepared to know this gentle giant for what he was. When Marcus called her to meet him in Tarsus, she went with every intention of winning him to her side and that of her son Caesarion.

Rather than land immediately, Cleopatra invited Marcus Antonius to dine with her on board her royal ship, intending to take full advantage of the situation to impress him with her wealth. As he stood on shore, waiting to board, he saw a splendid spectacle. There was the ship, with its silver oars and its great purple sails hanging in the windless evening: Cleopatra, robed as Venus, was reclining on a bed beneath a golden awning, surrounded by slave women dressed as nymphs and boys dressed as cupids The best Egyptian incense drifted in the still air and a magnificent feast was served. When Marcus commented on the splendour of the banquet, Cleopatra promptly brushed aside the comment and gave him all the dishes, cups, couches and embroideries as a gift. To those ashore it must have looked like the goddess *Isis* herself had descended to earth to feast with *Dionysus*.

The following evening, she again invited him on board providing an even more splendid feast, with gifts of couches, horses and slaves for all her guests. The third night she consented to dine on land with Marcus, casually accepting his coarser approach and, at the same time, captivating his heart. She ensured that he became fully aware of her power and wealth and that of Egypt. It was not long before Marcus agreed to aid her ambitions, mainly to form an alliance against Octavian and eventually overthrow him in favour of Caesarion. So keen was she to impress him that when he asked for advice on how to improve his table and explained the cost, she laughed and said it was nothing and that she could spend a fortune on a single meal, stating a sum equal to about £150,000. Marcus wagered that this was impossible and, as proof she arranged for an enormous banquet to be laid out. "But", exclaimed Marcus, "this is no more splendid than before" and he claimed it did not equal the amount specified. Cleopatra promptly ordered a cup of vinegar to be brought and ,taking off one of a pair of large pearl earrings threw it into the vinegar, in which it dissolved. The earring was valued at £75,000. To the astonishment of Marcus she quickly drank the vinegar. She was about to remove the other earring and do the same, but her wager was declared won.

Cleopatra stayed on in Tarsus a few weeks and then returned to Alexandria. Marcus followed her in the winter of

41BC, whilst in Rome his legal wife Fulvia and brother Lucius Antonius were preparing an attack on Octavian. Marcus was unhappy with the timing of this attack and was uncertain of the outcome. Whilst in Alexandria, he would try to raise troops, supposedly for his coming war with the Parthians; he too had Caesar's dream of conquering India. After a few weeks of luxurious living in Alexandria, the marriage of Cleopatra to Marcus Antonius was sanctioned by the Egyptian priests. As Cleopatra became pregnant with his child, Marcus was forced to go to Syria to face the Parthians who had allied with Syrian princes previously deposed. Just then, news reached Marcus that Fulvia and Lucius had been bettered and had fled from Rome.

In 40BC Cleopatra gave birth to twins, a boy and a girl, whom she named Alexandra and Cleopatra Selene. We know little of her over the next four years.

Marcus Antonius had sailed to Syria and found that most of the land was already in the hands of the Parthians. He then sailed to Ephesus and went on to meet up with Fulvia in Athens. After many quarrels, each blaming the other, Fulvia became sick and died. Marcus was quick to take political advantage of this to make peace with Octavian. A treaty was signed and sealed with the marriage of Marcus Antonius to Octavia, Octavian's sister, who would eventually become the grandmother of Nero. Marcus was then able to defeat the Parthians, the great victory increasing his popularity in Rome, whereas at that time Octavian was disliked and considered cruel. Marcus' plans were now to conquer the East and reaffirm his alliance with Cleopatra before returning to Rome to oust Octavian. Then he could proclaim himself 'King of the World'.

Cleopatra, on the other hand, was feeling let down and deserted. Marcus had been away a long time and she had been alone and uncertain. How could she be sure in trusting him, but, on the other hand, could she succeed without him? Her answer seemed to be to get him to formally marry her under Egyptian and Roman law and to formalise his opposition to Octavian by insulting Octavia. With this in mind she sailed again to Syria to see him in 37BC and met up with him in Antioch. She got him to agree to marriage and he took the formal title of Autocrator, or Absolute Ruler of the East, rather than the title of King of Egypt. He also agreed to make Caesarion his legal heir and gave, as a gift to Egypt, the lands of Arabia, parts of Jordan, Samaria and Galilee, the Phoenician Coast, Lebanon, the northern coast of Syria, part of Cilicia, Cyprus and part of Crete, as dominions. The Kingdom of Judea, ruled by Herod, was included in this. Cleopatra now had much of the land once owned by her predecessors, the XVIIIth dynasty Pharaohs. She, in turn, agreed to place her finance and the military might of Egypt at Marcus' disposal.

As Marcus marched towards his Parthian campaign, Cleopatra returned to Egypt via Damascus and Judea. In Judea Herod wanted to have her killed, but was persuaded by his advisors to leave her alone: instead he gave her safe escort and she agreed to rent him the lands.

Back in Alexandria, Cleopatra gave birth to her fourth child, a son of Marcus Antonius, named, by family tradition, Ptolemy. It was not long before she received word that the campaign in Syria had already failed and that Marcus was in desperate need of more funds, which she immediately provided. As the Romans retreated Marcus was deserted by the King of Armenia. The King of Pontus had already been captured. Marcus' own troops were reduced to less than twelve thousand men.

Marcus was so ashamed of his failure that he turned to wine. Cleopatra finally arrived herself, with vital food and provisions and found Marcus in desperate misery. She carried him back to Alexandria by boat and she may well have tried to dissuade him from fighting the Parthians in order to concentrate his efforts against Octavian: this would have been more consistent with her own ambitions.

Whilst recovering in Alexandria, Marcus heard news that Octavian had defeated Sextus Pompeius and that Lepidus (the third of the Triumvirate – Octavian and Marcus Antonius being the other two) had retired. This left Octavian in complete control of the West and of Roman Africa. Events took another turn when the King of Pontus, who had been captured in the Parthian war, arrived in Alexandria, on a mission for the King of Media. Media and Parthia, allies against Marcus, had now started to quarrel: Media sought the aid of Marcus to fight Parthia. Despite protest from Cleopatra, Marcus was determined to take advantage of this and put down Parthia. Octavian then sent his sister, Octavia, to meet Marcus in Greece. She was accompanied by 2000 legionaries. This was probably an attempt by Octavian to pick a quarrel, since Marcus had already left Egypt and was sailing back to Syria with Cleopatra. Cleopatra must have been quite perturbed by this, still unsure to which wife Marcus would show ultimate loyalty.

In the winter of 35BC, Marcus was finally persuaded to return to Alexandria in preparation for an early war with Octavian. But the next spring he returned to Syria and demanded a meeting with the King of Armenia. This was ignored, so Marcus promptly marched on and captured Armenia, declaring it a Roman province. He also arranged for the marriage of Princess Iotapa, daughter of the King of Media, to his little son, the twin, Alexandra Helios.

Octavia, now feeling insulted, returned to Rome, but refused to be the cause of war between her brother and her husband. Marcus held his 'Triumph over Armenia' in Alexandria, where he showed mercy to the captured King Artavasdes and his family, who, by Roman custom, would normally have been paraded and executed. He bestowed upon Cleopatra the title of Queen of all the domains he had given her, making the thirteen year old Caesarion co-regent, with the title 'King of Kings'. He gave Armenia to his own son, Alexandra Helios. To Cleopatra Selene he gave Libya, Cyrenaica and much of North Africa. He also donated many books to the Alexandrian Library, amongst which was a collection of books from the kings of Pergamum, at a great and colourful ceremony called the 'Donations of Alexandria', in 34BC.

Towards the end of 33BC Marcus Antonius and Cleopatra collected together their forces and allies and headed for Ephesus in preparation for war with Octavian. They arrived with 200 Egyptian ships and hundreds more from Rome, as well as untold supporters. These included: Bocchus, King of Mauritania; Tarcondimotus, Ruler of Upper Cilicia; Archelaus, King of Cappadocia; Philadelphus, King of

Paphlagonia; Mithridates, King of Commagene; Sadalas and Rhoemetalces, Kings of Thrace; Amyrntas, King of Galatia. It is uncertain whether all of these leaders knew exactly what they were about to fight for, but, to them, it seemed better to fight with Marcus than to incur his wrath. Marcus had a lot of support in Rome itself, while Octavian, who had shown himself to be cruel and ruthless, was largely disliked. Octavian, however, confidently announced that anyone wishing to side with Marcus Antonius should leave Rome immediately and about four hundred senators left to join Marcus at his headquarters in Ephesus. They left behind some seven to eight hundred senators who either sided with Octavian, or remained neutral. Although war had not been officially declared, it was inevitable. However, the presence of Cleopatra and her forces in Marcus' camp caused considerable dissent amongst the newly arrived senators, who began to insist that she retire into the background leaving the residence to Caesarion, whose claim they saw as legitimate. Cleopatra argued that her fleet would fight harder if she remained and that finances would be obtained more easily if she was present and so she stayed. It may have been that she mistrusted Marcus, who she saw as having already deserted her once and it may have seemed that he was only plotting to increase his own power. Roman support began to dwindle and it was rumoured that she had put an evil spell on Marcus.

Soon Octavian issued a formal declaration of war against Cleopatra, but notably not against Marcus Antonius. Marcus felt extremely confident and somewhat foolishly left four legions in Cyrene and another three in Syria. He sat in Greece with about 110,000 foot soldiers and 12,000 horsemen, as well as several hundred ships and Cleopatra's warships. Octavian had at least two hundred and fifty warships, 80,000 foot and 12,000 horse soldiers, but was very short of food and cash to pay them. Yet Cleopatra could have supplied the armies on Egyptian grain alone; she had untold wealth at her disposal in Egypt.

As time passed, dissent grew and desertions increased, as the Marcus camp became suspicious that he had become subservient to the Queen . Many of his supporters continued urging him to send her back to Alexandria. When he tried to do so, it led to a prolonged and bitter argument with her.

In addition, several events occurred which were seen as bad omens. A statue which Marcus had erected at the Acropolis in Athens, portraying himself as Bacchus, the god of wine, was torn down by a sudden hurricane. At Patrae, the Temple of Hercules, ancestor of Marcus, was struck by lightning and a town founded by him on the East coast in Italy had been destroyed by an earthquake. His forces were badly reduced by disease: the land at Atrium, where they were based, was becoming worn and filthy and Cleopatra's ready money was dwindling.

Eventually Cleopatra reluctantly agreed to leave, but Marcus became so frightened by her anger that he feared for his life. One evening, aware of his fear, Cleopatra took some wine and, first drinking some herself, passed the cup to Marcus. Before he could drink it, she placed in it some flowers from a wreath in her hair. As he was about to drink, she then quickly knocked it from his hand, explaining how it was poisoned by her wreath, saying "I could have killed you at any time, if I could have done without you!".

On August 28th Marcus decided to attack Octavian's fleet and create an exit route for Cleopatra, using twenty thousand legionaries and two hundred archers on his ships. However, the next day a powerful storm blew up which postponed the attack two days. The situation deteriorated further as Dellius and Amyrntas deserted Marcus's camp with their knowledge of his plans.

The sea battle commenced on September 1st. Straight away it was seen that, although Marcus had more and larger ships, those of Octavian were smaller and faster and fought with fire and missiles, avoiding direct ramming. It took only three to four hours before Octavian had control of the sea battle and , as a wind towards Egypt blew up, Cleopatra saw that defeat was inevitable. Finally, in shame, she obeyed Marcus' orders and sailed towards Egypt. Marcus, devastated already, panicked when he learned that his Queen was sailing off. He rushed after her but, although she allowed him aboard, she refused to see him. It is said that he sat in misery for three days, until Cleopatra's ladies in waiting finally persuaded her to see him in her cabin, where a romantic reunion took place. They learned then that the entire fleet at Actium had been destroyed and 5000 men killed, but that the land army still stood firm.

As Cleopatra landed in Egypt and made her way back to Alexandria, Marcus stayed in a Roman garrison at ParÊtonium, one hundred and sixty miles to the West. Here he received news that his forces had been defeated and that they had surrendered to Octavian after learning that Marcus had fled. Octavian had received the submission of the whole of Greece except Corinth, and the North African legions had joined him.

Cleopatra, in Alexandria, began to pull herself together after the defeat and may well have felt that she was better rid of Marcus, who was now little more than a drunken outlaw. Her main concern was for the safety of Egypt, herself and her children and to keep down any possibility of civil unrest when the population heard of the defeat. Marcus seems to have decided to live in isolation with his wine, whilst nearly all the kings who had helped him were being dethroned by Octavian. One exception was Herod of Judea, who first went to Egypt to try to persuade Marcus to assassinate Cleopatra and failing this, then went to Octavian himself to beg for mercy. Cleopatra was expecting an invasion by Octavian soon and decided to try to get some sort of alliance with India and the Eastern nations. She gained some time as Octavian was forced to return to Rome to put down disturbances.

Caesarion was nearly seventeen and about to officially enter manhood and become King. It seems that Marcus returned to the palace in Alexandria and organised that his son, Antyllus, by his Roman wife Fulvia, should also be declared of age. An attempt was made by Cleopatra and Marcus to rekindle their relationship. The birthday celebrations were tremendous: it would have been hard to believe that the two rulers had recently suffered such a disastrous defeat and that invasion was imminent. It was unfortunate that Marcus was unable to stop celebrating and resorted to drinking alcohol all day. News arrived that Octavian had returned to Asia Minor and was preparing to invade Egypt.

Cleopatra spent a lot of her time trying to perfect poisons, experimenting on criminals in her dungeons, seeking a poison which would be quick, painless and fatal. She had decided that she would never allow herself to be captured and paraded in shame in Rome. She sent her son, Caesarion, eastwards to the port of Berenice with a large purse, telling him to prepare to sail to the East and befriend the Kings of India. She intended to bargain with, or fight, Octavian, who was already in control of Syria and had penetrated Egypt as far as Paraetonium, where Marcus had stayed in his drunken solitude.

Octavian was determined to get Marcus' head but preferred to see Marcus assassinated by Cleopatra, or his suicide, to an execution. He proclaimed that he would tear down the walls of the city, if necessary, to get Marcus. Cleopatra was ready to take her own life if she had to and prepared rooms upstairs in her mausoleum as living/dying quarters, where she heaped up untold gems and gold ready to spoil in flames.

Marcus decided to fight rather than sit out a long siege. He marched and sailed ready to meet Octavian's forces, but was again disillusioned to see most of his forces simply go over to the enemy with no fight at all.

Marcus was left virtually alone and powerless. In a panic he rushed back to the palace shouting that the Queen had betrayed him, which of course she hadn't. Cleopatra was terrified of his sword and rushed to her mausoleum with her two best ladies-in-waiting where they drew the heavy bolts across the door. She waited only to see how Octavian would react towards her before killing herself. She had selected the bite of the asp snake as her way out of life.

Although she survived, Marcus heard news of her death and tried to take his own life by driving a sword up through his chest. He bled severely, but did not immediately die; he passed into unconsciousness. When Cleopatra, in turn, learned of this she ordered his body brought to her on a stretcher. The ladies had to draw back the heavy bolts on the door, so she and her two servants could try to pull the very heavy body up through a window, with ladders from below. They carried the unconscious and blood-soaked body to a bed, where he regained consciousness. Marcus urged Cleopatra to seek terms with Octavian and then died in her arms.

Cleopatra beat her breast in despair. She was determined to end her life now, but Octavian's men arrived outside and, tricking her into a conversation through the bolted door, sneaked in through the upper window and captured her. Octavian intended to display her in Rome, threatening that should she take her own life, then he would kill her children, Caesarion and Cleopatra Selene.

The body of Marcus Antonius was given to Cleopatra and it was placed in a tomb near her mausoleum. Octavian found Marcus Antonius' other son, Antyllus, hidden in a temple. He had been betrayed by his teacher Theodorus. Octavian had Antyllus killed . The evil-minded Theodorus was himself crucified by Octavian when it was discovered he had stolen a jewel from around the dead boy's neck.

Cleopatra became very sick and frail with distress, living in her mausoleum again and, after some days, she was visited by Octavian. When she saw him she jumped from her bed, almost naked and black and blue from self-inflicted bruises begging him to allow Caesarion to keep his throne. Although Octavian promised her mercy, it was apparent to her that he did intend to put her on show in Rome, to humiliate her in his 'Triumph' celebrations; again she decided to end it all by poison. She requested that she be allowed to make sacrifice at Marcus' tomb: later she returned to her mausoleum where she bathed and plaited her hair, ate a fine meal and then wrote a note to Octavian, asking that she should be buried next to Marcus. She then sent away her guards and servants and, realising that her dynasty was at an end and that her children would be slaughtered, she took an asp, which she either had already hidden or had smuggled in with figs, and forced it to bite her (as the story tells). Octavian, seeing the note, rushed down, but arrived too late to find Cleopatra and one of her ladies already dead, the other lady living long enough to proclaim her mistress's glory.

Octavian did in fact bury Cleopatra with full honour besides Marcus Antonius. He also sent word to Berenice to bring back Caesarion, under false promises. Caesarion, acting on advice of his mentor, Rhodon, returned to Alexandria where he was promptly executed. Octavian said that there was no room in the world for two Caesars. (Remember Octavian was Julius' nephew and Caesarion was Julius' son). Thus died the last of the Egyptian Pharaohs.

With the last of the Ptolemies dead, Octavian seems to have declared himself heir to the throne of Egypt. Inscriptions on temple walls recognised him as King of Upper and Lower Egypt, Son of the Sun, Caesar, Living for Ever, Beloved of *Ptah* and *Isis*. He also took the title Autocrator. His descendants would be Emperors of Rome and Kings of Egypt and still called Pharaoh.

In fact Egypt was regarded as the personal property of the Emperor of Rome, rather than a province in the usual sense. Octavian appointed a governor, Cornelius Gallus, who ruled Egypt from 30 to 29BC and great changes were introduced into the way the country was to be run. Although the same official posts were kept, Egypt came under Roman Law and had no king or capital city of its own. The main purpose of Egypt became to supply Rome with endless quantities of grain and to pay taxes.

16

DAILY LIFE IN ANCIENT EGYPT

We know that people were living in Egypt thirty thousand years ago and that since then there was an ice age when people moved South. They drifted back to the area around Giza about nine thousand years ago. There are few remains from before then, to associate with any major civilisation, except possibly the Sphinx. The argument over the age of the Sphinx continues today. Recent information on the weathering features of the carving itself and on the surrounding structures, published by John West is generally denied by Egyptologists who seem content with their own version of human history. So whilst we are certain of the climatic changes which caused populations to shift, we are uncertain about who these people were. If, as West suggests, the Sphinx is a lot older (7 to 8 thousand years), then it is a product of some civilisation and its technology about which we know nothing. If, on the other hand, there is some other explanation of their weathered appearance then we are still left with the question of how the Sphinx and pyramids were constructed and why. Whatever the age of the monuments they are surely the result of some long lost technology or magic and a huge question mark still hangs over the time before the unification of Egypt under Menes/Narmer/Scorpion.

One thing does seem certain; whoever lived in Egypt before the first dynasty, were excellent and keen astronomers, basing their religion on their observations of the movements of the stars, possibly over many thousands of years. Ancient Egyptian religions attached great importance to stellar events and it seems that great building efforts were put in to recreate the sky on the ground, at Giza. Upon examination of the layout at Giza and comparison with the appearance of the sky around 2500BC, it is difficult to deny that Giza is a map of the heavens at that date. Tremendous importance must have been attached to the building of these massive monuments, either simply for the glory of the Pharonic ego, as some message to future generations or as a scene of initiation into secrets. It is fairly certain that the pyramids were not simply huge tombs; even if the Pharaoh's body was placed in the tomb temporarily, no such bodies have ever been found. The tremendous work erecting these structures must have been a controlling factor in the policies of Egypt, as the belief in the next life must have governed the everyday practices of the people.

Another powerful influence on Egypt was its comparative isolation, at least along the Nile, from other countries across huge expanses of unfriendly desert. People tended to travel up and down the Nile, rather than across the desert. The whole of life in Egypt was dependent on the Nile and the annual flooding and its accurate prediction. Pharaohs could fall if they could not meet their responsibility of producing the ideal flood. The Nile itself was worshipped as the god *Hapi*.

Although life throughout the three thousand or so years of the Egyptian Empire was constantly changing, one thing we can be quite sure of, the people at the top, with the power and wealth, always had better living standards than those at the bottom who could only rely on the generosity, or lack of greed, of their leaders. Nothing new there!

In fact, life for the people in Egypt remained much the same for many thousands of years. Before Egypt acquired televisions, cars, electricity and all the modern day technology, it would have been quite hard for a lost time-traveller landing in Egypt to know exactly which century they had landed in. When Amelia B Edwards visited the country just over one hundred years ago, she remarked how little it must have changed since the time of the Pharaohs: she was talking about the main tourist places and even today many other parts of the country are still the same. As she said, we would certainly expect it to be a lot more changed than it is!

Egyptian men today are very much the same colour and build as those we see in paintings on the walls of tombs (that is the workers, not the Pharaohs to whom the ancient artists may well have been unduly generous). The farmers still take water from the Nile using the shaduf, a lever system and they still tip it into hand-dug irrigation channels. They plough and sow the fields using the same tools, probably descendants from the same oxen. People still eat mostly with the fingers, pouring water over their hands for washing before meals, from ewers which appear the same as in ancient paintings, into identical basins. Water is served to guests in exactly the same type of jars as Cheops used four thousand years ago, with flowers in the jars' necks. Even one of the favourite dishes served is the same, spicy minced meat stuffed into cucumbers! Musicians, girl dancers and fools still perform at banquets at the lower end of the hall. Little boys in the South still wear their hair in side-locks exactly the same as the boy Ramesses II and girls dress the same for parties. On the whole, life for the poor is unchanged.

The most powerful people in all the Egyptian periods were mostly men, usually the Pharaoh and the High Priests. Although these too were affected in times of famine, they usually got the best to eat, the best fabric, the most leisure, etc.. Below them would be their immediate families and companions, the heads of the armed forces, magicians and scribes to the royal court, the local rulers called Nomarchs and their families, skilled craftsmen and, at the bottom of the list, soldiers, workers, tomb diggers and finally the slaves when they existed.

Of course the Pharaoh and courtiers would always be seen in the very best of clothes and ceremonial gear, while the slaves would be lucky to get a loincloth. From the earliest times in our story, 5000BC, mankind in Egypt was using animal pelts. The poorer the people the coarser their clothing. Fortunately the weather was warm with little rain, but nights were cold in the desert. As time progressed, they learned to use flax and hemp for clothing. Sandals were made from reed and the better ones from leather. The Pharaohs often wore wigs made from human hair. Jewellery was worn by many people throughout the ages and the hierarchy got the best of the available gold, silver and semi-precious stones, often imported, such as turquoise and lapis lazuli. Necklaces and combs made of stones from 5000BC, have been found at an old Neolithic site called Beni-Salama.

From about 4000BC developments in Upper Egypt and

Lower Egypt were probably slightly different, although our view of their lives is totally dependent on what has been found, since nothing was being written at that time, at least as far as we know. In Lower Egypt traces of low mud huts and stone vases have been unearthed at Merimba. In Upper Egypt at El-Badari, un-warlike stone tools, thin bowls and polished stone figurines from this early or archaic period have been discovered.

From earliest times mankind survived by hunting. Ancient legends tell that man learned, from *Osiris*, to grow crops such as wheat and barley, to use sickles and flails and to mill the cereals and make baskets and mats out of grasses. There are tomb paintings of farmers using a winnowing fan. An early invention, still used along the Nile today, was the shaduf, a simple lever system to raise water from the river to irrigate the land in trenches. In Upper Egypt early man domesticated dogs and goats and, in Lower Egypt, kept sheep and oxen. Pigs, the animal associated with the god *Seth*, were bred in the North. Fishing nets were made from papyrus and reeds.

Our knowledge of lifestyles during the early dynastic times is marginally better. By 3000BC a lot of ideas had been brought to Egypt by its new masters and the differences between North and South evened out. The Pharaohs introduced their own gods and started building temples, although both the gods and the temples were very much for them, rather than for the common folk. It is probable that each individual house would have had its own statues or wall paintings of the preferred gods and that the gods were probably only prayed to when needed. For instance when the time for the inundation was due, Hapi, the Nile god, would be appeased.

Our knowledge of what the ancients ate comes from remains found in old rubbish tips – one man's rubbish becomes another man's archaeological treasure! – and from paintings on the walls of tombs, which they had been making for hundreds of years. From these scraps of information we gather that they grew and ate onions, garlic, leeks, beans, lentils, lettuce, gourds, dates, figs, cucumbers, melons, grapes (used as raisins and to make wine)and barley and wheat for beer and bread. They do not seem to have had any citrus fruit at all. They also collected honey from bees, ate fish, quails and ducks (probably raw),as well as geese, oxen, sheep and goats. So you can see they had a good range of food, but of course, this was when the Nile flooded to the best level and there was plenty of fertile land. In other times there were extreme shortages and famine when plenty of people died of starvation and disease. Life expectancy for the average person was not long, usually about thirty years. The Pharaohs, not surprisingly, usually lived longer, healthier lives.

People generally lived in houses made from mud-bricks, which were made by mixing mud, straw and pebbles in buckets and pouring the mixture into wooden frames which would be left to dry in the sun. Inside the house the walls were plastered and sometimes painted. The few windows were small and glassless. Richer people had larger houses with stairs leading up to the roof and sometimes a pool stocked with small fish. Small charcoal fires were used for cooking. Some of the information on the design of houses has come from tombs; a small model of a house, called the 'soul house', was made for the use of the dead person in the afterlife and placed in the tomb.

Finds of ancient necklaces made from feldspar (green) and carnelian(orange) from the desert, show us that not everyone had to work equally hard in the fields. Some artisans must have been rewarded for their special skills.

Many small items have been found which give us an insight into what the people did in their spare time. Carved and polished stone vases would be seen in the home. People who could afford it, liked to dress up and throw parties. Slate palettes, often cut into the form of an animal, were used to grind ores for green and grey-black eye paint, worn by both men and women and a rough form of lip-paint . Travelling barbers roamed the land looking for hair to cut and beards to shave. Women used to curl their hair using heated tongs. Henna was often used to colour the hair or the skin. An old song from a tomb wall said 'Put myrrh on your head and dress up in beautiful clothes'.

Entertainment at parties, banquets and official functions,

was provided by musicians, dancers and acrobats, also seen in tomb paintings. Amongst the musical instruments we can see they had five-stringed harps, bronze cymbals, rattles, clappers and, in later times, lyre and lute.

Children and adults too, played games. The popular games we know of were a form of leap-frog called 'Khuzza Lawizza'. Boys played at being soldiers and girls played with dolls. They also had model animals, balls and spinning tops. Later on, in the times of Tutankhamun and Ramesses the Great, the Pharaohs and nobility played a game called 'Senet', which involved throwing small sticks. These served as dice; the idea was to move one's pieces around a board, capturing spaces or sending one's opponent's pieces backwards. The first of the two players to get all his pieces off the board at the end was the winner. There is a beautiful painting of Tutankhamun playing with his Queen and an intact game of senet was found in his tomb by Howard Carter. You can buy Senet in shops today, although it's not quite as grand as Tutankhamun's version. Another game they played was called 'Snake', which involved moving stones around a coil; the first person to reach the centre being the winner. In addition to these pastimes there would have been storytelling around a fire or under a tree, which is how fables survived long before writing. Some researchers today believe that these stories contained great hidden knowledge to be passed down from generation to generation until such a time that they could, once again, be understood and that such a time is now.

The ordinary people did not have temples or churches to go to, so the main gods of the Pharaohs and priests were not important in everyday life. Only priests and kings went to the temples, except on special ceremonial occasions when the people would turn out to watch the processions. Priests had titles like First, Second or Third 'God's Servant' and lower ones were 'Pure Ones' or 'God's Fathers'. They mostly shaved their heads and served the statues of the gods in inner sanctums. Ceremonies involved the burning of incense and special oil lamps and the scattering of sacred water from the sacred lake within the temple grounds, for purification. Offerings of food were left for the gods to eat, if they wanted to. Some priests would spend their whole lives serving at a particular temple, conducting or helping with the many sacred festivals and ceremonies that differed depending on location and which god was worshipped. Other priests resided at mortuary temples, making sure that daily offerings were made and that the place was kept clean.

In some cases the worship of a dead Pharaoh continued for many years. At Giza the sacred rites were performed in the temple in worship to Khafre (Cheophren), the son of Khufu (Cheops) and builder of the second largest pyramid there, as long as two thousand years later! The cult of Khafre was older then than Christianity is now! The people were all preoccupied with surviving in the afterlife.

The land either side of the Nile is fertile and green, a garden of Eden or paradise compared with the surrounding barren deserts and the people were very attached to it. No matter how poor you were, how hard life was, or how hungry you were, you were always far better off than you would be out there in the hot hell of the desert; this concept applied to the underworld too and people tried to ensure that the afterlife was as pleasant as Egypt by preparing their tombs.

It is certain that Egyptians would have spent a large part of their lives preparing for their afterlife journey and they believed that you had to take your necessities and luxuries with you beyond the grave. In pre-dynastic times, burials were in shallow pits, maybe covered with a mound long since swept away by wind and sand. Personal items which belonged to the deceased were left in the pit, such as a comb, a tool, a cup or a piece of jewellery. Because the sand was so dry the body became dehydrated and therefore preserved.

This natural process was so good that one particular body has lasted six thousand years and recently been found, together with traces of ginger hair. Needless to say he has been nicknamed 'Ginger'. Later the Egyptians went to great length to preserve their dead bodies, especially those of the Pharaohs, using mummification techniques, as they believed the body would be needed again. Tombs were decorated with spells to help the Pharaoh pass all the tests and tombs of nobles were decorated with scenes of life, or the best of it.

The tombs were also representations of the house or palace of the deceased and it was common practice for family or descendants to take daily offerings of food and wine to help their ancestors survive in the underworld and to win their blessings; these were left outside at a nearby mortuary chapel. It was believed that the dead person's spirit would then travel out of the tomb for the refreshments. It must have been a major moral dilemma for the Pharaohs in later times, when there had been so much tomb robbing and destruction of the precious and vital mummies of their forefathers going on. The mortuary chapel became a good pointer to the whereabouts of the body and treasures and so decisions had to be made to change this. At the Valley of the Kings the decision was implemented by Tuthmosis I, who placed his tomb in the valley and his chapel several miles away on the other side of a hill, thus increasing the hardship and length of the journey his soul would have to make. Not that it did much good, since the tombs built in the valley were all robbed, except one, that of Tutankhamun and it looks like an attempt was made at that too. The people used to pray to their ancestors for gifts or help and so it became like a two-way bargain. The people fed the spirits of the dead and the dead, in turn, helped the living. It was believed that if the spirit was not fed, it would have to eat filth. There is a story that one man asked his ancestors for so much and was so disappointed that he went to the tomb and shouted at them that he was not going to feed them any more!

It was the priests who did most of the reading and writing and taught the boys who would become the future nobility, scribes, generals, architects and potentates, so you can imagine the powerful position that priests were in.

Most people turned to magic to help solve their problems, illnesses and hardships. Papyri have been found which show skills in medicine and knowledge of anatomy. They contained writings about the importance of the heart and how to take the pulse. They also had remedies for eye problems, tumours and gynaecological problems. Unfortunately, though, there were many ailments they could do nothing for, for example an abscess. A mummy of a Princess has been found and, upon examination of the remains, it looked like the cause of death had been toothache. People believed that sickness was caused by worm-like creatures which had got into the body. We know that the ancients employed the use of plants, herbs and berries such as juniper from the Lebanon and cannabis, to make medicines.

Examinations and analysis of hair and tissue from New Kingdom mummies, conducted at Manchester University in 1996, revealed traces of both nicotine and cocaine. This remarkable discovery, with modern-day contamination ruled out, has led to speculation of exactly how well travelled the Ancient Egyptians were. There is no evidence that tobacco or coca were grown in Egypt; could it be that the sailed to South America and back? Were they officials or were they ancient drug smugglers? Maybe we will never know.

The most powerful man in the Kingdom, below the Pharaoh, was the Vizier He was often a member of the Pharaoh's own family in the early days or selected from amongst nobility, priests or powerful land owners. Sometimes there was a separate Vizier for Upper and Lower Egypt.

The Vizier's responsibilities were many, ranging from organising the Pharaoh's day and appearances, to employing palace staff and bodyguards. He issued receipts and took daily reports from numerous subordinates. He co-ordinated reports from the Nomes, sealed documents of state and controlled access to archives and libraries. He also supervised all legal matters and even supervised the felling of trees. He had to deal with all territorial disputes within two months, or within 3 days if within his own town. He was usually the closest and most trusted man to the Pharaoh, knowing privileged secrets and partaking in royal decisions. He also was Chief Justice.

The legal system in Ancient Egypt was such that each city had its own council of elders, called a Saru, or later, a Kenbet, which advised on policing matters to a tribunal or court, called the Zazat. All serious crimes went to the Great Kenbet at Memphis. The most senior court was that of the Vizier. An inscription reads 'Audience is not given to the man at the back before the man at the front' – that is to say, they had a system of queues. The main concern of the Vizier was the will of the Pharaoh and not justice. Tuthmosis III, in a speech to his newly appointed Vizier Rekhmara, said to him "To be a Vizier requires not mildness but firmness. You must not take sides with the Saru or Zazat or make any man a slave. When a petitioner comes from Upper or Lower Egypt you must look thoroughly into his case and act in such a way that he has his rights. Remember also that an official must live with his face uncovered (meaning that the public were entitled to know his secrets). The wind and the water report all that he does. Look on your friend as a stranger and a stranger as your friend. An official who acts in this way will hold his post a long time. Do not send away any petitioner unheard and do not brusquely reject what he says. If you refuse him, tell him why. A man with grievance likes his tale to be heard even more than he wants it put right. Do not fly into a rage with a man wrongfully. Fly into a rage when rage is necessary; a real magistrate is always feared. If he is feared it makes the court procedure more impressive. But if people are scared out of their wits by him, it can do his reputation a great deal of harm. People won't say of him "There's a fine fellow". You will be respected in your profession if you act strictly according to the dictates of justice. When a man is an official he should act according to the rules laid down for him. Happy is the man who does what he is told! Never swerve from the letter of justice, whose tenets are familiar to you. Look what happens to a presumptuous official: Pharaoh sets the timid above the presumptuous. Act therefore in accordance with the rules laid down for you".

It seems to me, the author, that there are words of wisdom in this that many a modern day politician or leader should consider carefully.

Sometimes a Vizier would become so powerful that he would inherit the throne. Amenemhat was a Vizier of Mentuhotep and later became Pharaoh. Imhotep, the Vizier of Hosar and architect of the Step pyramid, became deified, received burial in a special tomb and was worshipped in Egypt for a thousand years.

The Chancellor was almost as powerful a man as the Vizier. He was also called the 'Director of the Seal' and dealt with complicated economic and trading problems, collecting taxes and handling the treasury and storehouses. Since taxes were paid in kind (that is, a man paid a percentage of what he produced), these storehouses must have been used and since many products were perishable, they had to be distributed, exported, or preserved quickly.

Around the Pharaoh there was many companions, often honoured men, who stayed at the palace at the Pharaoh's expense. These had titles such as 'Unique Friend', 'King's Companion', or a title descriptive of some job he may have been responsible for, such as 'Director of the King's Dress', 'Director of Oils', 'Keeper of the King's Wigs', 'Royal Sandal Bearer', etc.

The Pharaoh was pampered and educated from childhood into the belief that he was divine and usually, when an adult, acted so. They must have emanated auras of power and certainly the majority of their servants were devoted.

Here is a translation of an inscription found at Abydos, in a tomb which belonged to a man called Weni, a courtier at the time of Pepy I, in the sixth dynasty. This shows the satisfaction and honour a man might have felt in serving his king. It reads :

"I was born and brought up in the reign of King Teti. My first post was that of superintendent of royal tenants, but King Pepy made me a groom of the bedchamber. I was then promoted to the rank of King's Friend and made a supervisor of the King's Pyramid City. The King next elevated me to a judgeship, for he loved me with his whole heart, more than any other of his subjects. I discussed state secrets in the sole company of the vizier. I dealt in the King's name in matters relating to the harim and the six great courts of justice, for I was dearer to the King than any other noble, dignitary or subject. I begged his sacred majesty to bring me a white limestone sarcophagus from Tura and he ordered the chancellor to set sail with mariners and labourers to fetch it for me. It arrived with its lid, a door, a false door, lintels, foundations and an offering table. The King had never done anything of the kind before for any other subject. He did it because I pleased him. When I was a judge I was promoted Unique Friend and a chief superintendent of the royal tenants, over the heads of four other superintendents. I did exactly what the King wanted, on escort duty, in planning Royal Progresses, in waiting attendance. I continually took care to act in such a way that the King would praise me. When secret proceedings were taken in the harim against the queen, the King brought me in to hear. There was nobody else there, just me. There was no vizier or nobleman; just me. When it came to recording the case in writing, I did it with one other judge. And I started life as a mere superintendent of tenants. Before the King called me in no one had previously had the opportunity to hear secrets of the royal harim. This was because the king had a higher opinion of me than he had of all his other officials, councillors and servants".

It seems that most Pharaohs from the time of Narmer to the time of the early Ptolemies, commanded such great respect. Certainly they inspired or forced the building of the tremendous monuments which stand in Egypt to this day. Inscriptions on tomb walls suggest that many of the Pharaohs were much loved by those close to them. Even the Pharaohs who became unpopular after their reign, such as the female Hatshepsut and the so-called heretic Akhenaten, commanded great devotion whilst on the throne. Egyptian history tells how stories of the divine nature and origin of the Pharaohs had been passed down since times almost forgotten, from the gods who ruled after the year Dot, though the mysterious Followers of *Horus*, to the earthly kings who were the living *Horus*.

VISITING THE MONUMENTS TODAY

1. Giza and the Pyramids

The Great Pyramid and the Sphinx at Giza, just on the outskirts of Cairo, is the obvious place for most modern day tourists to head for. It was already famous at the times of Alexandra the Great and of the Romans, when tourists poured into Egypt to see the monuments which were already ancient 2000 years ago.

One catches one's first glimpse of the pyramids either from the train going to Cairo from Alexandria, or from some high point in Cairo. Many people have seen plenty of pictures of the pyramids, but until one gets close it is impossible to really appreciate their immensity, whatever comparison with St Paul's Cathedral or a football pitch we have read. The ground area is 14 acres.

As one approaches along the road to Giza, passing the modern hotels, one is able to catch glimpses and, sure enough, they begin to look big. From that point on they just seem to get magnified, until the Great Pyramid itself lies before you. If you try to take a photograph of it with your friend, you will realise the size! It is impossible, because to get the whole monument in the frame your friend appears like a dot, but to get your friend in the frame all you will be able to capture is the bottom one and a half levels of stone blocks!

Then the surprises will start. There's not one pyramid, not three, but nine and on the distant horizon across the desert there are more! Now be careful when you ask yourself 'Which is the biggest?', for the one which looks the bigger of the two main pyramids is actually the second biggest – that of Khephren. This is simply because it was built on slightly higher ground but, in fact, it is several feet shorter. Khephren's pyramid is the one with the remains of the original outer covering still visible near the top.

When you do get up close to the Pyramids they truly are remarkable in their size and appearance. Remember these were built at least four thousand five hundred years ago, if not fouteen thousand. You may be surprised to see that they are not smooth sided either, but consist of very many huge and uneven blocks of stone. This is because the outer casing of white granite was removed, centuries ago, to build a major mosque, that of the Sultan Hassan, as well as houses in Cairo.

Last century it became a challenge to climb the sides, but today it is illegal. Apparently it is not too difficult a task, if you know the best route, but if you lose your footing it is almost impossible to stop yourself falling all the way to the bottom and to certain death, hundreds of feet below.

What is now left of Cheop's pyramid stands 480 feet high, with sides measuring 730 feet, a total ground area of over 530,000 square feet. It is a long walk around it, especially on a hot and dusty day and many people choose not to do it.

If you are lucky enough to arrive on a day when it is open, you can buy a ticket for a small fee and go inside, climbing up and down the wooden ramps with your head bent, through the ancient ascending corridor to see the King's Chamber. The King's Chamber is built of red granite blocks, each weighing about twenty tons and which must have been put there during the building process, since they are too big to go through the corridors. These blocks are fitted together so accurately that it is not possible to pass a credit card between them. Not bad for a civilisation which did not yet have the wheel, or metal tools! That in itself is a monumental feat of engineering. Now another surprise; the chamber is bare, except for an empty sarcophagus and there is nothing is painted on the walls (except a little graffiti). There are only really three things which can be said about this room; it is big, made of stone and, apart from you, empty, and in that there may well lie a clue. All you find is yourself.

Close by you can see the second large chamber, slightly smaller, called the Queen's Chamber, although this is a misnomer since it had nothing to do with any queens. It may have been the original burial chamber for the Pharaoh, changed later during the building process – if indeed either chamber was ever intended for burials – no mummies were ever reportedly found.

There are various speculations on the reasons for building the pyramids; were they burial sites, symbolic representations of the original land as it was created out of the waters, initiation chambers, intergalactic landmarks, or simply monuments to glorify the Pharaoh's egos? In truth nobody really knows. The very existence of the pyramids poses so many mysteries as to attract theories from many sources. The reality is that we are unsure exactly when, how or why they were ever built.

Back outside the Great Pyramid and to the South, which you will clearly see on your walk around, is a modern building housing the Royal Boat. This was discovered by Karnel el-Mallakh in 1954 AD, in a pit in the ground, besides the pyramid. The pit was over 31 metres long and covered by 41 limestone blocks and contained the dismantled cedar wood boat in over one thousand pieces, each one marked by the makers. According to the markings and the stone, the pit had been sealed a few years after Cheop's death. It was put there, like everything put in tombs, to help in the underworld life. Whether or not Cheop's ever used it before or after his death is unknown, but it was extracted and reassembled in the 1950's, by Ahmed Youssef – it actually took fourteen years – and now stands in its special museum, along with a model. There is another unopened pit close by, to the West of the museum, containing another boat, but not in such superb condition.

The second of the three wondrous pyramids of this fourth dynasty is that of Cheop's son, Khephren or Cheophren. This is the one with some of the original outer casing still at its apex and was first opened by Belzoni in 1818 AD. Inside he found a 'burial chamber' containing a granite sarcophagus, but no mummy, which could make one ask whether the pyramid was ever built for burying the Pharaoh. The lid of the coffin was cracked and inside were some bones of cattle! Again you may be able to enter and see for yourself. There are many books devoted entirely to the pyramids and questioning their origins, as well as going into great depth about the measurements and the special mathematical relationships which can be found, so I do not intend to elaborate here, except to say that considering the age in which they were built the accuracy of the measurements is remarkable.

Outside the pyramid of Khephren is a Valley Temple, the remains of which were discovered by Mariette in 1853 and cleared of sand. It is actually quite well preserved and is a good example of a Valley temple which was where the ceremonies of the Embalming of the Pharaoh were re-enacted. There were twenty-three statues of Khephren found here and they are now in Cairo Museum.

At the end of the Valley Temple stands one of the most enigmatic and fascinating monuments of all time; the Sphinx, which the Arabs call 'The Father of Fear'. For years it has remained buried in the sands which are constantly blowing in from the desert, although it has been uncovered several times that we know of. Tuthmosis IV, in 1390BC, whilst resting against the giant head which was protruding from the sands, fell asleep and dreamt that the Sphinx spoke to him asking that he clear away the sand and promising greatness for the Pharaoh, in return. Tuthmosis duly ordered his men to clear the sand and recorded the feat on a stele which he left between the paws of the Sphinx, which we now call the 'Dream Stele'. Tuthmosis IV certainly became a very great man. The Sphinx was cleared on several more occasions, especially in Greco-Roman times and in more modern times by Caviglia in 1817 AD, when he found the fragmented beard and uraeus (the sacred symbol worn on the Pharaoh's brow, in the form of a cobra alone or with a vulture, symbolising dominion over both Upper and Lower Egypt).

The work of clearing the sand was continued by Mariette, Maspero and Brigsch and again by Baraize between 1923 and 1936 AD. When you see the size of the monument you will appreciate the size of the sand-clearing task. Nowadays, every day workmen go out with brushes and shovels to clear the sand which has blown in overnight, to make sure it remains clear for tourists.

Although the Sphinx is generally considered to have been built by workers at the same time as Khephren's pyramid, not everyone agrees. Certainly at one time it seems to have been used as a place of worship, as an altar has been found, but this may well have been added later. Khephren was worshipped as a god, in Egypt, up to two thousand years after his death. Unlike the pyramids which were constructed out of huge stone blocks transported from elsewhere, the Sphinx was carved out of solid bedrock with stones cut away from the sides to build walls. John Anthony West, an American and amateur Egyptologist, together with a geologist, has examined the weathering of the Sphinx and nearby structures over the last ten or so years and has discovered that the weathering patterns are different and that the weathering of the Sphinx is inconsistent with the supposed age of 4500 years. They say that it has clearly been worn by the prolonged flow of water, whereas the nearby mastabas have not. Since there has been little rain since the time of Khephren, this poses an interesting problem for the archaeologists. However, they do know that the weather there has not always been as dry as it is now and that just over 5000 years ago it was very different, with lots of rain and quite plush vegetation. It seems that people lived in the area long before the Pharaohs arrived on the scene. In fact there is evidence of human habitation up to 30,000 years ago, but people left the area about 12,000 years ago when the ice age hit what was to become Egypt. In fact Mr West postulates that the Sphinx is almost 12,000 to 15,000 years old, up to three times older than previously thought! Although he has some support he does go on to suggest that the unknown civilisation which built the Sphinx originated on Mars and does tend to lose support in this, although it is just as valid a theory as any other! Recently the facial features of the Sphinx have been compared, using computerised forensic identification techniques, with the features of the known statues of Khephren and it must be said, the match is not good. It may well be that the enigmatic face is not that of Khephren at all, or that it has been re-carved since it was first made. There are also theories which still require complete investigation, that there could be underground tunnels leading from the Sphinx to the pyramids.

The third of the major pyramids at Giza is that of Cheop's grandson, Menkaure, whom the Greeks called Mycerinus. There is evidence that this was restored during the XXVIth dynasty. It is written that Menkaure, unlike his grandfather Cheops and his father Khephren, was a pious and just man and that he was given only six years to rule by the gods and so stayed awake day and night to prolong his life on earth.

The third pyramid was opened using gunpowder, by Vyse, in 1838 AD. Within the second chamber, he found a sarcophagus without a lid, but, once again, no mummy. The sarcophagus was sent by ship to England, but the ship sank in the Mediterranean and the sarcophagus was lost, probably for ever. The lid of a wooden coffin was inscribed with the name Menkaure and is now in the British Museum; however this seems to have originated from the XXIVth dynasty, a long, long time after Khephren. Human bones found in the pyramid have been radio-carbon dated as coming from Christian times. Vyse also apparently found an iron plate measuring 0.124 x 4 x 1 inches in the supposed ventilation shaft. This would be the only evidence of iron from this time and would necessitate the shifting of the date of the Egyptian Iron Age back some 2000 years; it is unlikely to have been placed there since the building of the pyramid; access to the shaft was impossible before Vyse forced his way in. Yet another mystery.

The Valley Temple outside the pyramid has been excavated and a superb triad showing Menkaure with *Hathor* and a Nome deity, and a beautiful statue of Menkaure with Queen Khamerernebty II, were found and now stand in Cairo Museum.

There are six more smaller pyramids at Giza, referred to as the 'Queen's Pyramids', in various conditions. Human remains have been found and may be those of a Princess. There are also two small boat pits nearby.

Scattered around the pyramids at Giza is the Necropolis or burial grounds, containing a very large number of tombs of Pharaohs' families and nobility. Almost all are closed to the public, although a little backsheesh and a good torch can be very rewarding. The previously undisturbed tomb of Queen Hetepheres, wife of Snorfu and mother of Cheops, was discovered under limestone gravel, by Reisner in 1925 and contained some beautiful Royal Treasures. These included gold vessels, razors, knives, a toilet box, vases with traces of kohl and perfumes, jewellery made from malachite, lapis lazuli and turquoise, armchairs, a bed and a carrying chair, all of which are now in Cairo Museum. The sarcophagus was, once again, empty although there was an alabaster chest containing internal organs! There are many more tombs to the West and South of the Great Pyramid and rock cut tombs to the South East of Khephren's, all extensively excavated over the last century. That is, of course, not to say that there are not more, yet unfound!

Around the pyramids you will see the inevitable third world hasslers, but in Egypt these men are of a superior type to those in many eastern countries who will never take no for an answer. One golden rule is never to show even the slightest interest in what they offer unless you may consider buying, the second rule is to barter. Bartering is an essential part of everyday life, the people enjoy it and it earns you respect as well as ridiculous bargains. The usual process involves the salesman showing you his wares, in the city many items, but out in the desert, on the West bank at Luxor, often only one item, to try to capture your interest. Beware! If you ask "How much?", even though it may be out of curiosity, it is taken as a sign that you are interested enough to buy. Remember, to these people you are the rich man and they are often just trying to earn their daily bread. But once you have shown an interest, the next question they will try to ask is how much do you think it's worth and, let me say now, that it is always far, far more than what they want, if you base your ideas on the western world. So, your offer ought to be low. Don't be afraid of going so low that you will insult him, but obviously be realistic. Offer him about a tenth of what you would pay in Europe. He will then give you his 'best price', which does not mean his lowest; you will come up, he will come down, until you reach a compromise, a sale is made and everyone is happy. But, you may find he then asks you for a 'present for me' and that is up to you. One thing is sure; the experience is fun. If you have the time, you can get some interesting souvenirs and gifts to take home, but beware of offers of items said to have come from Pharaohs' tombs. More than likely they did not come from the tombs but have been made locally, albeit by the same techniques and similar tools as those used in Pharonic times, and aged cleverly with sand and cold tea or coffee; on the other hand if genuine, it is illegal to export them.

Another point to remember throughout your time in Egypt is that a simple smile is a key to many doors! Also, do not forget that backsheesh is a way of life; this is a small gift, often given before any service is done, to guides, tomb guards or hotel room cleaners and it ensures good service. A pound or two is plenty and it is normal to give a good tip at the end too.

You will, at the pyramids, be approached by Bedouins offering camel rides. Often this means getting on the camel, riding twenty yards to see the pyramids – usually a good viewpoint which you could have walked to – and the camel man asking to use your camera to take your photo. Don't worry, you can trust him with your camera, he has probably handled more that week than you have in your life! But, agree on the price before you get on the beast. Then you will pay about five or six Egyptian pounds; otherwise, if you leave it until you climb down, he'll ask you for twenty or thirty and you'll have a terrible job trying to pay less!

In the vicinity of the pyramids you will find plenty of merchants selling their wares and often the camel man will try to take you there, usually under the pretence of a cup of tea or cola. You'll get your tea and see some nice items and, even if you leave without buying, it will be a pleasant break from the dusty desert. You may be offered exotic concentrated perfumes pressed neat from flowers and told how 'Chanel' come to Egypt to buy, taking back to France to dilute with alcohol. You will certainly be offered samples and sure enough they are strong and free of alcohol. Look at the vendor's book and see the names of the film stars who have bought from him in the past. Strangely enough, many of the stars seemed to have visited all of the stores. You will be offered statuettes, rings, books, vases of alabaster and papyrus paintings, each vendor insisting their's is real and others fakes, like papyrus made from banana leaves. Unless you become an expert, it is difficult to tell. None of it is genuinely Pharonic and yet even a banana leaf painting is something of a souvenir. No harm is likely to come to you amongst these gentle and friendly people.

One final word on Giza; one evening, if you are there,

take a warm blanket (it is cold in the desert at night, believe me) and take a taxi or bus out to Giza again, for the Superb Sound and Light Show, the Son et Lumiere. During the show you can hear tales of the builders of the pyramids and watch as the pyramids and Sphinx are lit by many-coloured lights. It is not exactly a technicolour show but ought not to be missed.

2. Cairo Museum.

There are several guides to Cairo Museum on the market, including the one published by the museum itself and on sale at the ticket office. All I will say here is that the museum contains well over 100,000 items and that however long you spend there, you will not see it all. In any case, after a while one tends to just walk past most exhibits and only remember a few. If you have time for more than one visit, make it, otherwise it may be best to head for the rooms which interest you most.

The museum sells a catalogue of the exhibits, set out in order of the various rooms and corridors.

The Treasure of Tutankhamun is an obvious exhibition to head for and will be well worth your while. The few mummies on display may not be as exciting as one may imagine, except the odd interesting mummy of a cat or crocodile. There are thousands of statues and statuettes, jewellery, coffins, pyramid capstones, sections of hieroglyphic wall inscriptions, stele, Pharaohs' furniture and personal items and so much more, many of which are mentioned elsewhere in this book. There are also on sale posters, postcards, books, alabaster, papyrus, small pyramids and statuettes, rings and so on. There is a small refreshment place for that much needed tea or cola. All in all it is a must to visit the museum at least once; it covers the whole of Egyptian history from predynastic to Roman and certainly helps one to contemplate some of this vast expanse of time.

3. Saqqara and Memphis

From Cairo it is easy to reach Saqqara by taxi, by tour operator's bus, or by train and donkey. There is so much to see there that it is essential to start early, before it gets much too hot, and to get there the quickest way; that is by taxi; the driver will wait for you and bring you back. Once again do not forget to agree the price before getting in the car.

At Saqqara there are many impressive pyramids and, although smaller than Cheops' or Khephren's, they are themselves quite massive and older and look older too. This is thought to be the site of the first pyramid known to have been built, by the architect Imhotep, for the Pharaoh Hosar, also called Hozar, Hozer, Zosar, Djosar and so on, in different works. This is the Step Pyramid and was built, we think, about 2630BC, over 4500 years ago and seems to have developed from the idea of putting one mastaba on top of another. You can certainly see how it was built in layers and imagine once again how much physical effort it must have taken, as well as inspiration.

Surrounding the pyramid is a temple complex and within this was found the pyramid of Sekhemkhet. Nearby are the pyramids of Usekef, Isesi, Teti, Pepy I, Pepy II, Khabi, Merenre and Unas or Wenis as he is called on the new plaque there. The pyramid of Unas is the one which was repaired by Khaemwese, son of Ramesses II and where he left his inscription. It was opened by Maspero in 1881. Several of the pyramids were found to contain 'Pyramid Texts' or magic formulas painted on the inner walls to ensure the success of the *Kha* or spirit double of the Pharaoh in the afterlife. There are also two smaller pyramids of Queens, Neit and Input, also with texts.

The whole area around here is devoted to tombs, from the Early Dynastic, Old Kingdom and New Kingdom. It is not certain whether these were used for the physical burial of the Kings or whether the tombs at Abydos were, both being inscribed. There are, however, many tombs of famous nobles and courtiers, such as Ti, the Old Kingdom Overseer of Pyramids and Sun Temples, and Maya, the New Kingdom Overseer of the Treasury under Tuthmosis and Hatshepsut. There is also a tomb inscribed for Horemheb, probably made before he was Pharaoh; he had another made for him in the Valley of the Kings after he was crowned.

Not very far from here lies the massive Serapeum, the Cemeteries of Sacred Animals. Let's go back about one hundred and fifty years to the time when the famous archaeologist Mariette visited Saqqara. We can read what he wrote; '...it is possible the Serapeum would still be lost under the sands of the necropolis of Saqqara. One day, however, being attracted to Saqqara by my Egyptological studies, I perceived the head of a sphinx showing above the surface...close by lay a libation table on which was engraved a hieroglyphic inscription to *Apis-Osiris*. Then that passage in Strabo (the Greek historian of 25BC, who had written about the Serapeum) came to my memory and I knew that beneath my feet lay the avenue leading to the long and vaguely sought Serapeum'.

Mariette then quietly organised a large group of workmen to start carefully digging and unearthed two rows of one hundred and forty-one sphinxes in situ, a total of 600 feet long, leading to the cemetery. This task took four years! Inside he found twenty-four huge sarcophagi of bulls, three of which were inscribed, 13 to 14 foot long, one being inscribed with the recognisable name of Cambyses. The Ancient Historian Plutarch had written a story that Cambyses once ordered his priests to bring before him the God *Apis*. In those days a specific bull was chosen by its markings, to represent the physical manifestation of the god *Apis*, who was worshipped. When the priests brought the bull, Cambyses drew his dagger 'in a fit of rage and contempt and stabbed the animal in its thigh'. Plutarch's story told that the animal died and the priests secretly buried it in the Serapeum, but the inscription found by Mariette clearly stated that this sarcophagus belonged to that very same bull, which had survived for four years into the reign of Darius. The Serapeum had, unfortunately, been raided by early Christians and much destroyed, but this mummy and several treasures were found by Mariette. Unfortunately for him, he was recalled to France and had to bury his treasure. A competitor found it, by bribing local people, and stole it.

The Sacred animal cemeteries were centres of pilgrimage for centuries. They contained mummies of hawks, ibis, baboon and jackal, as well as the Serapeum itself. It was that prolific builder, Ramesses II, who started the rock cut underground galleries, and Nectanebo II who added the avenue of human headed sphinxes. You may remeber reading of the confusion between Ramesses II and III and Nectanebo I.

4. Other Pyramids

There are over eighty pyramids in Egypt and it would take a long time to see them all in anything but a fleeting way. From Saqqara one can see the Pyramids of Giza and also the two pyramids of interest at Dahshur. The third dynasty Pharaoh Huni started his pyramid here and it was completed by his son, Snorfu, the first Pharaoh of the fourth dynasty. As it was being built, someone must have realised that the angles were wrong, making it less stable. So the angles were changed half way-up, giving it the bent appearance from a distance, and thus its modern name ' The Bent Pyramid'. There is a small chamber inside and Valley Temple buildings. Nearby is another pyramid built by Snorfu, father of Cheops, called the 'Northern Stone Pyramid' or 'Red Pyramid', visible from Saqqara in the distance, with the angles of a true pyramid, at 430.

The pyramid of Amenemhat III, (well one of his two), called the 'White Pyramid', stands at Dahshur, excavated by De Morgan in 1894, when he found jewellery belonging to two princesses. Amenemhat's other pyramid, 'The Black Pyramid' stands near Hawara. It is a little further from Cairo, but still a pleasant day trip; you can see the state of subsidence which may have forced the Pharaoh to build his other one at Dahshur. If you wander around the site you may well see unearthed human skulls from the many tombs placed there.

At el-Lisht, on the site of the ancient capital of Amenemhat I, It-towy, there are the pyramids of Amenemhat I and Senusert I, the 'Southern Pyramid', where Maspero found fragments of inscribed alabaster objects with the King's name and, in 1894, Gauthier and Jèquier found a statue of Senusert I. At Hawara there arealso the few remains of the 'Labyrinth'.

At Meidum there lies the pyramid of Huni, which hardly looks like a pyramid at all, but was probably the first try at building a true pyramid in an eight-stepped process. It was probably finished by Snorfu. The tombs of *Ra*-hotep and his wife Nofret, whose impressive statues stand in Cairo Museum, were found here.

5. Tell el-Amarna

This modern town was the site of the ancient capital built by the heretic Pharaoh Akhenaten, who changed the state religion to *Aten*, the Sun Disk, in the XVIIIth dynasty. Much of his building work was destroyed by his successors, in the same way that he destroyed much of his predecessors'. But this ancient city, in the Hermopolitan Nome, was widespread and contained temples, palaces, administrative quarters and houses on the East bank of the Nile and areas for cultivation on the West. To the East there are rock cut tombs of officials and courtiers. The tomb built for Akhenaten himself was probably never used.

6. Abydos

Travel further South down the Nile and you will reach Abydos, the ancient centre for the cult of *Osiris* and stopping point for cruises in our times. The last ruler of predynastic Egypt may have been buried here, but this has not been proved. However, important prehistoric sites surround Abydos.

Abydos, called Abdew and Balliana, was the main site for pilgrimage in Ancient Egypt. Much the same as the Moslem's aim of reaching Mecca in his lifetime, the people of Ancient Egypt tried to visit Abydos. They also tried to enable themselves to travel there after their earthly life had ended, burying boats in or near there tombs, or having them painted on the walls, so that they could make the journey along the Nile.

Abydos is equated with the worship of *Osiris*. During the Old Kingdom, *Re* was considered an immortal king. But later, during the Middle Kingdom, *Osiris* became more important, offering a chance of immortality to folk other than the Pharaoh.

At Abydos, Ramesses II built a temple to Seti I and Merne*ptah* built an unusual L-shaped temple. There are chapels dedicated to many gods, including *Ptah*, *Re-Herekhte* and *Amun*, and *Isis*, *Osiris* and *Horus*. The temple also contains a mound which may have been once surrounded by water, as well as a subterranean chamber with no reliefs or inscriptions.

The Osireion, an imitation of a royal tomb, was also built here as a cenotaph to *Osiris*, which incorporated an island, surrounded by water, symbolic of the original land which came out of the Waters of Creation.

Throughout much of the time of the Pharaohs, Abydos was the site of the performance of an annual mystery play, a re-enactment of the *Osiris* myth. A mystery play is so-called because it relates to a mystery religion, that is a religion in which there are secret initiations. The play which involved scenes of the killing of *Osiris* by *Seth* and the subsequent battle between *Seth* and his nephew *Horus*, may have been quite realistic and bloodthirsty scenes.

7. Thebes/Luxor

Luxor is a 'modern' city – on Egyptian standards. It is one of the main tourists attractions in Egypt, within easy reach of Karnak, the Valley of the Kings, Ramesseum, Colossi of Memnon, Luxor Temple and many more sites. There are also flights to Abu Simbel and Aswan and flights and buses and taxis to Edfu, Esna, Kom Ombo and Aswan. There are good top quality hotels with swimming pools, plenty of sunshine and it is cheap and friendly, the ideal place for a couple of weeks as a base for investigating Upper Egypt. The history of Thebes spans thousands of years. Karnak Temple itself took over a thousand years of building by a lot of different Pharaohs.

The ancient name was Waset, renamed Thebia by the Greeks, known as Thebes of the Thousand Gates. It was the capital in the XIIth and XVIIIth dynasties. It has been a tourist centre off and on for more than two millenniaand you can find the occasional graffiti left by ancient Greeks, Romans and Persians

Karnak Temple, just up the road, was known as Ipet-isut, 'The Most Sacred of Places'. Dedicated to the triad of *Amun*, *Mut* and *Khonsu*, it is the largest temple ever built anywhere in the world and contains many small temples, halls, obelisks, statues and a Sacred Lake. There was an avenue of human headed sphinxes, built by Amenophis III and modified much later by Taharka and the Ptolemies which lead all the way back to Luxor Temple, in the centre of town, an avenue which was followed in times of great ceremonies, described below. Inside Karnak is the Great Temple of *Amun*, the impressively columned Hypostyle Hall, papyrus and lotus shaped columns and the remains of the Temple of *Aten*, built by Akhenaten and Tutankhamun, but later dismantled by their successors. There is a Temple of Montu, the god of war. In the southern enclosure is a Temple of Mut, where hundreds of statues of the lioness goddess *Sekhmet* were found. In 1902 a cachette was discovered containing 779 large stone statues and over 17,000 bronze. It is a most majestic site, with many superb inscriptions and several fine obelisks, put there by Hatshepsut and by Tutankhamun, and worthy of more than one visit.

In the evening there are Sound and Light shows, when you are shown around in groups, with amplified explanations of the various sections and halls and a final lecture whilst you sit on seats overlooking the well lit Sacred Lake. Once again I remind you it is cold at night, so wrap up well. If you get the opportunity, go!

Luxor Temple stands in the heart of the town, beside the Nile and within easy reach of the big hotels. This is the area where you will find the horse drawn carriages to take you for rides, and donkey men seeking trade for the West Bank. The rickety old ferry leaves from near here. The Temple was known in olden days as 'The Southern Harem of *Amun*', *Amun* taking the form of the fertility god *Min*. In Pharaonic times, every year saw the great festival of Opet at the time of the inundation, with great prayers for the best Nile flood level to make the ground fertile again. A large and beautiful statue of the god *Amun* was brought to Luxor Temple from Karnak Temple, down the Avenue of Sphinxes which joined the two. Luxor Temple is mainly constructed on top of an older site and built in the main by Amenophis III and Ramesses II, although added to by many other Pharaohs. Ramesses left some interesting inscribed pylons showing the Battle of Kadesh and his struggle with the Hittites. The Temple is a lot smaller than Karnak, but just as imposing.

Just up the road is a small museum, worth a visit and nearby a small bazaar.

8. The West Bank Monuments at Luxor

One can visit the monuments on the West Bank, after taking the ferry which runs continually back and forth, always crowded with locals and tourists, then by bus, taxi, or donkey. Although bus can be easier, taxi gives you more freedom to stay longer at places you like, while donkey-riding is more adventurous; by donkey you will ride along fields, over hills, follow the routes taken by the ancient workmen when they went to dig tombs in the valleys and may even get to see the inside of your guide's house and meet his family. Arriving above the Temple of Hatshepsut at Dier el-Bahari is particularly rewarding when riding a donkey. But whichever way you decide to do the tour, arrange the price first. Your first stop will probably be to see, briefly, the Colossi of Memnon, so named by the Greeks. These are the only remains of the Funerary Temple of Amenophis III. Pieces from here were taken by the Pharaoh Merneptah to build his own. Some time ago, at least 200 years, there was an earthquake and the huge statues, which once stood either side of what must have been a very impressive temple, were badly cracked. Ever since then they have reportedly made strange singing sounds at dawn and gathered a lot of superstitious tales; but modern scientists explain this as internal vibrations caused by temperature changes.

The Ramesseum is yet another amazing achievement of the work forces of Ramesses II. It is a less crowded monument than most and worth a look. There is a massive head, on its side on the ground, once part of a colossal figure. There are also some good wall reliefs of the Battle of Kadesh, depicting Ramesses himself.

At Medinet Habu there is the Temple of Ramesses III, with wall reliefs showing the Pharaoh and the 'Sea Peoples'. There is also a temple built for Tuthmosis III.

The Temple of Seti I, completed after his death by his son Ramesses II, contains a series of what can be described as family portraits. The Kings of Ancient Egypt often worshipped their ancestors as forms of *Osiris* and this can be seen clearly here. You can see Seti I worshipping Ramesses I crowned as *Osiris*, and Ramesses II worshipping the now dead Seti I! There is a strong family resemblance throughout. There is also a bas-relief of Queen Tuaa, the mother of Ramesses the Great.

At Dier el-Bahri you can see the Temple built for Hatshepsut, in several tiers, in the XVIIIth dynasty, partly cut into the hillside. Wall scenes here depict the claim of Hatshepsut that she was born of a divine coupling, the young female Pharaoh-to-be being suckled by the goddess *Hathor* in the form of a cow, as well as her later expeditions South to the distant Land of Punt (maybe Ethiopia), to bring back incense and semi-precious stones.

Nearby lies the ruined village of the workmen for the Valley of the Kings and Valley of the Queens. There are several tombs and those of Pachedu and Sennedjem contain some very appealing and interesting wall paintings. The village consisted of seventy terraced houses and their lower walls still stand, so you can see how little space they were allotted, compared with the space allowed for temples

9. The Valley of the Kings

This is the one place on the West Bank which nearly all tourists are bound to visit, in particular the tomb of Tutankhamun. However, there are plenty of other tombs, many worth seeing. The Valley itself, as one approaches, is dominated by the pyramid shaped mountain peak which may have led the Pharaohs of the XVIIIth dynasty to pick this place for their tombs. It is very dry and dusty and there is a small refreshment post that has been there for years. It was once rebuilt when they found out it was on top of tombs!

The valley is known to the Arabs as Bab-el-Molûk, which means 'The Gate of the King' and is probably derived from the original name in Ancient Egyptian. It was visited by tourists over 2500 years ago.

Sixty-two tombs have been found here so far, nearly all Royals but with one or two New Kingdom nobles. The only one found intact was that of Tutankhamun, which even today contains the boy's mummy. Hundreds of thousands of tourists descend the steps down into Tutankhamun's last resting place, carefree of rumours of curses upon desecrators of the tomb. It is a fact that several of the original workmen and scientists who first entered, including Carnarvon himself, died not long afterwards, but if there ever was an active curse it must have worn out years ago, because now nobody seems to be adversely affected. It would be quite silly to go to the valley and miss out this tomb, although it is not the best one: try to see the tomb of Seti.

Many of the other tombs are interesting, particularly that of Seti I, which has some really incredible decorations and is the deepest tomb. Wall paintings tell us a lot about Ancient Egypt, or rather the perfect image which the Pharaohs wanted to create for themselves, to take to the afterlife. There are many painted spells to enable the deceased to successfully pass the tests of the underworld, scenes and writings called The Books of the Dead. The normal pattern of tomb decorations is to depict all the scenes of the passage of the deceased Pharaoh through the underworld and this is represented beautifully in the tomb of Seti I. The tomb is the deepest one in the valley and runs to a depth of about 180 feet. You descend down steps and pass through chambers to the burial chamber, which is symbolic of the dead Pharaoh's journey. In Seti's tomb you see phenomenal paintings, columns of hieroglyphs, ceilings full of stars, strange demons on the walls. Finally the Pharaoh arrives at the end of his journey and stands before *Osiris* to witness his soul weighed against a feather, in the presence of *Anubis, Thoth, Sobek* and all the gods. Also in the tomb, in a side chamber known as the Chamber of the Cow, is the story of the Destruction of Mankind by *Sekhmet*, after *Re* became so angry.

Every tomb so far found was previously broken into by tomb robbers, even Tutankhamun's was disturbed. Tomb Robbing, although highly illegal and punishable by death, became very popular in the times of Ramesses IX and and X and no matter what was done, however many false doors and however deep the tombs were cut, the robbers still gained entry. In fact very few tombs now contain a sarcophagus. Tutankhamun's escaped because after the robbers were disturbed and the tomb resealed, the entrance became blocked and covered by rubble from a tomb cut out later, higher in the cliff. Thus the tomb became lost, until Howard Carter came along in the twentieth century A.D, nearly 3500 years later. But not only did the robbers take the treasures, they also damaged the mummies in their greed or need for more, digging beneath the cloth for rings and amulets. So eventually Ramesses decided enough was enough and, to save the mummies of his ancestors he removed them and stashed them in a secret hideaway, the tomb of Amenophis II and in the tomb of a person we do not yet name, called Tomb 55. This cache of mummies was rediscovered by Loret in 1898 AD.

A couple of non-royals are buried in this valley too. Namely Yuya and Thuya, the parents of Tiye, wife of Amenophis III. Their gold coffins and some treasure was found by Davis in 1905. A major difference between the tombs of the Pharaohs and those of the non-royal nobles lies in the decorations. In the latter the wall painting show many scenes of everyday life, whereas the Pharaohs seem to have been concerned only with the afterlife experiences. The nobles' tombs are very beautiful and should not be missed. They show scenes of fishing, fouling, hunting, winnowing, wine-making, family scenes, funeral scenes, singing and dancing, musicians and acrobats and workers of all types. We have gained a wealth of understanding of life in those days from these superb coloured paintings, although it is fairly certain that only the best aspects are portrayed and only in a perfect way.

In an adjacent valley, now called the Valley of the Queens, there is the tomb of Nefertari, the beloved and glorious wife of Ramesses II, with some truly magnificent wall paintings. However, these paintings are an example of the twentieth century devastation caused by endless thousands of tourists, whose very breath has caused the damage. Chemicals in the breath have started to crystallise on the paint and also salts from the rocks above have started crystallising under the paint. This has led a team of experts to conduct a massive rescue and repair operation, so the tomb has been closed to the public for some time.

10. Esna, Edfu, Kom Ombo and Aswan

I have grouped these places together, not because of any lack of interest, but because they can all be visited in one day by taxi from Luxor. Esna Temple is from the Greco-Roman Period and has a series of texts on its columns which show the calendar of festivals held in those days. Edfu was dedicated to *Horus* and *Hathor*. It was built at the site of an ancient town called Dbot, which was known in Greco-Roman times as Apollopolis Magna, the capital of the second Nome of Upper Egypt. The remains here make the temple the best preserved in Egypt and it looks very new compared with most of what you will have seen so far. The wall shows the conflict of *Horus* and *Seth* and the creation of the world. Kom Ombo is a 'double temple', dedicated to the crocodile god, *Sobek* and *Hathor* and *Khonsu* in the one half and *Horus the Elder* with *Tasenetofret*, the good sister form of *Hathor*, in the other. It used to be the capital of the Ombite Nome and was strategically important in Ptolemaic times. The Temple was built by the Ptolemies and added to by the Romans

At Aswan you can visit Elephantine Island and see the Nilometer spoken about by Strabo. Strabo wrote 'The Nilometer is a well built of regular hewn stones on the bank of the Nile, in which is recorded the rise of the stream, not only the maximum but also the minimum and average rise, for the water in the well rises and falls with the stream. On the side of the well are marks, measuring the height sufficient for the irrigation and other water levels. These are observed and published for general information. This is of importance to the peasants for the management of water, the embankments, the canals and so forth and to the officials on account of the taxes, for the higher the rise of water, the higher are the taxes'.

There are steps going down and marking from the Roman Period can be seen. It was used again in 1870 A.D, but today it is useless because of the Dam. South of Elephantine are the ancient quarries where the Egyptians cut their hard stone for building the monuments. Many carving were done there and in fact two were left unfinished, a huge one of *Osiris* and an unfinished obelisk which may well have become the largest obelisk ever cut if it had been completed. Probably the Pharaoh died before it was finished, or maybe invaders from the desert drove the workers away. There are many tombs of nobles nearbyat Qubhet el-Hawa.

11. Abu Simbel

To get to Abu Simbel the only sensible way is to fly and flights can be taken from Luxor. Abu Simbel has two rock-cut temples, both built by Ramesses II. They are amongst the most spectacular monuments in Egypt today. The Great Temple was dedicated to *Ptah, Amen-Re, Re-Harakhte* and Ramesses II, who deified himself. It contains walls scenes depicting his battle in Kadesh and scenes of the wars against Syria, Libya and Nubia. There is a stele commemorating the marriage of Ramesses to a Hittite princess, ending the conflict. It was cleared of sand in the early nineteenth century AD, when it attracted interest of Burckhardt, Belzoni, and Lepsius and Mariette. A small temple was also discovered by Amelia B Edwards in 1874. The Smaller Temple was dedicated to *Hathor* and Ramesses' favourite wife, Nefertari, whose tomb in the Valley of the Queens I mentioned.

In AD 1964 to 1968 an incredible thing happened to these temples – they were moved. This was done by UNESCO, so that they would not be submerged under the waters of the Aswan Dam. The temple was cut into large blocks, carefully marked, transported and put back together again. Large concrete domes were also built to replace the hill into which the original temple had been cut. Today the new site of these temples are visited by thousands of tourists who have taken a short flight from Aswan or Luxor. It is well worth a visit to see the colossal statues and to marvel at the technological capabilities at the time of Ramesses II and those we have now.

GLOSSARY

Alabaster	A calcite, white or yellow, used for building, vases, eyes in statues, occurring in the desert East of the Nile.
Amethyst	A semi-precious stone, which the Egyptians obtained from Nubia.
Amulet	A charm made of stone, gold, glass, bronze or wood, used as a magical protection, often inserted within a mummy wrapping.
Ankh	A hieroglyphic sign consisting of a letter T shape with a pear shape on top, meaning 'life', often depicted held in the hand of a god or goddess, as seen in tomb and temple paintings and relief.
Ba	The soul of the deceased.
Bas-relief	A manner of decorative carvings used in temples, created by cutting away the background so that the figurine stands out from the wall.
Carnelian	A reddish-brown semi-precious stone from Nubia.
Canopic Jar	A jar into which the internal organs were placed for preservation after extraction from the body of the deceased during mummification, sometimes bearing an inscription. The heart was not placed in a jar but replaced within the cadaver.
Cartouche	A painted oval shape in which the hieroglyphics of the five royal names and titles of the Pharaoh were written or carved, probably originally representing the universe.
Colossus	A huge statue of a Pharaoh or god.
Cuneiform	A form of ancient writing using symbols, used in Mesopotamia, Sumeria, Babylon, Assyria, etc.
Dahibeyeh	A boat used for transport on the Nile, particularly the Royal Dahibeyeh.
Demotic	An everyday script used after the 7th century bc.
Dynasty	A family of rulers, usually blood relatives, but sometimes also related to consecutive dynasties, created by Manetho the historian, for convenience of dividing Egyptian History into convenient periods of time.
Feldspar	A green stone used for beads or jewellery and amulets.
Heb-Sed	A festival of rejuvenation, celebrated by a Pharaoh after his first 35 years of reign and thereafter at random, of unknown origin but possibly symbolic of the pre-dynastic custom of slaying an old and feeble King. A time in which the Pharaoh would (in theory) prove his physical and mental capabilities.
Hieratic	A simplified form of hieroglyphic writing, used mostly for legal and business documents and for record keeping.
Hieroglyphics	An ancient script appearing in Egypt after the archaic about 3000 bc, consisting of pictures with phonetic values and ideograms.
Hypostyle	A style of close columns supporting a temple roof, representing plant growth, sometimes a lotus or papyrus.
Ka	The spirit of the deceased which Ancient Egyptians believed lived on as a double of the living person after death, requiring food and drink to be provided by descendants and worshippers, as offerings.
Lapis Lazuli	A blue stone from Afghanistan, much valued in Egypt for jewellery.
Malachite	A green stone from Sinai, used for production of eye-paint and painting.
Manetho	A historian-priest who lived at Sebynnytos, in the Delta, in the 3rd century bc. He wrote 8 books including a History of Egypt, of which only fragments remain. He devised the dynastic system.
Mastaba	The shape of the Old Kingdom tombs at Giza and Saqqara, meaning in Arabic 'bench' and consisting of constructions below and above ground. The architect Imhotep, in the time of the Pharaoh Hosar (Dozar), placed mastabas on top of each other and created the first pyramid structure, the Step Pyramid, still standing today, at Saqqara.
Mortuary	A Temple, often part of a burial complex but in the New Kingdom separate, in which rituals were performed to ensure the continued well-being of the deceased.
Mummy	A preserved body prepared by dehydration and then wrapped in chemically soaked linen, the internal organs having been removed for separate conservation.

Natron	A natural compound consisting of sodium carbonate and sodium bicarbonate, used for dehydration in the preparation of a mummy.
Nomarch	A local, sometimes powerful, ruler of a Nome.
Nome	A region of Ancient Egypt normally subservient to the Pharaoh, but with separate a local ruler, often with its own patron gods.
Obelisk	An upright, pencil-like stone, carved in one piece, topped by a pointed pyramidion, connected with the Solar Cult. Found in Temples of Karnak and Luxor. Made from granite from Aswan. Today samples can be seen in London (Cleopatra's Needle), Paris, Istanbul and the USA.
Oblation Table	A stone offering table used in temples.
Pantheon	A group of gods.
Papyrus	A reed-like plant growing along the Nile, used for making paper, boats, ropes and sandals. Symbolising renewal.
Pharaoh	King of Egypt, originally meaning 'Great House'.
Pylons	Two great towers at the main entrance to a temple, sometimes supporting flag poles.
Pyramidion	A small stone pyramid shape at the top of an obelisk, symbolic of the sun's rays.
Pyramid texts	Magic formulae placed inside 6th dynasty pyramids at Saqqara, used to aid the deceased in the afterlife trials and dangers.
Red Land	The desert area around the Nile.
Rock Tomb	A tomb cut out of rock in the Middle Kingdom, probably used as an attempt to prevent tomb robbery.
Rosetta Stone	A stele found at Rosetta by the troops of Napoleon, dating from the reign of Ptolemy V (196 bc), bearing an inscription in three languages, one of which was hieroglyphic and which enabled the translation of hieroglyphs by Champollion. Now in the British Museum.
Sarcophagus	A coffin-like container for a mummy, although many royal sarcophagi found have been empty. Often carved out of stone and inscribed with magical formulae. On the outside often with painted eyes to enable the deceased to 'see out'.
Scarab	An amulet or item of jewellery in the shape of a scarab beetle or dung beetle, considered holy and magical, called in Egyptian 'Kheper' which meant 'Come into existence', because of the unknown way in which the beetles appeared out of the desert sand (actually from eggs).
Sea Peoples	A collective term for various Mediterranean sea-faring tribes, who tried to invade Egypt during the reigns of Merneptah and Ramesses II.
Serapeum	An underground complex of galleries at Saqqara, discovered in 1850 ad, by Mariette, containing the sarcophagi of 64 mummified Royal Bulls, regarded as incarnations of the god Apis.
Shaduf	Still used in Egypt today, a system consisting of a lever and weight, which enables water to be raised from the Nile and poured into irrigation trenches.
Stele	A rectangular stone on which inscriptions were carved, usually commemorating a specific event.
Sherd or Shard	Fragments of pottery often used for writing.
Uraeus	Sacred symbol worn on the brow of the Pharaoh. The word is derived from the Greek word 'ouraious', meaning cobra. The uraeus was usually made of gold and depicted the cobra goddess Edjo either alone or with the vulture goddess Nekhbet. It symbolised rule over Upper Egypt and Lower Egypt.
Ushabati	Carved mummiform figures placed in tombs as slaves in the underworld. Literally 'Answerers'.
Vizier	Chief Minister, often also Chancellor, for a Pharaoh. Often a member of the Royal Family. Responsible for the general running of the Kingdom.

PHARAOHS IN ORDER OF DYNASTY

0	Narmer	Horus Narmer/Meri-Nar
0	Zekhen	
1	Menes – Scorpion	Aha/Horus Aha/Meni
1	Djer	Zer /Iteti?/Athothis?
1	Wadj/Djet?	Udadji?/Iterty?/Uenephes
1	Den	Udimu?/Usaphaidos
1	Adjib	Enezib?/Miebidos?/Anedjib
1	Semerkhet	Semempses, Zoser-TI/Teti
1	Qa'a/Ka-aa	Bieneches
1	Meryet-Nit Queen	
2	Hetepsekhemwy	Buzau/Boethos
2	Re'neb	Kakau/Kaichos
2	Ninetjer	Neteren /Banentiru /Binothris
2	Peribsen	Sekhemib/Uaznes/Tlas
2	Kha'sekhemwy	Zazai/Cheneres
2	Sened	Sendji/Sethenes
2	Neterka	Chaires
2	Neterkara	Nephercheres
2	Khasekhem	Huzefa /Neferkasokar/Sesochris
3	Zanakht	Nebka
3	Hosar	Djoser/Hozar/Hoser
3	Sekhemkhet	Horus Sekhemkhet
3	Kha'ba	Horus Kha'ba
3	Huni	
4	Snofru	Snefru
4	Khufu	Cheops/Suphis
4	Ra'djedef	Djedefre
4	Khafre	Cheophren/Khephren/Chephren
4	Menkaure	Mycerinus
4	Shepseskaf	
5	Userkaf	Weserkaf
5	Sahure	
5	Neferirkare Kakai	Kakai
5	Shepseskare	Ini
5	Ra'neferef	
5	Niuserre	Izi
5	Menkauhor	
5	Djedkare	Izezi/Isesi
5	Unas	Unis/Wenis
6	Teti	
6	Pepy I	Pepi I
6	Merenre	Nemtyemzaf
6	Pepy II	Pepi II
7	Neferkare'	
8	!	
9	Merykare	
9	Khety	
10	Ity	
11	Inyotef I	
11	Inyotef II	Imhotep II
11	Inyotef III	Imhotep III
11	Mentuhotep I	Mentuhotpe/Montuhotep
11	Mentuhotpe II	Mentuhotep II
11	Mentuhotpe III	Mentuhotep III

11	Mentuhotep IV	
12	Amenemhat I	
12	Senwosret II	Senusret II/Sesostris II
12	Senwosret III	Senusret III/SesostrisIII
12	Amenemhat III	
12	Amenemhat IV	
12	Nefrusobk	Nefersobek (Queen)
12	Amenemhat II	
12	Senwosret I	Senusret I/Sesostris I/Userten
13	Wegaf	
13	Neferhotep I	
13	Sebekhotpe IV	
13	Sebekhotpe V	
13	Amenemhat V	
13	Harnedjheriotef	
13	Amenyqemau	
13	Sebekhotep I	Sobekhopte I
13	Sobekhotep II	Amenemhat Sobekhotep
13	Sebekhotep III	Sebekhopte III
13	Hor	
13	Amenemhat VII	
13	Khendjer	
13	Mentuemzaf	
13	Dedumose I	Dudimose I
13	Dedumose II	
13	Neferhotep III	
13	Iayib	
13	Ay	
13	Sihathor	
13	Sekhemkare	
13	Sehetepibre	
13	Iufni	
13	Sankhibre	
13	Smenkhkare	
13	Sehetepibre	
13	Sewadjkare	
13	Nedjemib(..)re	
13	Sedjef(..)kare	
13	(..)kare Inyotef	
13	(..)set	
13	Renseneb	
13	Smenkhkare Mermesha	
13	Sebekhotep VI	Sobekhotep VI
13	Sankhrenesewadjtu	
13	Mersekhemre Ined	
13	Sewadjkare	
13	Sebekhotep VII	
14	!!	
15	Salitis	Shalek?
15	Sheshi	
15	Apachnan	Khyan/Khian
15	Apophis	Aphosis/Apepi
15	Assis Khamudi	
15	Bnon	
15	Iannas	
16	!!!	
17	Kamose	Kamosis

215

17	Inyotef V	
17	Tao II	Djehuti'o II/Sequenenra II
17	Sebekemzaf I	
17	Nebireyeraw	
17	Sebekemzaf II	
17	Ta'o I	Djehuti'o I
17	Segnere III	
17	Seqenenre' III	
18	Ahmose	Amophis
18	Amenhotep I	Amenophis I
18	Tuthmosis I	Thutmosis I
18	Tuthmosis II	Thutmosis II
18	Tuthmosis III	Thutmosis III
18	Hatshepsut	Hatchetsut
18	Amenhotep II	Amenophis II
18	Tuthmosis IV	Thutmosis IV
18	Amenhotep III	Amenophis III
18	Akhenaten	Amenophis IV/Ikhenaton
18	Smenkhkare	
18	Tutankhamun	Tutankhaten
18	Aya	Ay; Eye
18	Haremheb	Horemheb
18	Amenmasse	
19	Ramesses I	Ramsis I
19	Seti I	Sethos I
19	Merneptah	
19	Seti II	Sethos II
19	Siptah	
19	Queen Twosre	Tausert
19	Ramesses II	Ramsis II/Ramses the Great.
20	Ramesses VII	Ramsis VII
20	Sethnakhte	Setnakht
20	Ramesses III	Ramsis III
20	Ramesses IV	Ramsis IV
20	Ramesses V	
20	Ramesses VI	Ramsis VI
20	Ramesses VIII	Ramsis VIII
20	Ramesses IX	Ramsis IX
20	Ramesses X	Ramsis X
20	Ramesses XI	Ramsis XI
20	Herihor	
21	Pinedjem I	Paynedjem I
21	Psusennes I	
21	Osorkon	Osorkon the Elder
21	Siamun	
21	Har-Psusennes II	
21	Amenennisu	
21	Amenope /Amenemopet	
21	Piankh	
21	Masaharta	
21	Djedkhonsefankh	
21	Menkheperre	
21	Smendes	
21	Pinudjem II	
21	Psusennes II	
22	Takelot II	
22	Sheshonq III	Shoshenk III/Shishak ??

22	Osorkon II	
22	Pami	
22	Sheshonq V	Shoshenk V
22	Osorkon V	
22	Sheshonq I	Shoshenk I
22	Osorkon III	
22	Sheshonq II	Shoshenk II
22	Osorkon IV	
23	Pedubaste I	
23	Peftjau'awybast	
23	Takelot III	
23	Rudamun	
23	Iuput II	
23	Shoshenk IV	
24	Bocchoris/Bakenranef	Bakenranef
24	Tetnakhte	
25	Shabaka	
25	Shebitku	Shabataka
25	Taharqa	
25	Tantamani	Tanwetamani
25	Kashta	
25	Piye	Pi'ankh
25	Alara	
26	Psammetichus I	Psamtik I
26	Necho II	
26	Psammetichus II	Psamtik II
26	Apries	Wahibra/Hphra
26	Amasis II	
26	Psammeticus III	Psamtik III
26	Ameris (Governor)	
26	Tefnakht II	
26	Nekauba	
27	Cambyses	
27	Darius I	
27	Xerxes I	
27	Artaxerius I	
27	Darius II	
28	Amyrtaios	
29	Nepherites I	
29	Psammuthis	
29	Hakoris	
29	Nepherites II	
30	Nectanebo I	
30	Teos	
30	Nectanebo II	
31	Artaxerxes III	Ochus
31	Arses	
31	Darius III Codoman	
31	Khababash	
32	Alexander III	Alexander the Great
32	Philip Arrhidaeus	
32	Alexander IV	
33	Ptolemy I	Soter I
33	Ptolemy V	Epiphanes
33	Cleopatra VII	Mark Anthony & Queen Cleopatra
33	Ptolemy XV	Caesarion
33	Ptolemy III	Euergetes I

33	Ptolemy IV	Philopator
33	Ptolemy VI	Philometor
33	Ptolemy VII	Neos Philopator
33	Ptolemy XI	Alexander II
33	Ptolemy XII	Neos – Dionysos – Auletes
33	Ptolemy XIII	
33	Ptolemy XIV	
33	Cleopatra III	
33	Ptolemy IX	Soter II Lathyros
33	Ptolemy X	Alexander I
33	Ptolemy II	Philadelphus
33	Harwennofre	
33	'Ankhwennofre	
33	Harsiese	
33	Antiochus IV	Epiphanes
33	Ptolemy VIII	Euergetes II Physkon
33	Berenice IV	
34	Augustus	Octavian
34	Tiberius	
34	Gaius	Caligula
34	Claudius	
34	Nero	
34	Galba	
34	Otho	
34	Vespasian	
34	Titus	
34	Domitian	
34	Nerva	
34	Trajan	
34	Hadrian	
34	Antoninus Pius	
34	Marcus Aurelius	
34	Lucius Verus	
34	Commodus	
34	Septimius Severus	
34	Caracalla	
34	Geta	
34	Macrinus	
34	Diadumenianus	
34	Severus Alexander	
34	Gordian III	
34	Philip	
34	Decius	
34	Gallus	
34	Volusianus	
34	Valerian	
34	Gallienus	
34	Macrianus	
34	Quietus	
34	Aurelian	
34	Probus	
34	Diocletian	
34	Maximian	
34	Galerius	

ALPHABETICAL LIST OF PHARAOHS

Name	Period	Date	Dynasty
'Ankhwennofre	Ptolemaic	199	33
(..)kare Inyotef	II Int Period	1,700	13
(..)set	II Int Period	1,700	13
Adjib	Early	before 2,800	1
Ahmose	New Kingdom	1,539	18
Akhenaten	New Kingdom	1,352	18
Alara	III Int Period	780	25
Alexander III	Greco-Roman	332	32
Alexander IV	Greco-Roman	316	32
Amasis II	Sait	570	26
Amenemhat I	Middle Kingdom	1,937	12
Amenemhat II	Middle Kingdom	1,875	12
Amenemhat III	Middle Kingdom	1,817	12
Amenemhat IV	Middle Kingdom	1,772	12
Amenemhat V	II Int Period	1,700	13
Amenemhat VII	II Int Period	1,700	13
Amenennisu	III Int Period	1,040	21
Amenhotep I	New Kingdom	1,514	18
Amenhotep II	New Kingdom	1,427	18
Amenhotep III	New Kingdom	1,382	18
Amenmasse	New Kingdom	1,204	18
Amenope /Amenemopet	III Int Period	993	21
Amenyqemau	II Int Period	1,700	13
Ameris (Governor)	Late Period	715	26
Amyrtaios	Late Period	404	28
Antiochus IV	Ptolemaic	168	33
Antoninus Pius	Roman Emperor	138AD	34
Apachnan	II Int Period	1,604	15
Apophis	II Int Period	1,585	15
Apries	Sait	589	26
Arses	Persian II	338	31
Artaxerius I	Persian I	465	27
Artaxerxes III	Persia II	343	
Assis Khamudi	II Int Period	15	2
Augustus	Roman Emperor	30	34
Aurelian	Roman Emperor	270AD	34
Ay	II Int Period	1,664	13
Aya	New Kingdom	1,327	18
Berenice IV	Ptolemaic	58	33
Bnon	II Int Period	1,633	15
Bocchoris/Bakenranef	III Int Period	720	24
Cambyses	Persian I	525	27
Caracalla	Roman Emperor	198AD	34
Claudius	Roman Emperor	41AD	34
Cleopatra III	Ptolemaic	11	33
Cleopatra VII	Ptolemaic	51	33
Commodus	Roman Emperor	180AD	34
Darius I	Persian	52I	27
Darius II	Persian I	424	27
Darius III Codoman	Persian II	335	31
Decius	Roman Emperor	249AD	34
Dedumose I	II Int Period	1,700	13

Dedumose II	II Int Period	1,700	13
Den	Early	before 2,800	1
Diadumenianus	Roman Emperor	218AD	34
Diocletian	Roman Emperor	218AD	34
Djedkare	Old Kingdom	2,388	5
Djedkhonsefankh	III Int Period	1,046	21
Djer	Early	before 2,900	1
Domitian	Roman Emperor	81AD	34
Gaius	Roman Emperor	37AD	34
Galba	Roman Emperor	68AD	34
Galerius	Roman Emperor	293AD	34
Gallienus	Roman Emperor	253AD	34
Gallus	Roman Emperor	251AD	34
Geta	Roman Emperor	209AD	34
Gordian III	Roman Emperor	238AD	34
Hadrian	Roman Emperor	117AD	34
Hakoris	Late Period	393	29
Har-Psusennes II	III Int Period	959	21
Haremheb	New Kingdom	1,323	18
Harnedjheriotef	II Int Period	1,700	13
Harsiese	Ptolemaic	131	33
Harwennofre	Ptolemaic	205	33
Hatshepsut	New Kingdom	1,473	18
Herihor	New Kingdom	1,080	20
Hetepsekhemwy	Early	before 2,700	2
Hor	II Int Period	1,700	13
Hosar	Early	2,630	3
Huni	Early	2,599	3
Iannas	II Int Period	1,633	15
Iayib	II Int Period	1,674	13
Inyotef I	I Int Period	2,074	11
Inyotef II	I Int Period	2,064	11
Inyotef III	I Int Period		11
Inyotef V	II Int Period	1,640	17
Ity	I Int Period	2,060	10
Iufni	II Int Period	1,700	13
Iuput II	III Int Period	754	23
Kamose	II Int Period	1,555	17
Kashta	III Int Period	760	25
Kha'ba	Early	2,603	3
Kha'sekhemwy	Early	before 2,650	2
Khababash	Persian II	332	31
Khafre	Old Kingdom	2,520	4
Khasekhem	Old Kingdom	before 2,650	2
Khendjer	II Int Period	1,700	13
Khety	I Int Period	2,134	9
Khufu	Old Kingdom	2,551	4
Lucius Verus	Roman Emperor	161AD	34
Macrianus	Roman Emperor	260AD	34
Macrinus	Roman Emperor	217AD	34
Marcus Aurelius	Roman Emperor	161AD	34
Masaharta	III Int Period	1,054	21
Maximian	Roman Emperor	286AD	34
Menes – Scorpion	Early	before 2,920	1
Menkauhor	Old Kingdom	2,396	5
Menkaure	Old Kingdom	2,490	4
Menkheperre	III Int Period	1,045	21

Name	Period	Date	#
Mentuemzaf	II Int Period	1,700	13
Mentuhotep I	Middle Kingdom	2,080	11
Mentuhotep IV	Middle Kingdom	1,944	11
Mentuhotpe II	Middle Kingdom	2,007	11
Mentuhotpe III	Middle Kingdom	1,956	11
Merenre	Old Kingdom	2,255	6
Merneptah	New Kingdom	1,213	19
Mersekhemre Ined	II Int Period	1,700	13
Meryet-Nit Queen	Old Kingdom	before 2,800	1
Merykare	I Int Period	2,090	9
Narmer	Early	before 3,000	0
Nebireyeraw	II Int Period	1,632	17
Necho II	Sait	610	26
Nectanebo I	Late Period	380	30
Nectanebo II	Late Period	360	30
Nedjemib(..)re	II Int Period	1,700	13
Neferhotep I	II Int Period	1,696	13
Neferhotep III	II Int Period	1,700	13
Neferirkare Kakai	Old Kingdom	2,446	5
Neferkare'	Old Kingdom	2,150	7
Nefrusobk	Middle Kingdom	1,763	12
Nekauba	Late Period	688	26
Nepherites I	Late Period	399	29
Nepherites II	Late Period	380	29
Nero	Roman Emperor	54AD	34
Nerva	Roman Emperor	96AD	34
Neterka	Old Kingdom	before 2,650	2
Neterkara	Old Kingdom	before 2,650	2
Ninetjer	Early	before 2,700	2
Niuserre	Old Kingdom	2,416	5
Osorkon	III Int Period	984	21
Osorkon II	III Int Period	924	22
Osorkon III	III Int Period	883	22
Osorkon IV	III Int Period	730	22
Osorkon V	III Int Period	735	22
Otho	Roman Emperor	69AD	34
Pami	III Int Period	783	22
Pedubaste I	III Int Period	818	23
Peftjau'awybast	III Int Period	740	23
Pepy I	Old Kingdom	2,289	6
Pepy II	Old Kingdom	2,246	6
Peribsen	Early	before 2,650	2
Philip	Roman Emperor	244AD	34
Philip Arrhidaeus	Greco-Roman	323	32
Piankh	III Int Period	1,074	21
Pinedjem I	III Int Period	1,070	21
Pinudjem II	III Int Period	990	21
Piye/Pi'ankh	III Int Period	747	25
Probus	Roman Emperor	276AD	34
Psammetichus I	Sait	664	26
Psammetichus II	Sait	595	26
Psammeticus III	Sait	525	26
Psammuthis	Late Period	394	29
Psusennes I	III Int Period	1,040	21
Psusennes II	III Int Period	969	21
Ptolemy I	Ptolemaic	304	33
Ptolemy II	Ptolemaic	285	33

Ptolemy III	Ptolemaic	246	33
Ptolemy IV	Ptolemaic	221	33
Ptolemy IX	Ptolemaic	116	33
Ptolemy V	Ptolemaic	205	33
Ptolemy VI	Ptolemaic	180	33
Ptolemy VII	Ptolemaic	145	33
Ptolemy VIII	Ptolemaic	170	33
Ptolemy X	Ptolemaic	107	33
Ptolemy XI	Ptolemaic	80	33
Ptolemy XII	Ptolemaic	80	33
Ptolemy XIII	Ptolemaic	51	33
Ptolemy XIV	Ptolemaic	47	33
Ptolemy XV	Ptolemaic	44	33
Qa'a/Ka-aa	Early	before 2,800	1
Queen Twosre	New Kingdom	1,188	19
Quietus	Roman Emperor	260	34
Ra'djedef	Old Kingdom	2,528	4
Ra'neferef	Old Kingdom	2,419	5
Ramesses I	New Kingdom	1,295	19
Ramesses II	New Kingdom	1,279	19
Ramesses III	New Kingdom	1,184	20
Ramesses IV	New Kingdom	1,153	20
Ramesses IX	New Kingdom	1,126	20
Ramesses V	New Kingdom	1,147	20
Ramesses VI	New Kingdom	1,143	20
Ramesses VII	New Kingdom	1,136	20
Ramesses VIII	New Kingdom	1,129	20
Ramesses X	New Kingdom	1,108	20
Ramesses XI	New Kingdom	1,099	20
Re'neb	Early	before 2,700	2
Renseneb	II Int Period	1,700	13
Rudamun	III Int Period	757	23
Sahure	Old Kingdom	2,458	5
Salitis	II Int Period	1,640	15
Sankhibre	II Int Period	1,700	13
Sankhrenesewadjtu	II Int Period	1,700	13
Scorpion – see menes	Archaic		
Sebekemzaf I	II Int Period	1,634	17
Sebekemzaf II	II Int Period	1,630	17
Sebekhotep I	II Int Period	1,700	13
Sebekhotep III	II Int Period	1,700	13
Sebekhotep VI	II Int Period	1,700	13
Sebekhotep VII	II Int Period	1,700	13
Sebekhotpe IV	II Int Period	1,685	13
Sebekhotpe V	II Int Period	1,678	13
Sedjef(..)kare	II Int Period	1,700	13
Segnere III	II Int Period	1,628	17
Sehetepibre	II Int Period	1,700	13
Sehetepibre	II Int Period	1,700	13
Sekhemkare	II Int Period	1,700	13
Sekhemkhet	Early	2,611	3
Semerkhet	Early	before 2,800	1
Sened	Early	before 2,630	2
Senwosret I	Middle Kingdom	1,917	12
Senwosret II	Middle Kingdom	1,842	12
Senwosret III	Middle Kingdom	1,836	12
Septimius Severus	Roman Emperor	193	34

Seqenenre' III	II Int Period	1,500	17
Sethnakhte	New Kingdom	1,186	20
Seti I	New Kingdom	1,294	19
Seti II	New Kingdom	1,200	19
Severus Alexander	Roman Emperor	222AD	34
Sewadjkare	II Int Period	1,700	13
Sewadjkare	II Int Period	1,700	13
Shabaka	Late Period	716	25
Shebitku	Late Period	702	25
Shepseskaf	Old Kingdom	2,472	4
Shepseskare	Old Kingdom	2,426	5
Sheshi	II Int Period	1,622	15
Sheshonq I	III Int Period	945	22
Sheshonq II	III Int Period	895	22
Sheshonq III	III Int Period	835	22
Sheshonq V	III Int Period	773	22
Shoshenk IV	III Int Period	720	23
Siamun	III Int Period	978	21
Sihathor	II Int Period	1,685	13
Siptah	New Kingdom	1,194	19
Smendes	III Int Period	1,069	21
Smenkhkare	New Kingdom	1,341	18
Smenkhkare	II Int Period	1,700	13
Smenkhkare Mermesha	II Int Period	1,700	13
Snofru	Old Kingdom	2,575	4
Sobekhotep II	II Int Period	1,700	13
Ta'o I	II Int Period	1,625	17
Taharqa	Late Period	690	25
Takelot II	III Int Period	860	22
Takelot III	III Int Period	764	23
Tantamani	Late Period	664	25
Tao II	II Int Period	1,565	17
Tefnakht II	Late Period	696	26
Teos	Late Period	365	30
Teti	Old Kingdom	2,323	6
Tetnakhte	III Int Period	727	24
Tiberius	Roman Emperor	14AD	34
Titus	Roman Emperor	79AD	34
Trajan	Roman Emperor	98AD	34
Tutankhamun	New Kingdom	1,336	18
Tuthmosis I	New Kingdom	1,493	18
Tuthmosis II	New Kingdom	1,481	18
Tuthmosis III	New Kingdom	1,479	18
Tuthmosis IV	New Kingdom	1,392	18
Unas	Old Kingdom	2,356	5
Userkaf	Old Kingdom	2,465	5
Valerian	Roman Emperor	253	34
Vespasian	Roman Emperor	69	34
Volusianus	Roman Emperor	251	34
Wadj/Djet?	Early	before 2,800	1
Wegaf	II Int Period	1,783	13
Xerxes I	Persian I	486	27
Zanakht	Early	2,649	3
Zekhen	Early	before 2,950	0

BOOKLIST

Title	Author	Category
A Biographical Dictionary of Ancient Egypt	Rosalie D & David A E	General
A Dictionary of Egyptian Civilisation	Posener G.	General
A Guide to Religious Ritual at Abydos	David A. R.	Religion
A History of Ancient Egypt	Grimal N	General
A History of Egypt under the Ptolemaic Dynsasty	Bevan E.	Ptolemy
A Test of Time	Rohl D	Exodus, dating, III Intermediate Period
A Thousand Miles up the Nile	Edwards Amelia B.	Travel
After Tutankhamun	Reeves V.C. N.	New Kingdom
Akhenaten, Pharaoh of Egypt	Aldred C.	Akhenaten
Akhenaten's Egypt	Thomas A. P.	Akhenaten
An Ancient Egyptian Herbal	Manniche l.	Medicine
An Ancient Egyptian Hieroglyphic Dictionary in Two Volumes	Wallis Budge E.A	Hieroglyphics
Ancient Egypt, it's Culture and History	Manchip White J. E.	General
An Introduction to Ancient Egypt	James T G H	General
Ancient Egypt	David A. R. and A. E.	General
Ancient Egypt – Eyewitness Series	Collection	General
Ancient Egypt – Onomastica	Gardiner A.	Language
Ancient Egyptian Literature	Lichtheim M	Literature
Ancient Egyptian Masonry	Engelbach R Clark S.	Building
Ancient Egyptian Paintings	Davies N.	Art
Ancient Egyptian Religion	Cerny J.	Religion
Ancient Egyptian Religions	Frankfort	Religion
Ancient Lives: The Story of the Pharaohs' Tombmakers	Romer J	General
Ancient Materials and Industries	Lucas A.	General
Ancient Records of Egypt	Breasted J. H.	General
Archaic Egypt	Emery W.B.	Predynastic and dynasty 1
Atlas of Ancient Egypt	Baines J & Malek J	General
Atlas of Mysterious Places	Various	General
Beyond the Pyramids	Kennedy D.	Travel
Blue Guide to Egypt	Various	Travel
British Egyptology	Wortham J.	Travel
China and Japan, Myths and Legands	MacKenzie D.	Far East
Cities of the Dead	Paine M.	Fiction
Cleopatra	Bradford E.	Cleopatra; Greco-Roman; Ptolemy
Cleopatra.	Grant M.	Cleopatra; Greco-Roman; Ptolemy
Death in Ancient Egypt	Spencer A. J.	Mummies; Religion
Development of Religion and Thought in Ancient Egypt	Breasted J. H.	Religion
Discovering Ancient Egypt	Rosalie David A.	General
Drawings from Ancient Egypt	Peck W. H.	Art
Egypt after the Pharaohs	Bowman A.	Romans etc
Egypt before the Pharaohs	Hoffman	Pre-dynastic
Egypt in Nubia	Emery W. B.	Nubia
Egypt of the Pharaohs	Gardiner A. H.	General
Egypt to the end of the Old Kingdom	Aldred C.	Pre-dynastic;
Egypt under the Ptolemaic Dynasty	Bevin E.	Cleopatra; Ptolemies;
Egyptian Antiquities in the Nile Valley	Balkie	Discoveries

Title	Author	Subject
Egyptian Architecture	Petrie	Architecture: Art; Petie.
Egyptian Art	Aldred C	Art
Egyptian Gods and Myths	Thomas A. P.	Mythology
Egyptian Grammar	Gardiner A. H.	Specialised Language
Egyptian Kingdoms	David A R	General
Egyptian Legends and Stories	Seton M. V. & Williams	Legends; Religion
Egyptian Life	Stead M	General
Egyptian Magic	Wallis Budge E. A.	Religion
Egyptian Magic.	Jacq C	Religion
Egyptian Medicine	Reeves C.	Medicine
Egyptian Mummies	Andrews C.	Mummies; Religion
Egyptian Mummies	Adams B.	Mummies
Egyptian Mysteries	Lamy L.	Religion
Egyptian Mythology	Ions V.	Mythology
Egyptian Myths	Hart G	Mythology, Religion
Egyptian Painting in the Middle Kingdom	Terrace H.	Art; Middle Kingdom
Egyptian Pyramids and Mastaba Tombs	Watson P.	Pyramids and tombs
Egyptian Sculpture	Murray M.	Art
Egyptology	Putnam J.	General
Evidence Embalmed	David A. R. & Tapp E.	Religion
Exploring the World of the Pharaohs	Hobson C	General
Faces of the Pharaohs	Partridge R. B.	Mummies
Fingerprints of the Gods	Hancock G.	Mystery; Pyramids;
Flinders Petrie, A Life Of Archeology	Drower M S	Biography
Footsteps	Brice Norman	General
From Exodus to King Akhnaton	Velikovsky I.	New Kingdom, Exodus, Akhenaten
From Fetish to God in Ancient Egypt	Wallis Budge E A	Religion
Gods of the Egyptians	Wallis Budge E A	Religion
Great Ones of Ancient Egypy	Brunton W.	General
Great Tombs of the First Dynasty	Emery W.	Tombs; Religion; 1st dynasty
Hieroglyphs	Katon & Mintz	Language
Hieroglyphs and the Afterlife	Forman W. & Quirke S.	Hieroglyphics; Religion
Hieroglyphs, the Writing of Ancient Egypt	Katan N J & Mintz B	Hieroglyphics
Iknaton, Legend and History	Giles F. J.	Akhenaten; Legends; Religion
Imhotep	Hurry J. B.	Pyramids
In the Shadow of the Pyramids	Malek & Forman	Pyramids; Tombs; Old Kingdom
Keeper of Genesis	Bauval R & Hancock G.	Origins; Sphinx; Great Pyramid
Kings and Queens of Ancient Egypt	Brunton W.	General
Kingship and the Gods	Frankfort H.	Religion
Life in Ancient Egypt	Strouhal E.	General
Life in Egypt under Roman Rule	Lewis N.	Romans
Life under the Pharaohs	Cottell L.	General
Loadstone	Harbinson A.	Fiction
Luxor and its Temples	Blackman A. M.	Luxor; Karnak; Temples
Manetho	Weil R.	Manetho the Ancient Historian
Middle Kingdom Art in Ancient Egypt	Aldred C.	Art; Old Kingdom
Moses, Pharoah of Egypt	Ahmed Osman	New Kingdom; Biblical; Moses
Mummies	Paterson & Andrews	Mummies
Mummies and Human Remains	Dawson W. R. & Gray P.	Mummies

Title	Author	Category
Mummies, Myth and Magic in Ancient Egypt	El Mahdy	Magic
Myth and Symbol in Ancient Egypt	Clark R.T.Rundle	Religion
Myths and Legends – Egypt	Collection	Legends; Religion
Name of the Beast	Easterman D.	Fiction
Narrative of Operations and Recent Discoveries	Belzoni G.	Discoveries; Pyramids; Tombs
New Light on Ancient Egypt	Maspero G.	History
Nubia under the Pharaohs	Trigger B.	Nubia
Oedipus and Akhnaton	Velikovsky I	Akhenaten
Old Kingdom Art in Ancient Egypt	Aldred	Art; Old Kingdom
Osiris and the Egyptian Revolution	Wallis Budge E A	Religion Medici Soc
Penguin Guide to Ancient Egypt	Murname	Travel and General
Peoples of the Sea	Velikovsky I	New Kingdom
Pharaoh Triumphant, the Life and Times of Ramesses II	Kitchen K A	New Kingdom
Pharaohs and Pyramids	Hart G	Pyramids
Predynastic Egypt	Adams B.	Pre-dynastic
Principles of Egyptian Art	Schafer H.	Art
Ptolemaic Alexandria	Fraser P. M.	Ptolemy
Pyramids	Pratchett T.	Fiction
Pyramids and Progress	Ward J	Pyramids
Pyramid Prophesies	Toth M.	Mystery
Pyramid Power	Toth M.	Mystery
Queens of the Pharaohs	Cottell L.	General
Ramses II and His Time	Velikovsky I	Ramesses II
Ramses the Great	Freed R.	New Kingdom
Riding the Desert Trail	Selby B.	Travel
River God	Smith W.	Fiction
River in the Desert; Modern Travels in Ancient Egypt	Roberts P W	Travel
Saqqara, the Royal Cemetary of Memphis	Lauer	Tombs; Saqqara
Secrets of the Great Pyramid	Tompkins P	Great Pyramid
Serpent in the Sky	West J A	Origins, Pyramids
Social Life in Ancient Egypt	Petrie	Discoveries
Sphinx	Cook R.	Fiction
Stranger in the Valley of the Kings	Osman A.	Tombs; Valley of Kings
Technology in the Ancient World	Hodges H.	Pyramids
The Ancient Egypt Texts	Faulkner R O	Translations
The Ancient Egypt Texts (reissued)	Faulkner R O	Translations
The Ancient Egyptians' Religious Beliefs and Practice	David A. R.	Religion
The Art and Architecture of Ancient Egypt	Stevenson-Smith W.	Art; Architecture
The Art of Ancient Egypt	Ross	Art
The Arts in Ptolemaic Egypt	Noshy I.	Ptolemy; Art
The Attitude of the Ancient Egyptians to Death and the Dead	Gardiner A. H.	Religion
The Battle of Actium	Carter J. M.	Romans; Cleopatra
The Bent Pyramid	Fakhry A.	Pyramids
The Boat beneath the Pyramid	Jenkins N	Pyramids
The Birth of Civilisation in the Near East	Frankfort H.	General
The British Museum Book of Ancient Egypt	Quirke S & Spencer J	General
The Burden of Egypt	Wilson J. A.	General
The Buried Pyramid	Goneim M. Z.	Pyramids
The Conflict of Horus and Seth	Griffiths J.G.	Religion; Mythology; Origins

Title	Author	Subject
The Complete Tutankhamun	Reeves N	Tutankhamun, Kingdom, Tombs
The Death of Gods in Ancient Egypt	Sellers J B	Religion
The Development of the Egyptian Tomb down to ... Cheops	Reisner J. A.	Tombs; Old Kingdom; Pyramids
The Discovery of the Tomb of Tutankhamun	Carter H. & Mace A.C.	Discovery; Tutankhamun; Tombs
The Early Dynastic Period	Edwards	Old Kingdom; Archaic4
The Egyptians	Aldred	General
The Fort Cemetery at Hierakonpolis	Adams B.	Graves
The God Ptah	Holmberg & Sandman M.	Mythology
The Gods of Ancient Egypt	Watterson B.	Religion; Mythology
The Great Belzoni	Mayes S.	Biography
The Great Pyramid Decoded	Lemesurier P	Great Pyramid
The Great Pyramid Fact Sheet	Spencer A J	Great Pyramid
The Great Pyramid, Your Personal Guide	Lemesurier P	Great Pyramid
The Great Tomb Robberies of the 20th Dynasty	Peet	Tombs; New Kingdom
The Hermetica	Gilbert A G	Translation
The History of Egypt under Roman Rule	Milne J. G.	Romans
The History of Herodotus	Redfield R.	Greek Historian Herodotus' Writings
The History of the Giza Necropolis	Reisner	Tombs; Pyramids; Religion
The Intellectual Adventure of Early Man	Frankfort H.	General; Religion
The Legacy of Egypt	Glenville S. R. K.	General
The Life and Times of Akhenaten	Weigall A.E.P.G.	Akhenaten; Religion; New Kingdom
The Life and Times of Cleopatra, Queen of Egypt	Weigall A. E. P. G.	Cleopatra; Ptolemies; Romans
The Lost Pharaohs	Cottell L.	General
The Literature of the Ancient Pharaohs	Erman A.	Stories
The Nile and Egyptian Civilisation	Moret A.A. E. P. G.	General
The Old Kingdom in Egypt	Smith W.	Old Kingdom
The Origins of Osiris	Griffiths J.G.	Mythology
The Orion Mystery	Bauvel R & Gilbert A	Origins, Pyramids, Mythology
The Penguin Guide to Ancient Egypt	Murrane W.J.	Travel
The Phoenicians and the West	Aubet M E	Phoenicians
The Ptolemies of Egypt	Elgood P. G.	Ptolemy; Greco-Roman
The Pyramids	Fakhry A.	Pyramids
The Pyramid Builders of Ancient Egypt	David A. R.	Pyramids
The Pyramids of Egypt	Edwards I. E. S.	Pyramids
The Pyramids of Teotihuacan	Editor S A	Pyramids
The Ramasseum	Quibell J E	Ramesess II
The Reign of Tuthmose IV	Bryan B. M.	New Kingdom
The Riddle of the Pyramids	Mendelssohn K	Pyramids
The Rise and Fall of the Middle Kindom in Thebes		Winlock
The Royal Mecropolis of Thebes	Thomas E.	Tombs
The Royal Tombs of el-Armana	Martin	Tombs; Akhenaten; New Kingdom
The Royal Tombs of the First Dynasty	Petrie F.	Tombs; Archaic; Saqqara; Abydos
The Seventh Scroll	Smith W.	Fiction
The Sign and the Seal	Hancock G	Mystery fiction

Title	Author	Subject
The Sky Religion in Egypt	Wainwright G. A.	Religion
The Sons of Re	Rose J.	General
The Sphinx and the Megaliths	Iviny J	Sphinx
The Step Pyramid	Firth, Quibell & Lauer	Pyramids; Architecture; Saqqara
The Third Intermediate Period in Egypt	Kitchen K. A.	III Intermediate Period
The Tomb of Queen Ti	Davis T.	Tombs
The Tomb of Tutankhamun	Carter H. & Mace	Tombs; New Kingdom; Tutankhamun
The Traveller's Key to Ancient Egypt	West J A	Travel
The Valley of the Kings	Reeves C. N.	Tombs
The Warrior Pharaohs	Cottell L.	General
Thebes of the Pharaohs	Nims C. F.	Thebes; New Kingdom
Travels in Nubia	Burckhardt	Nubia
Tutankhamun	Desroches-Noblecourt C	Tutankhamun; Tombs
Tutankhamun, His Tomb and its Treasures	Edwards I.E.S.	Tutankhamun; Tombs
Tutankhamun's Treasure	Fox & Penelope	Tutankhamun; Tombs
Upper Egypt	Kamil J.	Upper Egypt
Valley of the Kings	Romer J	New Kingdom Tomb
Voices from Ancient Egypt	Parkinson R B	Hieroglyphics
Women in Ancient Egypt	Robins G.	Women
Who was Who in Egyptology	Dawson & Uphill	General

ACKNOWLEDGEMENTS

I would briefly like to thank several people who have helped produce this work. My first visit to Egypt was with Susan Beswick who shared the fascination with me and provided me with material during my time of preparation. Thanks also to Lesley James who also inspired deeper explanation into some aspects and helped me see through the eyes of others. In HMP Blantyre House I was helped and encouraged by Will Hutchinson, Earnest John Pennington, Ralph Dellow, Ingrid Travers and Dorritt. I would also like to thank Frontier Publishing and Michael Pryce for their help during the final stages. Finally I would like to thank all the Pharaohs who left such a wonderful wealth of mystery and magic, for us to unravel. May their bodies survive!

Index

A
Abdullah Al Mamun 87
Abu Simbel 24, 27, 204, 210
Abydos 26, 200, 203
Admonitions of the Prophet 101
Aha 28, 36, 73
Ahmose 104
Akhenaten 8, 28, 42, 127, 203
Akhetaten 203
Akhsenpaaten 128
Alexander of Macedonia 150, 161
Alexander the Great 150, 161
Alexandria 151, 155, 159
Amarna Letters 128
Amasis 147
Amelia B Edwards 180, 211
Amenemhat I 82, 202
Amenemhat III 81, 104
Amenesse 138
Amenhotep I 117, 202
Amenhotep III 22, 38, 126, 202, 209
Amenophis I 117
Amenophis III 22, 38, 126, 202, 209
Amenophis IV 8, 28, 42, 127
Ammenemes I 102

Ammenemes III 81
Amun 43, 57, 118, 123
Amun-Re 63, 118, 211
Ancient story 55, 63, 75, 78, 81, 100, 106, 109, 119, 145, 188, 189
Ankhwennofre 154
Anthony and Cleopatra 155
Antioch 170
Anubis 49, 208
Apis – Osiris 126, 201
Archaic Period 22
Arsinoe 153, 162
Artapanus 108
Artaxercius 149
Artaxerxes II Ochus 149
Aswan Dam 204, 210
Aten 42, 128, 203
Atlantis 35
Atrium 174
Atum 40
Auguste Mariette 25, 201
Autocrator 171
Avaris 119
Avenue of Sphinxes 205
Ay 132

B

Ba	70, 82
Bab-el-Molûk	232
Babylon	147
Badarian culture	33
Battle of Pharsalia	160
Battle of Qadesh	132, 205
Beer	63
Belzoni	193, 211
Beni Hassan	122
Beni-Salama	181
Bent Pyramid	77, 202
Berenice	152, 155, 157
Bes	49
Biban-el-Muluk	83
Black Pyramid	202
Boats	62, 78, 103, 163, 203
Bocchoris	146
Books of the Dead	114
British Museum	34, 81, 128, 159, 168
Brutus	168
Burckhardt	21, 24
Burial pits	34
Buto	37
Byblos	55

C

Cache of mummies	209
Caesarion	156, 177
Cairo Museum	19, 112, 122, 199
Calendar	166
Cambyses	147, 201
Camel rides	198
Canopic Jars	70
Cartouche	38, 74, 141
Caviglia	89
Champollion	25, 105
Chancellor	188
Chariots	119
Cheops	19, 77, 109
China	142
Cleopatra's Needle	165
Cleopatra II	152, 154
Cleopatra III	152, 154
Cleopatra Selene	170, 177
Cleopatra VII	44, 152, 155
Clothing	188
Cocaine	142
Coffin Texts	103
Colossi of Memnon	22, 126, 204
Cornelius Gallus	178
Cyprus	162

D

Dahibeyeh	165
Dahshur	77, 202
Darius I	148, 201
Darius III Codoman	149
Davison	89
Davison's Chamber	89
Demetrius	157
Den	73
Dier el-Bahari	101, 122, 206
Dion Cassius	159
Dionysus	32
Divine Votaress of Amun	145
Djosar	73, 98, 200
Double Crown	37
Dream Stele	194
Drovetti	24
Duat	57, 64
Dudimose	107
Dynasty 1	39, 97
Dynasty 2	98
Dynasty 3	74, 98
Dynasty 4	77
Dynasty 5	81, 99
Dynasty 6	81, 100, 189
Dynasty 11	102
Dynasty 12	81, 102
Dynasty 13	104
Dynasty 14	104
Dynasty 17	104, 116
Dynasty 18	81, 101, 105, 206
Dynasty 19	107
Dynasty 20	138, 139
Dynasty 22	144
Dynasty 25	146
Dynasty 26	146
Dynasty 27	147
Dynasty 28	148
Dynasty 31	150

E

Edfu	60, 204, 210
Elephantine	77, 210
Elysian Fields	65
Ennead of Heliopolis	40, 47
Ephesus	172
Epiphanes	152, 154
Esna	204, 210
Esna Temple	210
Euergetes	152, 153
Exodus	108
Eye of Horus	57

F

Fayum Lake	35
Festival of Drunkenness	63
First Intermediate Period	22, 100
Flavius Josephus	23
Florence Nightingale	25
Followers of Horus	188

G

G. Elliot Smith	31
Games	184
Geb	50
Ginger	34, 185
Gold of Valour	120
Golden Horus name	38
Golden Section	92
Great Pyramid	19, 73, 84, 191
Greaves, John	89
Greece	146, 150, 172

H

Hapi	76, 180

229

Haremheb	132	Khnum	51, 77, 124
Harwennofre	154	Khufu (Cheops)	19, 77, 109
Hathor	37, 58, 122, 211	King's Chamber	78, 88, 91, 192
Hatshepsut	8, 114, 116, 119, 122, 206	King Nebuchadnezzar II	147
Hawara	202	King Scorpion	28, 35
Heb-Sed	67	King Solomon	108
Heliopolis	40, 47	Kom Ombo	204, 210
Henry Salt	24		
Heracleopolis	101	**L**	
Herihor	143	Labyrinth	202
Hermopolis	76	Land of Punt	207
Herod	171, 175	Lapis Lazuli	181
Herodotus	21, 90, 147, 148	Late Period	22, 146
Hierakonpolis	34	Lathyro	158
Hieratic	25	Law	187
Hieroglyphs	23, 44, 74, 112, 208	Lepidus	171
Hittites	128, 135, 205, 211	Lepsius	211
Holy Bible	20, 106, 136	Libya	35, 144
Hor-Aha	28	Lisht	81, 202
Horse drawn chariot	119	Loret	116
Horus	37, 50, 55, 57, 190	Luxor	69, 204
Horus name	38, 139	Luxor Temple	205
Hosar	73, 98, 200		
How Did They Build IT?	93		
Howard Carter	26, 72, 129	**M**	
Howard-Hyse	90	Maadi	33
Huni	77, 202	Magic	108, 145
Hyksos	104	Mameluks	29
		Mamun	87
I		Manetho	9, 22, 31, 108, 146, 153
Ides of March	167	Marcus Antonius	158, 168
Imhotep	76, 188	Mariette	25, 201, 211
Imyotef	101	Maspero	26, 200
Inundation	205	Mastabas	43, 73
Iron Plate	86	Medinet Habu	139, 206
Isis	50, 55, 57	Meidum	75, 202
Israelites	144	Memphis	39, 47, 199
Items found within the Great Pyramid		Menes	28
of Giza	86	Menkaure	79, 90, 195
		Mentuhotep I Nebhepetre	101, 188, 206
J		Mentuhotep III	102
J.R.Hill	86	Mentuhotep IV	104
James Bruce	23, 141	Mercenaries	147
Japan	142	Merimba	33
Jerusalem	144	Merneptah	107, 138, 203
John Anthony West	8, 80, 85, 195	Middle Kingdom	22, 81, 203
Joshua	147	Min	50, 205
Judea	147	Minshat Abu Omar	33
Julius Caesar	160	Montu	52
Jupiter	167	Moses	20, 107, 136
		Mosque of the Sultan Hassan	78
K		Mud-brick houses	183
Kadesh	132, 205	Mummies	27, 69, 122, 201, 207
Kamose	105, 117	Musical instruments	181, 209
Karnak	116, 122, 204	Mut	205
Kenbet	187	Mycerinus	79, 90, 195
Kephri	63		
Kha	40, 43, 70, 78, 200	**N**	
Kharkady	63	Napoleon Bonaparte	24, 89, 105
Khaemwese	21, 136, 200	Naqada	26, 33
Khafre	81, 185	Narmer	28, 36, 73, 190
Khasekhemwy	38, 73, 98	Narmer Palette	36
Khephre	39	Naucratis	26, 147
Khephren	41, 51	Nebti name	38

Necho II	147	Ptolemy IV	152, 153
Nectanebo I	139, 149	Ptolemy IX Soter II	152, 155
Nectanebo II	142, 149, 201	Ptolemy V Epiphanes	115, 152, 154
Nefertari	29, 134, 209	Ptolemy X Alexander I	152
Nefertiti	42, 128	Ptolemy XI Alexander II	152, 154
Neith	58	Ptolemy XII	154, 157
Nekhebet	38	Ptolemy XIII Auletes1	152, 155, 157
Nero	170	Ptolemy XIV	152, 155
New Kingdom	22, 71, 97	Ptolemy XV	152, 156
Nilometer	23, 33	Punt	207
Nomes	76, 98, 181, 187	Pyramid of Khephren	24, 27, 199
Northern Stone Pyramid	202	Pyramid Texts	104, 200
Nubia	76, 128, 144, 147		
Nun	40, 52, 63	**Q**	
		Qadesh	133, 205
O		Quarries	210
Obelisk	122, 205	Queen's Chamber	78, 85, 192
Octavia	170	Queen's Pyramids	196
Octavian	158, 168	Queen Ahhotpe	117
Ogdoad of Hermopolis	42	Queen Berenice	152, 155, 157
Old Kingdom	22, 203	Queen Hetepheres	27, 196
On	40	Queen Nefertari	29, 134, 209
Orion	79, 96	Queen Tiye	72, 126, 136, 209
Osiris	31, 55, 204, 206	Queen Twosre	138
P		**R**	
Palermo Stone	27	Ra	38, 46, 63
Papyrus	44, 78, 106, 186	Radiocarbon dating	15
Papyrus of Ourmai	148	Ra-Harakhte	58, 63
Parthians	167	Ra-hotep	202
Pelusium	160	Ramesses I	132
Peoples of the Sea	139, 206	Ramesses II	24, 67, 75, 132, 134, 201
Pepy I	100, 189, 200		204, 206
Pepy II	100, 123, 200	Ramesses III	139
Peribsen	73, 98	Ramesses IV	141
Persians	148	Ramesses V	142
Petrie	26, 129	Ramesses the Great	24, 67, 75, 132, 134
Pharos	150, 163	Ramesses VI	150
Pharos Lighthouse	153, 160	Ramesses X	142, 208
Philadelphus	152	Ramesseum	206
Philometer	152, 154	Re	38, 46, 63
Philopator	152, 153	Red Crown	36
Pinedjem I	143	Red Pyramid	202
Pi-Ramesse	106, 132	Red Sea Canal	147, 163
Pleny the Elder	23	Re-Harakhty	211
Plutarch	23, 201	Reisner	26, 196
Pompey	157, 160, 165	Rekhmara	188
Pottery	33	Robert Hay	25
Potter's Wheel	99	Robert Schoch	85
Pre-dynastic	33	Rohl	108
Prenomen	38	Roman	22, 24, 154
Priests	98, 118, 143, 165	Rosetta stone	18, 105, 154
Prophecy of Neferti	102	Rudolf Gantenbrink	85
Psammetichus I	146		
Psammeticus III	146	**S**	
Psamtik	146	Sacred Lake	205
Psusennes I	144	Sandals	181
Psusennes II	145	Saqqara	75, 100, 199
Ptah	40, 78, 211, 253	Sarcophagus	103
Ptolemaic Dynasty	152	Saru	188
Ptolemaic Period	22, 210	Scarab	64
Ptolemies	152	Scorpion	28, 35
Ptolemy I Soter1	152, 153	Sea Peoples	139, 206
Ptolemy III Philadelphus	152, 153	Second Intermediate Period	22

231

Sedge and the Bee	38	The Descending Passage	91
Sekhmet	63, 205	The first time	31
Senet	184	The Grand Gallery	91
Senwosret I	81, 102, 202	Thebes	104, 188, 142, 204
Senwosret II	81, 103	Third Intermediate Period	22, 143
Senwosret III	103	Thomas Young	24
Septimus Severus	127	Thoth	41, 46, 123, 208
Seqenenre	105, 122	Tiy	209
Serapeum	25, 150, 201	Tobacco	142
Sesostris I	81, 102	Tomb of Tutankhamun	129, 184, 207
Sesostris II	81, 103	Tomb robbing	71, 127, 142, 208
Seth	33, 37, 46, 57, 138, 153	Toothache	122
Seth animal	33	Tourists breath	209
Sethnakhte	138	Triumvir	171
Sethos I (Seti I)	116, 132, 206	Turin Canon of Kings	24, 27
Sethos II (Seti II)	138	Turquoise	181
Seven Wonders of the Ancient World	150	Tutankhamun	72, 116, 184
		Tutankhaten	43, 128
Shabaka	144, 146	Tuthmosis I	119, 186
Shabaka Stone	40	Tuthmosis II	119
Shaduf	180	Tuthmosis III	38, 122, 188, 206
Shepseskaf	99	Tuthmosis IV	79, 114, 124, 194
Sheshonq I	144	Two Ladies' name	38
Sheshonq III	106, 144		
Shishak	106, 144	**U**	
Shu	41, 53	Unas	19, 21, 136, 200
Siamun	144	Unique Friend	189
Singing colossi	22, 127	Uraeus	37, 194
Size and comparison of size, of the			
Great Pyramid	86, 191	**V**	
Slaves	106, 135	Valley of the Kings	22, 26, 69, 129, 207, 263
Smendes	143		
Snorfu	77, 110, 196, 202	Valley of the Nobles	72
Sobehhotep IV	108	Valley of the Queens	72, 207
Sobek	208, 253	Velikovsky	139, 141, 149
Solomon	108	Ventilation' shafts	86
Sosigenes	166	Venus	166
Soter	152, 153	Vizier	44, 73, 187
Southern Pyramid	202	Vyse	196
Sphinx	9, 29, 73, 79, 124, 191		
Step Pyramid	73, 98	**W**	
Stone Age	14	Wadjet	54, 55
Strabo	22, 87, 201, 210	Walls of the Ruler	102
Stretching of the Cord	68	Wayman Dixon	86
Subterranean Chamber	71	Weighing of the soul	64, 208
Succession	37, 98	Wenis	19, 21, 136, 200
Sultan Hassan	88, 192	Westcar papyrus	109
Sun Temples	100, 200	White Crown	36, 57, 59
		White Pyramid	202
T		Wigs	181
Table at Saqqara	27	William Stukely	24
Table of Karnak	27, 146	William Warburton	24
Taharka	146	**X**	
Tanis	142	Xerxes I	148
Tantamani	146		
Tao I	105	**Y**	
Tao II	105	Yuya and Thuya	209
Tarsus	169		
Tefnut	41, 53	**Z**	
Tell el-Amarna	128, 203	Zazat	188
Temple of Zeus Ammon	150	Zep Tepi	31
Teos	141	Zosar	75, 98, 200
Teti	188, 200		
The Ascending Passage	91		